Prentice Hall
LITERATURE
Timeless Voices, Timeless Themes

English Learner's Companion
Teacher's Edition

THE AMERICAN EXPERIENCE

Prentice
Hall

Upper Saddle River, New Jersey
Glenview, Illinois
Needham, Massachusetts

Copyright © 2002 by Pearson Education, Inc., Upper Saddle River, New Jersey 07458. All rights reserved. Printed in the United States of America. This publication is protected by copyright, and permission should be obtained from the publisher prior to any prohibited reproduction, storage in a retrieval system, or transmission in any form or by any means, electronic, mechanical, photocopying, recording, or likewise. For information regarding permission(s), write to: Rights and Permissions Department.

ISBN 0-13-063687-8

3 4 5 6 7 8 9 10   06 05 04 03 02

Acknowledgments

Grateful acknowledgment is made to the following for permission to reprint copyrighted material:

Sandra Dijkstra Literary Agency for Amy Tan
"Mother Tongue" by Amy Tan. Copyright © 1989 by Amy Tan. First appeared in THREEPENNY REVIEW.

Rita Dove
Rita Dove, "For the Love of Books," first published as part of the INTRODUCTION TO SELECTED POEMS, Pantheon Books/Vintage Books, © 1993 by Rita Dove.

Farrar, Straus & Giroux, Inc.
"The First Seven Years" from THE MAGIC BARREL by Bernard Malamud. Copyright © 1950, 1958 and copyright renewed © 1977, 1986 by Bernard Malamud.

Harcourt Brace & Company
"A Worn Path" from A CURTAIN OF GREEN AND OTHER STORIES, copyright 1941 and renewed 1969 by Eudora Welty. "Everyday Use" from IN LOVE & TROUBLE: STORIES OF BLACK WOMEN, copyright © 1973 by Alice Walker.

W. W. Norton & Company, Inc.
From "Civil Disobedience" reprinted from WALDEN AND CIVIL DISOBEDIENCE by Henry David Thoreau, edited by Owen Thomas. Copyright ©1966 by W. W. Norton & Company, Inc.

Scribner, a division of Simon & Schuster, Inc.
"The Far and the Near" from DEATH TO MORNING by Thomas Wolfe. Copyright 1935 by Charles Scribner's Sons; copyright renewed © 1963 by Paul Gitlin. "In Another Country" from MEN WITHOUT WOMAN by Ernest Hemingway. Copyright 1927 by Charles Scribner's Sons. Copyright renewed 1955 by Ernest Hemingway.

Sterling Lord Literistic, Inc.
"The Crisis, Number 1" by Thomas Paine from CITIZEN TOM PAINE. Copyright by Howard Fast.

Syracuse University Press
"The Iroquois Constitution" from PARKER ON THE IROQUOIS: IROQUOIS USES OF MAIZE AND OTHER FOOD PLANTS; THE CODE OF HANDSOME LAKE; THE SENECA PROPHET; THE CONSTITUTION OF THE FIVE NATIONS by Arthur C. Parker, edited by William N. Fenton (Syracuse University Press, Syracuse, NY, 1981).

Viking Penguin, Inc., a division of Penguin Putnam, Inc.
"The Turtle (Chapter 3)" from THE GRAPES OF WRATH by John Steinbeck, copyright 1939, renewed © 1967 by John Steinbeck.

Note: Every effort has been made to locate the copyright owner of material reprinted in this book. Omissions brought to our attention will be corrected in subsequent editions.

Contents

© Pearson Education, Inc.

Part 2: Selection Summaries in English and Spanish With Alternative Reading Strategies 205

Unit 1: Beginnings—1750

Unit 2: A Nation Is Born (1750–1800)

Unit 3: A Growing Nation (1800–1870)

© Pearson Education, Inc.

Unit 4: Division, Reconciliation, and Expansion (1850–1914)

Unit 5: Disillusion, Defiance, and Discontent (1914–1946)

© Pearson Education, Inc.

Unit 6: Prosperity and Protest (1946–Present)

© **Pearson Education, Inc.**

To the Teacher

As you face the challenge of heterogeneous classes, you will find a wide variety of abilities and strengths among your students. This book is aimed at English learners who have difficulty with their grade-level textbooks. You can use it to keep your classes reading the same selections, but getting the instruction and reading support at the appropriate level. This book provides extended support for those students who need more guidance with reading strategies, literary analysis, and critical thinking skills.

Factors that Affect Reading Success

There are four key factors that influence students' ability to achieve reading success. These factors, alone and in combination, determine how well a student will learn, grow, and succeed as a reader. To understand the students in your classroom, consider these factors:

(a) **Kinds of Learners** Consider each student's background, previous learning experiences, and special needs. In addition to students who read fluently at grade level, you may find a mix of the following learning characteristics in your classroom:

- *Students who speak a language other than English at home* Unlike their fully fluent counterparts, these students often speak English only at school. This situation leaves them limited hours in which to learn the grammar, vocabulary, idioms, and other intricacies of English.

- *Students who have recently moved to this country* These students may be highly capable students without the specific language skills to function academically in English.

- *Students with learning disabilities* These students may have cognitive, behavioral, social, or physical challenges that make reading more difficult.

(b) **Kinds of Skills and Instruction** Students' reading ability is influenced by the skills they bring to the task. Students must master the skills of decoding, activating and building prior knowledge, and making connections among experiences and new information. Other factors include a student's knowledge of the English language and vocabulary, and a student's ability to apply reading comprehension strategies.

Active reading, including the practice of summarizing, questioning, setting a purpose, and self-monitoring, is key to successful reading. For those students who have not yet developed such skills, your classroom instruction is critical. You should model such skills and encourage students to practice them. Through practice, students should be able to internalize the strategies of active reading.

© Pearson Education, Inc.

(c) **Kinds of Texts** Just as students and their backgrounds and skills vary, so do the texts presented in a language arts curriculum. The grade-level language arts classroom curriculum traditionally addresses fiction, nonfiction, poetry, and drama. Each of these forms presents unique challenges to students. Each writer and selection also presents challenges in the difficulty of the concepts addressed or in the coherence of the writing. For example, you may find that students are more comfortable with narratives than with expository writing. Focused reading strategies that you model and reinforce can help students tackle texts that are more dense or difficult for them to master.

(d) **Classroom Environment** The classroom environment affects everything and everyone within it. Research suggests that students learn best in a friendly, respectful setting categorized by these criteria:

- Students feel a sense of safety and order.
- They feel comfortable taking risks.
- They understand the purpose and value of the tasks presented.
- Students have high expectations and goals for learning.
- They feel accepted by their teachers and peers.

Students performing below grade level may be especially self-conscious. Therefore, these criteria are key to helping students take full advantage of the opportunities the classroom affords. Set your classroom as a caring yet on-purpose environment that helps students achieve.

Researchers encourage teachers to be truthful with students about the work it will take to build and master abilities in the language arts. Tell your students that improving reading, writing, speaking, and listening takes a great deal of practice. You need to be prepared to provide direct instruction, guided practice, specific feedback, coaching, and more. Then, encourage your students to understand their responsibilities as active, self-directed learners as well.

The English Learner

English language learners are those students whose first language is not English. For these students, the challenge of an average language arts classroom looms large.

There are very few generalities to draw about this group of students, beyond their need to develop English fluency. Some are high functioning in their home language with a strong understanding of the routines and expectations of schools. Others are severely underschooled and therefore, they need to learn school routines, the vocabulary for studying English, and English itself. Some are not literate in their home language.

© Pearson Education, Inc.

For English learners, initial reading and writing will be slower because the students struggle with fluency. Consequently, the following conditions result:

- These learners may revert to poor reading strategies to accommodate difficulty with language. For example, they may not read in sentences and instead tackle each word individually.

- Students may have a cultural disadvantage because they have less relevant prior knowledge or background information. Even if students can decode the selection, they may have difficulty in constructing meaning from the text or simply relating to its topic.

- These students are less familiar with academic language—the language of directions, content analysis, and school routines.

English learners may benefit from a separate reading support classroom to help them master reading English. In a heterogeneous classroom, however, English learners will benefit from the specific steps you take to support them.

- Present extensive and dynamic pre-teaching instruction to help students meet the literacy challenge.

- Explain critical concepts and key vocabulary in advance. Particularly, focus on classroom activities that build conceptual and linguistic foundation.

- Show students text organizations.

- Model appropriate comprehension strategies.

- Provide a clear purpose for reading.

Overview of Components for Universal Access

The *Prentice Hall Literature: Timeless Voices, Timeless Themes* program includes an array of products to provide universal access. Fully integrated, these materials help teachers identify student needs or deficiencies and teach to the varying levels in a classroom, while providing the quality that literature teachers expect.

As your main resource, the *Annotated Teacher's Edition* provides a lesson plan for every selection or selection grouping. In addition to teaching notes and suggestions, it also includes cross-references to ancillary materials. Customize for Universal Access notes help teachers direct lessons to the following groups of students: special needs students, less proficient readers, English learners, gifted and talented students, and advanced readers. In addition to teaching notes and suggestions, it also includes cross-references to ancillary material such as the *Reader's Companion*, the *Adapted Reader's Companion*, and the *English Learner's Companion*.

The **Teaching Guidebook for Universal Access** gives you proven strategies for providing universal access to all students. In addition to its general teaching strategies and classroom management techniques, this component explains how the parts of the Prentice Hall program work together to ensure reading success for all student populations.

The **Reading Diagnostic and Improvement Plan**—part of the Reading Achievement System—provides comprehensive diagnostic tests that assess students' mastery of reading skills. The book also includes charts that help you map out improvement plans based on students' performance on the diagnostics.

You can use the **Basic Reading Skills: Comprehensive Lessons for Improvement Plan**—also part of the Reading Achievement System—to give instruction and practice that bring students up to grade level, enabling them to master the skills in which they are deficient. For each skill covered, you'll find the following materials:

- lesson plan with direct instruction

- teaching transparency

- blackline master for student application and practice

The **Reader's Companion** and **Reader's Companion Teacher's Edition** are consumable components of the Reading Achievement System. The books contain the full text of approximately half of the selections from the student book. Questions prompt students to interact with the text by circling, underlining, or marking key details. Write-on lines in the margins also allow for students to answer questions. You can use this book in place of the student book to help students read interactively. In addition, a summary and a reading-skill worksheet support every selection grouping in the student book.

© **PEARSON** Education, Inc.

The *Adapted Reader's Companion* and *Adapted Reader's Companion Teacher's Edition* are another set of consumable components of the Reading Achievement System. These books use the same format and contain the same selections as the *Reader's Companion*. However, the selections are abridged and appear in a larger font size. The questions are targeted toward special education students. You can use this book as a supplement to or in place of the student book for certain selections to enable special education students to experience the same literature and master the same skills as on-level students. These components also contain a summary and a reading-skill worksheet to support every selection grouping in the student book.

The *English Learner's Companion* and *English Learner's Companion Teacher's Edition* are a third set of consumable components of the Reading Achievement System. These books use the same format and contain the same selections as the *Reader's Companion*. Again, the selections are abridged and appear in a larger font size. The questions are targeted toward English learners. You can use this book as a supplement to or in place of the student book for certain selections to enable English learners to experience the same literature and master the same skills as students who are native English speakers. These components also contain summaries in English and Spanish, along with a reading-skill worksheet to support every selection grouping in the student book.

Listening to Literature Audiotapes and CDs These components feature professional recordings of every selection in the student book. To support student reading, you can play the selections, in part or in full, before students read them.

Spanish/English Summaries Audio CD Audio summaries in both English and Spanish are provided for every selection. You can play these selection summaries for struggling readers, special education students, and English learners before they read the actual texts.

Basic Language Skills: Reteaching Masters With the reteaching masters, you can provide basic-level instruction and practice on grammar and language skills.

Interest Grabber Videos These videos are an optional enrichment resource designed to provide background for a selection or otherwise motivate students to read the selection. There is a video segment for every selection or selection grouping in the student book.

About the *English Learner's Companion*

The *English Learner's Companion* is designed to support your students whose first language is not English. Its two parts offer different levels of support.

Part 1: Selection Adaptations with Excerpts of Authentic Text

Part 1 will guide English learners as they interact with half the selections from *Prentice Hall Literature: Timeless Voices, Timeless Themes.* This range of selections includes the more challenging selections, the most frequently taught selections, and many examples of narrative and expository writing. Part 1 provides pre-reading instruction, larger print summaries of literature selections with passages from the selection, and post-reading questions and activities.

The **Preview** page will help your students get the general idea of the selection and therefore be better equipped to understand it. Both written and visual summaries preview the selections before students read the adapted versions.

The **Prepare to Read** page is based on its parallel in *Prentice Hall Literature: Timeless Voices, Timeless Themes.* It introduces the same literary element and reading strategy addressed in the textbook and provides a graphic organizer to make the information more accessible.

The **selection** pages present the text in a larger font size. Interspersed among blocks of authentic text, the companion also provides summaries of episodes or paragraphs to make the selections more accessible to your students.

The **side notes** make active reading strategies explicit, asking students to look closely at the text to analyze it in a variety of ways. Notes with a *Mark the Text* icon prompt students to underline, circle, or otherwise note key words, phrases, or details in the selection. Notes with write-on lines offer students an opportunity to respond in the margin to questions or ideas. These notes offer focused support in a variety of areas:

> **Literary Analysis** notes provide point-of-use instruction to reinforce the literary element introduced on the Preview page. By pointing out details or events in the text in which the literary element applies, these notes give students the opportunity to revisit and reinforce their understanding of literature.

> **Reading Strategy** notes help students practice the skill introduced on the Preview page. These notes guide students to understand when, how, and why a strategy is helpful.

> **Stop to Reflect** notes ask students to reflect on the selection or on a skill they are using. By encouraging students to solidify their own thinking, these notes help to develop active reading skills.

 © Pearson Education, Inc.

Reading Check notes help students to confirm their comprehension of a selection. These notes help to make explicit a critical strategy of active reading.

Read Fluently notes provide students with concrete, limited practice reading passages aloud with fluency.

Vocabulary and Pronunciation notes address specific points of language development for English learners. For example, notes might explain English word parts, teach the multiple meanings of words, point out and show the pronunciation of new words, or ask students to make comparisons with English words and those in their home language.

English Language Development notes deal with concepts including spelling, grammar, mechanics, and usage. They call out for students the finer points of text written in English.

Culture Notes explain aspects of American culture that students new to the country might not understand. These notes, explaining traditions such as holiday celebrations and leisuretime activities, are especially helpful to students who may be able to read the selection fluently but not understand its context as well.

Background notes provide further explanation of a concept or detail to support student understanding.

The **Review and Assess** questions following the selection ensure students' comprehension of the selection. Written in simple language, they assess students' understanding of the literary element and the reading strategy. In addition they offer a scaffolded guide to support students in an extension activity based on either a writing or listening and speaking activity in the *Student Edition* of the grade-level textbook.

Part 2: Selection Summaries in English and Spanish with Alternative Reading Strategies

Part 2 contains summaries of all selections in *Prentice Hall Literature: Timeless Voices, Timeless Themes*. Summaries are provided in English and Spanish. These summaries can help students prepare for reading the selections. Alternatively, the summaries may serve as a review tool.

This section also includes alternative reading strategies to guide students as they read selections. The strategies may be useful for reviewing selection events and ideas or to reinforce specific reading strategies for students.

How to Use the *English Learner's Companion*

When you are planning lessons for heterogeneous classes, this companion reader offers you an opportunity to keep all the students in your class reading the same selection and studying the same vocabulary, literary element, and reading strategy but getting the support they need to succeed. Here are some planning suggestions for using the book in tandem with the grade-level volume of *Prentice Hall Literature: Timeless Voices, Timeless Themes*.

Use the *Annotated Teacher's Edition* and the *Student Edition* of the grade-level textbook as the central text in your classroom. The *Annotated Teacher's Edition* includes *Customize for Universal Access* notes throughout each selection. In addition, it identifies when use of the *English Learner's Companion* is appropriate.

TEACHING SELECTIONS INCLUDED IN PART ONE

PRE-TEACH with the Full Class

Consider presenting the* Interest Grabber *video segment. This optional technology product can provide background and build motivation.

Preview the selection. To help students see the organization of a selection, or to help them get a general idea of the text, lead a quick text pre-reading or "text tour" using the textbook. Focus student attention on the selection title, the art accompanying the text, and any unusual text characteristics. To build connections for students, ask them to identify links between the selection and other works you have presented in class, or to find connections to themes, activities, or other related concepts.

Build background. Use the Background information provided in the *Student Edition.* Whether explaining a historical time period, a scientific concept, or details about an idea that may be unfamiliar to students, this instruction presents useful information to help all students place the literature in context.

Focus vocabulary development. The student edition includes a list of vocabulary words included in the selection or selection grouping. Instead of attempting to cover all of the vocabulary words you anticipate your students will not know, identify the vocabulary that is most critical to talking and learning about the central concepts. However, for the words you do choose to teach, work to provide more than synonyms and definitions. Using the vocabulary notes in the *Annotated Teacher's Edition*, introduce the essential words in more meaningful contexts: for example, through simple sentences drawing on familiar issues, people, scenarios, and vocabulary. Guide students in internalizing the meanings of key terms through these familiar contexts and ask them to write the definitions in their own words. Look at these examples of guided vocabulary instruction:

© Pearson Education, Inc.

Point out the word *serene* and explain that it means "calm or peaceful." Then, provide the following scenarios and ask students to determine whether the situations are *serene* or not: an empty beach at sunset *(yes)*; a playground at recess *(no)*. You might also ask students to provide their own examples of *serene* situations.

Point out the word *interval* and explain that it means "the period of time between two events or points of time." Ask students to identify the interval between Monday and Wednesday *(two days)* and the interval between one Monday and the next Monday *(one week)*.

You might also take the opportunity to teach the prefix *inter-*, meaning "between." Then, discuss with students the following group of words:
interview (a meeting between two or more people);
interstate (between two or more states);
international (between nations);
intervene (to come between two sides in a dispute).

Introduce skills. Introduce the *Literary Analysis* and *Reading Strategy*, using the instruction in the *Student Edition* and the teaching support in the *Annotated Teacher's Edition.*

Separate the class. As students fluent in English begin reading the selection in the *Student Edition*, have English learners put their textbooks aside. Direct these students to the *English Learner's Companion* for further pre-teaching.

PRE-TEACH for English Learners Using the *English Learner's Companion*

Reinforce the general idea. Use the selection and visual summaries presented on the first page of every selection in the *English Learner's Companion*. These summaries will give students a framework to follow for understanding the selection. Use these tools to build familiarity, but do not use them as a replacement for reading.

Present audio summaries. The *Spanish/English Summaries Audio CD* can reinforce the main idea of a selection.

Reinforce skills instruction. Next, use the Prepare to Read page to reinforce the *Literary Analysis* and *Reading Strategy* concepts. Written in simpler language and in basic sentence structures, the instruction will help students better grasp these ideas.

Provide decoding practice. Because many English learners lack strategies for decoding bigger words, give them guided practice with the vocabulary words for the selection. Using the list, model a strategy for decoding polysyllabic words. First, show students how to break the word into parts and the put the parts back together to make a word.

> For the word *mimic*, ask students to draw a loop under each word part as they pronounce it.
>
> *mim ic*   *fright en ing*

Using this strategy, you can encourage students to look for familiar word parts and then break the rest of the word down into its consonant and vowel sounds. By building this routine regularly into your pre-teaching instruction, you reinforce a key reading skill for your students.

Prepare for lesson structure. To build students' ability to complete classroom activities, examine your lesson to see what types of language functions students will need to participate. Look at these examples:

> If students are being asked to make predictions about upcoming paragraph content in an essay, review the power of transition words that act as signals to meaning. Rather than teaching all transitions, limit your instruction to the ones in the passages. Identify the key transition words and point out their meaning. In addition, teach students some basic sentence patterns and verbs to express opinions. Model for students statement patterns such as:
>
> *I predict that . . .*
>
> *Based on this transition word, I conclude that . . .*

TEACH Using the *English Learner's Companion*

As students fluent in English in your class read the selection in the textbook, allow English learners to read the adapted version in the *English Learner's Companion*. Whenever possible, give these students individualized attention by pairing them with aides, parent volunteers, or student peers.

Set purposes and limits. To keep students focused and motivated, and to prevent them from becoming overwhelmed as they read a selection, clearly establish a reading purpose for students before assigning a manageable amount of text. Once you identify a focus question or a purpose, revisit the question occasionally as students read. You can do this with a brief whole-group dialogue or by encouraging students in pairs to remember the question. In addition, your effective modeling will also provide the scaffolding for students to begin internalizing these strategies for effective reading.

© Pearson Education, Inc.

Model your thinking. Describe and model strategies for navigating different kinds of text. Use the questions raised in the side notes as a starting point. Then, explain how you arrive at an answer. Alternatively, ask a student to explain his or her responses to classmates.

Reinforce new vocabulary. Present key words when they occur within the context of the reading selection. Review the definition as it appears on the page. Then, make the words as concrete as possible by linking each to an object, photo, or idea.

Build interactivity. The side notes in the *English Learner's Companion* are an excellent way to encourage student interactivity with the selections. To build students' ability to use these notes, model several examples with each selection. These are not busy work; they are activities that build fluency and provide the scaffolding necessary for student success.

Whenever possible, get students physically involved with the page, using *Mark the Text* icons as an invitation to use highlighters or colored pencils to circle, underline, or number key information. In addition, some students may find that using a small piece of cardboard or heavy construction paper helps to focus and guide their reading from one paragraph or page to the next.

Vary modes of instruction. To maintain student attention and interest, monitor and alternate the mode of instruction or activity. For example, alternate between teacher-facilitated and student-dominated reading activities. Assign brief amounts of text at a time, and alternate between oral, paired, and silent reading.

Monitor students' comprehension. As students use the side notes in the margins of the *English Learner's Companion*, build in opportunities to ensure that students are on purpose and understanding. Consider structured brief conversations for students to share, compare, or explain their thinking. Then, use these conversations to praise the correct use of strategies or to redirect students who need further support. In addition, this is an excellent chance for you to demonstrate your note-taking process and provide models of effective study notes for students to emulate.

Reinforce the reading experience. When students read the selection for the first time, they may be working on the decoding level. If time allows, students should read the selection twice to achieve a greater fluency and comfort level.

REVIEW AND ASSESS Using the *English Learner's Companion*

Reinforce writing and reading skills. Assign students the extension activity in the *English Learner's Companion*. Based on an activity presented the grade-level text, the version in the *English Learner's Companion* provides guided, step-by-step support for students. By giving students the opportunities to show their reading comprehension and writing skills, you maintain reasonable expectations for their developing academic competence in English.

Model expectations. Make sure that students understand your assessment criteria in advance. Provide models of student work whenever possible for them to emulate, along with a nonmodel that fails to meet the specified assessment criteria. Do not provide exemplars that are clearly outside their developmental range. Save student work that can later serve as a model for students with different levels of academic preparation.

Lead students to closure. To achieve closure, ask students to end the class session by writing three to five outcome statements about their experience in the day's lesson, expressing both new understandings and needs for clarification.

Encourage self-monitoring and self-assessment. Remember to provide safe opportunities for students to alert you to any learning challenges they are experiencing. Consider having students submit anonymous written questions (formulated either independently or with a partner) about confusing lesson content and process. Later, you can follow up on these points of confusion at the end of class or in the subsequent class session.

EXTEND Using the Student Edition

Present the unabridged selection. Build in opportunities for students to read the full selection in the grade-level textbook. This will allow them to apply familiar concepts and vocabulary and stretch their literacy muscles.

Play an audio reading of the unabridged selection. Use the *Listening to Literature Audiotapes* or *CDs*. Students may benefit from reading along while listening to a professional recording of the selection. Encourage students to use their fingertips to follow the words as they are read.

Invite reader response. When students have finished reviewing the selection—whether in the companion or in the grade-level textbook—include all students in your class in post-reading analysis. To guide an initial discussion, use the Respond question in the *Thinking About the Selection* in the textbook. You will find that questions such as the following examples will provide strong springboards for classroom interaction:

> **Respond:** What advice would you have given the mother and daughter? Why?

> **Respond:** What questions would you like to ask the writer about his experience?

> **Respond:** Do you find the boy's actions courageous, touching, or silly? Explain your answer.

Encourage students to explain their answers to these questions by supporting their ideas with evidence from the text or their own lives. In addition, invite students to respond to classmates' ideas. These questions will lead students

 © Pearson Education, Inc.

from simply getting the gist of a selection to establishing a personal connection to the lesson content.

Direct student analysis with scaffolded questions. When you are ready to move students into the Review and Assess questions, let your average-achieving students use the instruction and questions in the grade-level textbook. At the same time, encourage English learners to use the questions in the *English Learner's Companion.*

- Questions in the companion, written in more simple language and providing more explicit support, will be more accessible to these students. Students will be applying concepts and practicing strategies at their own level.

- Some English learners may be prepared to answer questions in the grade-level text. The two-part questions in the *Thinking About the Selection* section are written to build and support student analysis. First, students use lower-level thinking skills to identify information or to recall important details in a selection. For the second part, students use a higher-level thinking skill based on the answer to the first part.

Look at these examples of scaffolded questions from the grade-level textbook:

(a) Recall: Why does the boy tell his father to leave the sickroom?
(b) Infer: What does this reveal about the boy?

(a) Recall: Why does the boy think he will die?
(b) Infer: What is the meaning of the title?

Revisit and reinforce strategies. Recycle pre- and post-reading tasks regularly, so students can become more familiar with the task process and improve their performance. If they are constantly facing curricular novelty, English learners never have the opportunity to refine their skills and demonstrate improved competence. For example, if you ask them to identify a personality trait of an essential character in a story and then support this observation with relevant details in an expository paragraph, it would make sense to have them write an identical paragraph in the near future about another character.

Show students how to transfer skills. Consider ways in which students can transfer knowledge and skills gleaned from one assignment/lesson to a subsequent lesson. For example, discuss with students the ways in which they can apply new vocabulary and language strategies outside of the classroom. In addition, demonstrate the applicability of new reading and writing strategies to real-world literacy tasks. Include periodic writing tasks for an authentic audience other than the teacher: another class, fellow classmates, local businesses, family, etc.

Offer praise and encourage growth. Praise students' efforts to experiment with new language in class, both in writing and in speaking.

USING PART TWO

For selections that are not presented as adaptations in Part One, use the summaries and activities in Part Two to support your English learners.

PRE-TEACH

In addition to the pre-teaching strategies listed on page xvii, consider these strategies to accommodate English learners.

Provide students with a "running start." Use the selection summaries offered in the *English Learner's Companion.* These summaries, provided in English and Spanish, will give students a framework for understanding the selection to follow.

Build interest. To take full advantage of the summaries, ask students to write one or two questions that the summaries raise in their minds. Share these questions in a discussion before reading the full text.

TEACH

As your students read the full selection in the textbook, provide English learners with support and individualized attention by pairing them with aides, parent volunteers, or student peers. In addition to the suggestions on page xviii, consider these additional strategies.

Model your thinking for side-column questions. To help these students practice the *Literary Analysis* skill and the *Reading Strategy*, use the questions raised in the side notes as a starting point. If students have difficulty answering the questions, review the concept for students and model your thinking process. Look at these examples of modeling explicit thinking:

> ### Reading Strategy: Making Inferences
>
> Remind students that, in a work of fiction, a writer expects readers to make connections with what they already know or have read in an earlier passage. Show students how to make inferences based on the side-column question and the appropriate text. Look at this passage from a selection as an example:
>
> > "Mary, you oughta write David and tell him somebody done opened his letter and stole that ten dollars he sent," she said.
> >
> > "No mama. David's got enough on his mind. Besides, there's enough garden foods so we won't go hungry."
>
> Then, use language like this to model your thinking process:
>
> *I'm not sure whom the characters are talking about. There hasn't been any David mentioned in the story. What's this about a letter? First, I ask myself what information there is in the passage. Mama sounds like she cares about this person; it's probably a friend or a family member. David sends money to*

   © Pearson Education, Inc.

the family, so he must be in another place. I'll ask myself what I know from what I've already read. Do I know anything about characters who live far away? Earlier, Mama said the father worked in Louisiana so that he could support the family. Could David be the father? I think so! He probably sends his wages back to Mississippi. That's the part about the letter! Somebody opened up one of the letters and took the money.

Reading Strategy: Interpreting Poetic Language

In poetry, writers may describe an event in very different language from what they might use in writing an essay. Students can increase their understanding of poetry by learning to interpret poetic language. To help them, use the side notes and any marked texts to model your thinking process. Look at this example based on the following poetic lines:

> You crash over the trees,
>
> you crack the live branch—
>
> the branch is white,
>
> the green crushed,

Then, use language like this to model your thinking process:

I am not sure exactly what is being described in the last two lines. What do the colors mean? Why is the branch white? What is the author referring to by "green crushed"? I'll start by figuring out what I do know. This poem is about a storm. From the second line, I can figure out that lightning or wind has struck the tree and cracked a branch. Green is the color of leaves. When a storm cracks a branch, it may fall to the ground. The leaves are crushed by the fall; this must be "the green crushed." But branches aren't white; they're brown or gray. However, if they're cracked open, the wood inside is white. The storm has cracked the branch and exposed its white insides.

Use the Reading Check questions in the Student Edition. Consider pairing students, working with small groups, or setting brief instructional time for *Reading Check* questions that appear with every selection. These recall-level questions can be answered based on information in the text. Ask students to point to their answers in the selection before returning to reading.

REVIEW AND ASSESS

In addition to the suggestions on page xix, consider these additional strategies:

Build tests using the computer test bank. The computer test bank allows you to sort questions by difficulty level. Use this feature to generate tests appropriate to English learners.

Part 1

Selection Adaptations With Excerpts of Authentic Text

Part 1 will guide and support you as you interact with selections from *Prentice Hall Literature: Timeless Voices, Timeless Themes.* Part 1 provides summaries of literature selections with passages from the selection.

- Begin with the Preview page in the *English Learner's Companion.* Use the written and visual summaries to preview the selections before you read.

- Then study the Prepare to Read page. This page introduces skills that you will apply as you read selections in the *English Learner's Companion.*

- Now read the selection in the *English Learner's Companion.*

- Respond to all the questions along the sides as you read. They will guide you in understanding the selection and in applying the skills. Write in the *English Learner's Companion*—really! Circle things that interest you. Underline things that puzzle you. Number ideas or events to help you keep track of them. Look for the **Mark the Text** logo for help with active reading.

- Use the Review and Assess questions at the end of each selection to review what you have read and to check your understanding.

- Finally, do the Writing or the Speaking and Listening activity to extend your understanding and practice your skills.

Interacting With the Text

As you read, use the information and notes to guide you in interacting with the selection. The examples on these pages show you how to use the notes as a companion when you read. They will guide you in applying reading and literary skills and in thinking about the selections. When you read other texts, you can practice the thinking skills and strategies found here.

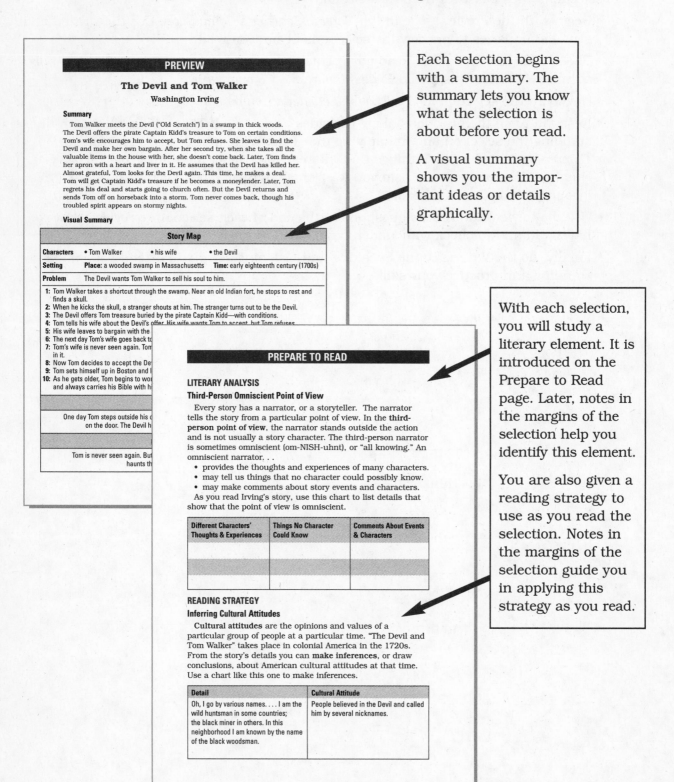

PREVIEW

The Devil and Tom Walker
Washington Irving

Summary

Tom Walker meets the Devil ("Old Scratch") in a swamp in thick woods. The Devil offers the pirate Captain Kidd's treasure to Tom on certain conditions. Tom's wife encourages him to accept, but Tom refuses. She leaves to find the Devil and make her own bargain. After her second try, when she takes all the valuable items in the house with her, she doesn't come back. Later, Tom finds her apron with a heart and liver in it. He assumes that the Devil has killed her. Almost grateful, Tom looks for the Devil again. This time, he makes a deal. Tom will get Captain Kidd's treasure if he becomes a moneylender. Later, Tom regrets his deal and starts going to church often. But the Devil returns and sends Tom off on horseback into a storm. Tom never comes back, though his troubled spirit appears on stormy nights.

Visual Summary

Story Map		
Characters	• Tom Walker	• his wife • the Devil
Setting	**Place:** a wooded swamp in Massachusetts	**Time:** early eighteenth century (1700s)
Problem	The Devil wants Tom Walker to sell his soul to him.	

1: Tom Walker takes a shortcut through the swamp. Near an old Indian fort, he stops to rest and finds a skull.
2: When he kicks the skull, a stranger shouts at him. The stranger turns out to be the Devil.
3: The Devil offers Tom treasure buried by the pirate Captain Kidd—with conditions.
4: Tom tells his wife about the Devil's offer. His wife wants Tom to accept, but Tom refuses.
5: His wife leaves to bargain with the
6: The next day Tom's wife goes back to
7: Tom's wife is never seen again. Tom in it.
8: Now Tom decides to accept the De
9: Tom sets himself up in Boston and
10: As he gets older, Tom begins to wo and always carries his Bible with h

One day Tom steps outside his on the door. The Devil h

Tom is never seen again. But haunts th

PREPARE TO READ

LITERARY ANALYSIS
Third-Person Omniscient Point of View

Every story has a narrator, or a storyteller. The narrator tells the story from a particular point of view. In the **third-person point of view**, the narrator stands outside the action and is not usually a story character. The third-person narrator is sometimes omniscient (om-NISH-uhnt), or "all knowing." An omniscient narrator. . .
• provides the thoughts and experiences of many characters.
• may tell us things that no character could possibly know.
• may make comments about story events and characters.
As you read Irving's story, use this chart to list details that show that the point of view is omniscient.

Different Characters' Thoughts & Experiences	Things No Character Could Know	Comments About Events & Characters

READING STRATEGY
Inferring Cultural Attitudes

Cultural attitudes are the opinions and values of a particular group of people at a particular time. "The Devil and Tom Walker" takes place in colonial America in the 1720s. From the story's details you can **make inferences**, or draw conclusions, about American cultural attitudes at that time. Use a chart like this one to make inferences.

Detail	Cultural Attitude
Oh, I go by various names. . . . I am the wild huntsman in some countries; the black miner in others. In this neighborhood I am known by the name of the black woodsman.	People believed in the Devil and called him by several nicknames.

Each selection begins with a summary. The summary lets you know what the selection is about before you read.

A visual summary shows you the important ideas or details graphically.

With each selection, you will study a literary element. It is introduced on the Prepare to Read page. Later, notes in the margins of the selection help you identify this element.

You are also given a reading strategy to use as you read the selection. Notes in the margins of the selection guide you in applying this strategy as you read.

© Pearson Education, Inc.

Text set in a narrow margin provides a summary of selection events or details.

Text set in a wider margin provides the author's actual words.

Use write-on lines to answer the questions. You may also want to use the lines for your own notes or for questions you have.

When you see this symbol, follow the directions to underline, circle or mark the text as indicated.

Questions after every selection help you think about the selection. You can use the write-on lines or charts to answer the questions.

◆ Stop to Reflect

What do you think will happen to Crowninshield? Why?

_____

_____

_____

◆ Reading Strategy

Circle two nicknames for the Devil that are used by people in Walker's area. From the nicknames, what do you **infer** that European colonists associated with the word *black*? Circle the letter of your answer below.

(a) good (c) poverty

(b) evil (d) boldness

◆ Literary Analysis

An **omniscient**, or all-knowing, **narrator** tells us the thoughts and attitudes of different characters. Circle Tom's wife's thoughts or attitudes about the treasure. Write one word to describe the wife.

_____

"He's just ready for burning!" said the black man, with a growl of triumph. "You see I am likely to have a good stock of firewood for winter."

"But what right have you," said Tom, "to cut down Deacon Peabody's timber?"

"The right of a <u>prior</u> claim," said the other. "This woodland belonged to me long before one of your white-faced race put foot upon the soil."

"And pray, who are you, if I may be so bold?" said Tom.

"Oh, I go by various names. I am the wild huntsman in some countries; the black miner in others. In this neighborhood I am known by the name of the black woodsman. . . ."

"The upshot of all which is, that, if I mistake not," said Tom, sturdily, "you are he commonly called Old Scratch."

"The same, at your service," replied the black man, with a half-civil nod.

♦ ♦ ♦

The Devil offers Tom Captain Kidd's pirate treasure if Tom agrees to his terms. Tom makes no decision. Instead he asks for proof that the Devil is who he says he is. So the Devil presses his finger to Tom's forehead and then goes off. When Tom gets home, he finds a black thumbprint burned into his forehead. He also learns of the sudden death of Absalom Crowninshield. Convinced he has met the Devil, he tells his wife all about it.

♦ ♦ ♦

All her <u>avarice</u> was awakened at the idea of hidden gold, and she urged her husband to <u>comply</u> with the black man's terms and

---

Vocabulary Development

prior (PRĪ uh) *adj.* previous; from before
avarice (A vuh riz) *adj.* greed
comply (kum PLĪ) *v.* go along with; agree to

REVIEW AND ASSESS

1. Circle the words that best describe Tom Walker.

greedy   loyal   loving   selfish   lazy

2. What happens to Tom's wife?

_____

_____

3. Complete these sentences to explain the bargain that Tom makes.

Tom agrees to _____

in exchange for _____.

4. What happens to Tom in the end?

_____

_____

5. **Literary Analysis** Show that the story uses **third-person omniscient point of view** by finding examples for the chart below.

Different Characters' Thoughts & Experiences:	Comments About Events & Characters:

---

from The Iroquois Constitution

Translated by Arthur C. Parker

Summary

This selection is an excerpt, or a section, from *The Iroquois Constitution.* Dekanawidah, who is an Iroquois prophet, speaks here of the Tree of Great Peace that gives shelter and protection to the Iroquois nations. He explains why and how the Five Nations, a group of five Iroquois tribes, should come together to form a union or confederacy for their common good.

Visual Summary

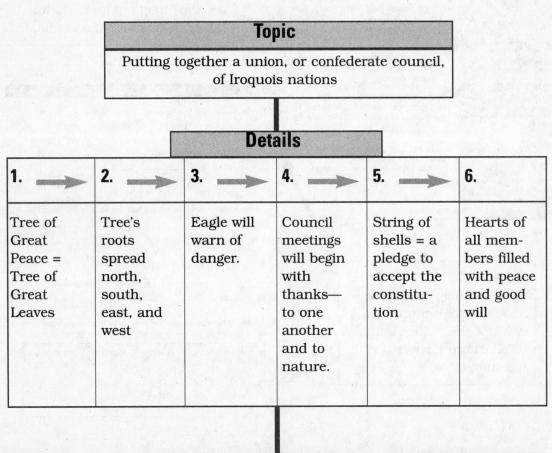

Topic

Putting together a union, or confederate council, of Iroquois nations

Details

1.	2.	3.	4.	5.	6.
Tree of Great Peace = Tree of Great Leaves	Tree's roots spread north, south, east, and west	Eagle will warn of danger.	Council meetings will begin with thanks— to one another and to nature.	String of shells = a pledge to accept the constitution	Hearts of all members filled with peace and good will

Main Idea Sentence

Members of the confederate council will be committed to peace for all people, for the present and for future generations.

© Pearson Education, Inc.

LITERARY ANALYSIS

Origin Myths

Origin myths are stories about beginnings. These stories are passed down from generation to generation. Many such stories were told and retold long before they were written down.

Origin myths may explain one or more of the following:
- customs, traditions, or social organizations
- natural landmarks such as high mountains
- events beyond people's control, such as earthquakes

This passage from the Iroquois Constitution tells about the founding of a social organization: the alliance between five different Native American nations or peoples.

READING STRATEGY

Recognizing Cultural Details

The ideas, customs, and skills of a particular people or group make up its culture. Literature often reflects the culture that produces it. As you read, **recognizing cultural details** can deepen your understanding. Notice references to objects, animals, or practices that tell you how the people of a culture live or think.

Use the chart below to record two details from the selection. Then tell what each detail tells you about the ideas, customs, or beliefs of the Iroquois.

Detail from the Iroquois Constitution	What It Reveals About Ideas, Customs, or Beliefs
EXAMPLE: planting and naming of the Tree of the Great Peace	• Iroquois put a high value on nature • names have great meaning
1.	
2.	

© Pearson Education, Inc.

_____

_____

_____

♦ Literary Analysis

Circle two words that show the nature of the Great White Roots in this **origin myth**. What can you tell from this passage about the purpose of the alliance?

_____

_____

♦ Culture Note

The speaker sometimes repeats words and concepts: for example, "seats," "feathery down of the globe thistle," and "Five Nations." The repetitions draw attention to the formal, serious nature of the speaker's words and actions. Write one other word or phrase that is repeated in this selection.

_____

_____

from The Iroquois Constitution
Translated by Arthur C. Parker

I am Dekanawidah and with the Five Nations[1] <u>confederate</u> lords I plant the Tree of the Great Peace. I name the tree the Tree of the Great Long Leaves. Under the shade of this Tree of the Great Peace we spread the soft white feathery down of the globe thistle as seats for you, Adodarhoh, and your cousin lords.

We place you upon those seats, spread soft with the feathery down of the globe thistle, there beneath the shade of the spreading branches of the Tree of Peace. There shall you sit and watch the council fire of the confederacy of the Five Nations, and all the affairs of the Five Nations shall be transacted[2] at this place before you.

Roots have spread out from the Tree of the Great Peace, one to the north, one to the east, one to the south and one to the west. The name of these roots is the Great White Roots and their nature is peace and strength.

♦ ♦ ♦

Other nations wishing to speak with the Five Nations will trace the roots to the tree. Peaceful and obedient people will be welcomed.

♦ ♦ ♦

Vocabulary Development

confederate (kon FED er it) *adj.* united with others for a common purpose

---

1. **Five Nations** the Mohawk, Oneida, Onondaga, Cayuga, and Seneca tribes. Together, these tribes formed the Iroquois Confederation.
2. **transacted** (trans ACT id) *v.* done.

© Pearson Education, Inc.

We place at the top of the Tree of the Long Leaves an eagle who is able to see afar. If he sees in the distance any evil approaching or danger threatening he will at once warn the people of the confederacy.

The smoke of the confederate council fire shall ever ascend and pierce the sky so that other nations who may be allies may see the council fire of the Great Peace . . .

◆ ◆ ◆

The Onondaga lords will open every council meeting by giving thanks to their cousin lords. They will also offer thanks to the earth, the waters, the crops, the trees, the animals, the sun, the moon, and the Great Creator.

◆ ◆ ◆

All lords of the Five Nations' Confederacy must be honest in all things . . . It shall be a serious wrong for anyone to lead a lord into trivial[3] affairs, for the people must ever hold their lords high in estimation[4] out of respect to their honorable positions.

◆ ◆ ◆

When a new lord joins the council, he must offer a pledge of four strings of shells. The speaker of the council will then welcome the new lord. The lords on the other side of the council fire will receive the pledge. Then they will speak these words to the new lord:

◆ ◆ ◆

Vocabulary Development

ascend (uh SEND) *v.* rise

3. **trivial** (TRIV i al) *adj.* unimportant.
4. **estimation** (es ti MA shun) *n.* opinion, judgment.

© Pearson Education, Inc.

◆ **Reading Strategy**

What role does the eagle play as a **cultural detail** for the Five Nations?

_____

_____

_____

◆ **Reading Strategy**

Circle the **cultural details** in the underlined passage that show why the smoke of the council fire will ascend to the sky.

◆ **Stop to Reflect**

What is one requirement for all the lords of the Five Nations?

_____

_____

_____

◆ **Read Fluently**

Read the bracketed passage aloud. Circle three words that name qualities a new lord should have.

◆ **Vocabulary and Pronunciation**

The expression *cast not over your shoulder behind you* means "don't discard or throw away." What does the underlined sentence mean?

_____

_____

_____

◆ **Reading Strategy**

What attitude about the future do the members of the speaker's **culture** have?

_____

_____

_____

_____

"With endless patience you shall carry out your duty and your firmness shall be tempered[5] with tenderness for your people. Neither anger nor fury shall find lodgement in your mind and all your words and actions shall be marked with calm <u>deliberation</u>. In all your deliberations in the confederate council, in your efforts at law making, in all your official acts, self-interest shall be cast into oblivion.[6] <u>Cast not over your shoulder behind you the warnings of the nephews and nieces should they chide[7] you for any error or wrong you may do, but return to the way of the Great Law which is just and right.</u> Look and listen for the welfare of the whole people and have always in view not only the present but also the coming generations, even those whose faces are yet beneath the surface of the ground—the unborn of the future nation."

Vocabulary Development

deliberation (di lib er A shun) *n.* careful consideration

---

5. **tempered** (TEM perd) *v.* made more moderate.
6. **oblivion** (uh BLIV i un) *n.* forgetfulness.
7. **chide** (CHĪD) *v.* criticize.

© Pearson Education, Inc.

1. What three actions does the speaker perform in the first paragraph? List them on the chart.

First Paragraph

Action 1: _____

Action 2: _____

Action 3: _____

2. Why is it important for an eagle to be placed at the top of the Great Tree?

_____

_____

3. According to the speaker, what attitude should the people have about their lords?

_____

_____

_____

4. **Literary Analysis:** An **origin myth** is a story about beginnings. What beginning does this decree help to explain?

_____

_____

5. **Reading Strategy:** When you **recognize cultural details**, you relate a literary selection to the culture that produced it. What do the qualities and conduct required of council lords tell you about Iroquois society and its values?

_____

_____

Listening and Speaking

A Dramatic Reading

The Iroquois Constitution describes how a new Iroquois lord should join the council. With two other students, plan a dramatic reading of this process.

1. Assign the roles

   • Who will play the role of Dekanawidah? This student will read all the main sections that have no quotation marks.

   _____

   • Who will play the role of a narrator? This student will read the sections that are indented and set off with diamonds.

   _____

   • Who will play the role of the speaker of the council? This student will read the last paragraph, which is in quotation marks.

   _____

2. Plan the reading.

   • What will you use as props, or items that you will hold during your dramatic reading?

   _____

   • Where will you sit, walk, or stand as you perform?

   _____

3. Rehearse your reading several times to learn your roles.

   • What changes do you need to make in your plan after your first rehearsal?

   _____

4. Present your reading to your class.
5. Answer your classmates' questions about the Iroquois Constitution or about your reading.

© Pearson Education, Inc.

from The Interesting Narrative of the Life of Olaudah Equiano

Olaudah Equiano

Summary

This excerpt, or section, from a slave narrative tells of the experiences of a young slave during the middle passage, or the trip across the ocean. Olaudah Equiano describes the horrors of the journey, telling of the sickening smells in the hold of the ship, where people are so crowded they can hardly turn around. He tells about the cruelty of the whites, who starve the captives and keep them in chains. When two captives jump overboard, preferring death to slavery, one is saved and then whipped badly for trying to escape. Equiano also tells of seeing flying fishes during the journey and of being shown how to use a quadrant, an instrument that determines the position of a ship. When they arrive in Bridgetown, the captives are put into small groups to be examined by people who plan to buy them.

Visual Summary

Main Idea

Filthy, crowded, cruel conditions on slave ships from Africa cause many slaves to die during the journey.

The smell of the ship is terrible.	The ship's crew is cruel.	Many slaves die.
perspiration	slaves are chained	some become sick from the filth and smells
no fresh air	crew refuses to share food	some jump into the sea
necessary tubs	slaves beaten for trying to escape	some suffocate from lack of fresh air

LITERARY ANALYSIS

Slave Narratives

In an autobiography, a writer tells the true story of his or her own life. A **slave narrative** is an autobiographical account of the life of a slave. Slave narratives are often written to show the horrors of slavery.

For example, Olaudah Equiano gives this description of the harsh conditions on the ship that brought him to Barbados:

> The shrieks of the women, and the groans of the dying, rendered the whole a scene of horror almost inconceivable.

As you read, look for other details that describe the horrors of the voyage.

READING STRATEGY

Summarizing

When your reading is challenging, it is often useful to **summarize** the main points. When you summarize, you use your own words to state briefly the main ideas and details of the text. A good summary is always much shorter than the original passage.

To summarize, make a diagram like the one shown, which summarizes Equiano's first paragraph. As you read, write notes like these to help you summarize Equiano's ideas.

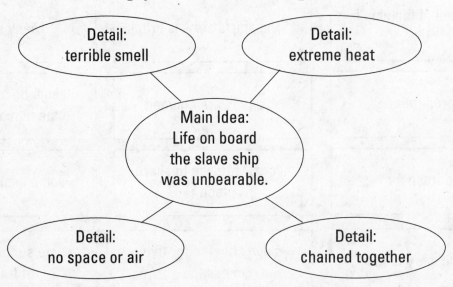

Summary: The heat, the foul air, the cramped quarters, and the chains all combined to make life on board the slave ship unbearable.

© Pearson Education, Inc.

from The Interesting Narrative of the Life of Olaudah Equiano

Olaudah Equiano

At last when the ship we were in, had got in all her cargo, they made ready with many fearful noises, and we were all put under deck, so that we could not see how they managed the vessel. But this disappointment was the least of my sorrow. The stench of the <u>hold</u> while we were on the coast was so intolerably <u>loathsome</u>, that it was dangerous to remain there for any time, and some of us had been permitted to stay on the deck for the fresh air; but now that the whole ship's cargo were confined together, it became absolutely <u>pestilential</u>. The closeness of the place, and the heat of the climate, added to the number in the ship, which was so crowded that each had scarcely room to turn himself, almost suffocated us. This produced <u>copious</u> perspirations, so that the air soon became unfit for respiration, from a variety of loathsome smells, and brought on a sickness among the slaves, of which many died—thus falling victims to the <u>improvident</u> <u>avarice</u>, as I may call it, of their purchasers. This wretched situation was again aggravated by the galling[1] of the chains, now become insupportable, and the filth of the necessary tubs, into which the children often fell, and were almost suffocated. The shrieks of the women, and the groans of the dying,

---

Vocabulary Development

loathsome (LOHTH suhm) *adj.* hateful

pestilential (pes ti LEN shuhl) *adj.* likely to cause disease

copious (KO pee uhs) *adj.* plentiful

improvident (im PRAH vuh duhnt) *adj.* shortsighted

avarice (AV uh ris) *n.* greed for riches

---

1. **galling** (GAWL ing) *n.* the creation of sores by rubbing or chafing.

◆ **English Language Development**

In modern English, a comma almost never divides the subject of a sentence from the main verb. What verb goes with the subject *ship* in the first sentence?

_____

_____

_____

◆ **Vocabulary and Pronunciation**

Many words in English have multiple meanings. The word *hold*, for example, can be a verb meaning "to have in one's hands." It can also be a noun meaning "the inside of a ship." What is the meaning of *hold* in the first paragraph?

_____

_____

_____

◆ **Literary Analysis**

Underline three details in this **slave narrative** that show the horrible conditions for the slaves on board ship.

◆ **Stop to Reflect**

Why would it have been in the interest of the slave traders to treat the slaves better?

_____

_____

_____

◆ **Reading Strategy**

Summarize the bracketed section in your own words.

_____

_____

_____

◆ **English Language Development**

The normal plural of *fish* in modern English is *fish*, not *fishes*. Using a dictionary, identify the plurals of the following nouns:

deer _____

tiger _____

wolf _____

sheep _____

◆ **Reading Check**

Underline the parts of the summary that show what some slaves do to escape the misery of the journey.

◆ **Read Fluently**

Read the bracketed passage aloud. Circle the two sights that attract Equiano's curiosity.

rendered the whole a scene of horror almost inconceivable.

◆　◆　◆

Equiano envied the fish of the sea for their freedom. During the voyage, he grew more fearful of the white slavers' cruelty.

◆　◆　◆

One day they had taken a number of fishes; and when they had killed and satisfied themselves with as many as they thought fit, to our astonishment who were on deck, rather than give any of them to us to eat, as we expected, they tossed the remaining fish into the sea again, although we begged and prayed for some as well as we could, but in vain.

◆　◆　◆

Some of the hungry slaves tried to get fish in secret. They were discovered and whipped. Then three desperate slaves jumped into the sea. The others were immediately put below deck. Two of the slaves drowned. The third was rescued and then beaten unmercifully.

◆　◆　◆

During our passage, I first saw flying fishes, which surprised me very much; they used frequently to fly across the ship, and many of them fell on the deck. I also now first saw the use of the quadrant;[2] I had often with astonishment seen the mariners make observations with it, and I could not think what it meant. They at last took notice of my surprise; and one of them, willing to increase it, as well as to gratify my curiosity, made me one day look through it. The clouds appeared to me to be land, which disappeared as they passed along. This heightened my wonder; and I was now more persuaded than ever, that I

---

2. **quadrant** (KWAH druhnt) *n.* an instrument used by navigators to determine a ship's position.

© Pearson Education, Inc.

was in another world, and that every thing about me was magic.

◆ ◆ ◆

The ship anchored off Bridgetown, the capital of the island of Barbados in the West Indies. Merchants and planters came on board to examine the slaves. The slaves on the ship were fearful, but some older slaves came from the land to reassure them. Finally, the slaves went ashore.

◆ ◆ ◆

We were underlined conducted immediately to the merchant's yard, where we were all pent up together, like so many sheep in a fold, without regard to sex or age. . . . We were not many days in the merchant's custody, before we were sold after their usual manner, which is this: On a signal given (as the beat of a drum), the buyers rush at once into the yard where the slaves are confined, and make choice of that parcel[3] they like best. . . .

◆ Stop to Reflect

In the last paragraph of this **slave narrative**, what is the effect of these details on the reader's emotions?

_____

_____

_____

_____

_____

_____

Vocabulary Development

conducted (kuhn DUHK tuhd) *v.* led

custody (KUHS tuh dee) *n.* keeping, possession

---

3. parcel (PAR suhl) *n.* group.

1. Why does Equiano blame the deaths of many slaves on the "improvident avarice" of the traders?

_____

2. What happens when the traders catch a number of fish?

_____

_____

3. What happens when the traders recover the slave who had jumped overboard?

_____

_____

4. **Reading Strategy:** When you **summarize** a passage, you use your own words to state briefly the main idea and the key details. Summarize the passage about the flying fish and the quadrant.

_____

_____

5. What do you think the details about the flying fish and the quadrant show about the young Equiano's personality?

_____

_____

6. **Literary Analysis:** The purpose of a **slave narrative** is often to show the horrors of bondage. What details in the description of life in the merchant's yard in Bridgetown contribute to this purpose?

_____

_____

 © Pearson Education, Inc.

Writing

A Museum Placard

Museum exhibits usually include **placards**, or signs that identify the items on display. Sometimes a large placard is placed at the beginning of an exhibit. The purpose of this placard is to introduce visitors to the exhibit and to educate them about it.

Recently, some museums have been presenting exhibits to show the historical facts of the slave trade. Write the introductory information for a placard that visitors will read at the beginning of an exhibit on the slave trade. On your placard, explain the sequence of events that happened to slaves like Olaudah Equiano.

Follow these guidelines to write your placard:

• Use the text of Equiano's narrative to gather facts. Also use library sources, such as encyclopedias and history books.

1. How were the slaves captured?

_____

2. What were the events during the voyage?

_____

3. What events happened after the slave ships landed?

_____

• Plan a graphic display for your placard like the one shown below. This graphic display organizes key events in time order.

Model: Organizing Events in Time Order		
How were the slaves captured?	What were the events during the voyage?	What events happened after the slave ships landed?

• Check that your placard gives information about the stages of the slave trade. Revise any confusing shifts in time order.
• Use a large piece of construction paper to create your placard. Display it on the bulletin board in your classroom.

from The General History of Virginia
John Smith

Summary

This excerpt, or section, from *The General History of Virginia* tells of the hardships of the Jamestown colony. Fifty colonists die between May and September. When Captain John Smith goes on an expedition, he and his men are attacked by Indians. Smith's life is spared because he gives the Indians his compass and because Pocahontas, Chief Powhatan's daughter, saves him. After six weeks as a captive, Smith is allowed to return to Jamestown. Pocahontas brings the settlers food, saving their lives.

Sequential Organizer

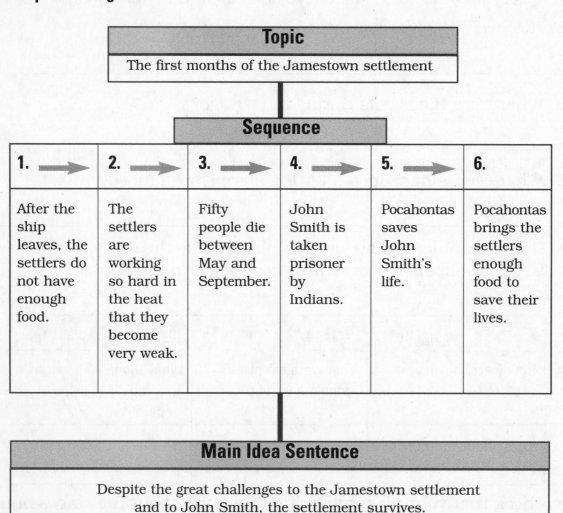

Topic
The first months of the Jamestown settlement

Sequence					
1.	2.	3.	4.	5.	6.
After the ship leaves, the settlers do not have enough food.	The settlers are working so hard in the heat that they become very weak.	Fifty people die between May and September.	John Smith is taken prisoner by Indians.	Pocahontas saves John Smith's life.	Pocahontas brings the settlers enough food to save their lives.

Main Idea Sentence
Despite the great challenges to the Jamestown settlement and to John Smith, the settlement survives.

© **Pearson Education**, Inc.

LITERARY ANALYSIS

Narrative Accounts

A **narrative account** tells the story of real-life events. Some historical narratives, including *The General History of Virginia*, are firsthand accounts, also called primary sources. John Smith actually lived through the events that he describes. For example, Smith tells here about his responsibilities in the new colony:

> The new President and Martin, being little beloved, of weak judgment in dangers, and less industry in peace, committed the managing of all things abroad to Captain Smith . . .

Other historical narratives are written by people who did not experience the events. The writers of these accounts depend on research, rather than on firsthand observation. These narratives are called secondary sources.

Firsthand accounts, or primary sources, are valuable for historians because the writers are close to the story. On the other hand, because of the writer's personal involvement, firsthand accounts are not always objective. As you read, look for factual information that Smith saw or heard firsthand. Also think about whether the information is objective.

READING STRATEGY

Breaking Down Sentences

You can increase your understanding of a text by **breaking down sentences**. Consider one part of a sentence at a time. Look at a long sentence, and separate its most important parts from the difficult language until you get to the main idea.

The most important parts of any sentence are the *who* and the *did what*. The *who* is the subject. The *did what* is the main verb.

As you read, use the diagram below to help you figure out the meaning of long, complicated sentences.

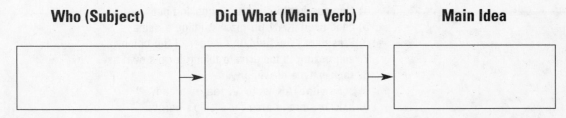

Who (Subject)	Did What (Main Verb)	Main Idea

© Pearson Education, Inc.

from The General History of Virginia
John Smith

What Happened Till the First Supply

Being thus left to our fortunes, it fortuned[1] that within ten days, scarce ten amongst us could either go[2] or well stand, such extreme weakness and sickness oppressed us. And thereat none need marvel if they consider the cause and reason, which was this: While the ships stayed, our allowance was somewhat bettered by a daily proportion of biscuit which the sailors would <u>pilfer</u> to sell, give, or exchange with us for money, sassafras,[3] or furs. But when they departed, there remained neither tavern, beer house, nor place of relief but the common kettle.[4] Had we been as free from all sins as <u>gluttony</u> and drunkenness we might have been canonized[5] for saints, but our President[6] would never have been admitted for engrossing to his private,[7] oatmeal, sack,[8] oil, aqua vitae,[9] beef, eggs, or what not but the kettle; that indeed he allowed equally to be distributed, and that was half a pint of wheat and as much barley boiled with water for a man a day, and this, having fried some twenty-six weeks in the ship's hold,[10] contained as many worms as grains so that we

Read Fluently

Read the bracketed passage aloud. How do things change after the ships leave?

_____

_____

_____

English Language Development

In the underlined clause, the word *if* has been omitted. Rewrite that part of the sentence using the word *if*.

_____

_____

_____

Vocabulary Development

pilfer (PIL fer) *v.* steal

gluttony (GLUT un nee) *n.* habit of eating too much

---

1. **fortuned** *v.* happened.
2. **go** *v.* be active.
3. **sassafras** (SAS uh fras) *n.* a tree, the root of which was valued for its use as medicine.
4. **common kettle** communal cooking pot.
5. **canonized** (KAN uh nizd) *v.* made a saint.
6. **President Wingfield,** the leader of the colony.
7. **engrossing to his private** taking for his own use.
8. **sack** *n.* type of white wine.
9. **aqua vitae** (AK wuh VI tee) *n.* brandy.
10. **hold** *n.* storage area for a ship's cargo.

 © Pearson Education, Inc.

might truly call it rather so much bran than corn; our drink was water, our lodgings castles in the air.

◆ ◆ ◆

That summer fifty colonists die, and another President is elected. Suddenly the fortunes of the settlers change. The Indians bring them food. Smith blames the hard times on the colonists' ignorance. They thought the sea journey would take two months and it took five. So supplies run short.

◆ ◆ ◆

<u>Such actions have ever since the world's beginning been subject to such accidents, and everything of worth is found full of difficulties, but nothing so difficult as to establish a commonwealth so far remote from men and means and where men's minds are so untoward[11] as neither do well themselves nor suffer others. But to proceed.</u>

The new President and Martin, being little beloved, of weak judgment in dangers, and less industry in peace, committed the managing of all things abroad[12] to Captain Smith, who, by his own example, good words, and fair promises, set some to mow, others to bind thatch, some to build houses, others to thatch them, himself always bearing the greatest task for his own share, so that in short time he provided most of them lodgings, neglecting any for himself. . . .

◆ ◆ ◆

Leading an expedition on the Chickahominy River, Smith and his men are attacked by Indians. Smith is held prisoner for six or seven weeks. Several times he is on the point of being killed. However, he gains the favor of the Indian leader, who finally brings him to Powhatan.

◆ ◆ ◆

---

11. **untoward** *adj.* stubborn.
12. **abroad** *adv.* outside the perimeter fence.

© Pearson Education, Inc.

from The General History of Virginia **21**

◆ **Reading Check**

Why is the corn spoiled?

_____

_____

_____

◆ **English Language Development**

"Castles in the air" is a phrase that has become a proverb in English, meaning "imaginary schemes." Give an example of a proverb or traditional saying in your native language.

_____

_____

_____

◆ **Reading Strategy**

Break down the underlined **long sentence**. Circle the part of the sentence that states the main idea.

◆ **Literary Analysis**

Circle two phrases in this part of Smith's **narrative account** that might be examples of reporting that is not objective.

_____

_____

_____

_____

_____

Smith uses a number of archaic, or old-fashioned, words that are no longer current in English, such as *whereat*. Use the context to determine the meaning of this word and write the meaning below.

_____

_____

_____

Why do you think Powhatan does not kill Smith?

_____

_____

_____

At last they brought him to Werowocomoco, where was Powhatan, their Emperor. Here more than two hundred of those grim courtiers stood wondering at him, as he had been a monster, till Powhatan and his train had put themselves in their greatest braveries.[13] Before a fire upon a seat like a bedstead, he sat covered with a great robe made of raccoon skins and all the tails hanging by. On either hand did sit a young wench[14] of sixteen or eighteen years and along on each side the house, two rows of men and behind them as many women, with all their heads and shoulders painted red, many of their heads bedecked[15] with the white down of birds, and a great chain of white beads about their necks.

At his entrance before the King, all the people gave a great shout. The queen of Appomattoc was appointed to bring him water to wash his hands, and another brought him a bunch of feathers, instead of a towel, to dry them; having feasted him after their best barbarous manner they could, a long consultation was held, but the conclusion was, two great stones were brought before Powhatan: then as many as could, laid hands on him, dragged him to them, and thereon laid his head and being ready with their clubs to beat out his brains, Pocahontas, the King's dearest daughter, when no <u>entreaty</u> could prevail, got his head in her arms and laid her own upon his to save him from death; <u>whereat</u> the Emperor was contented he should live to make him hatchets, and her bells, beads, and copper, for they thought him as well of all occupations as themselves.[16]

◆   ◆   ◆

Vocabulary Development

entreaty (en TREE tee) *n.* plea or prayer

---

13. **braveries** (BRAY vuh reez) *n.* fine dress.
14. **wench** *n.* young woman.
15. **bedecked** (bee DEKT) *v.* decorated.
16. **as well . . . themselves** capable of making them just as well as they could themselves.

© Pearson Education, Inc.

Powhatan and Smith become friends. The Indian king offers to sell the colonists land in exchange for guns and a grindstone. Smith returns to Jamestown and sends cannons and a millstone back to Powhatan. When some of the colonists try to turn back to England, Smith prevents them by force. He is also able to defeat a plot against him by the President and some other settlers.

◆ ◆ ◆

Now every once in four or five days, Pocahontas with her attendants brought him so much provision that saved many of their lives, that else for all this had starved with hunger.

His <u>relation</u> of the plenty he had seen, especially at Werowocomoco, and of the state and bounty of Powhatan (which till that time was unknown), so revived their dead spirits (especially the love of Pocahontas) as all men's fear was abandoned.

Thus you may see what difficulties still crossed any good endeavor; and the good success of the business being thus oft brought to the very period of destruction; yet you see by what strange means God hath still delivered it.

◆ **Vocabulary and Pronunciation**

In English, the word *relation* can mean "a person in the same family" or "an account or a telling." Which meaning of the word is used in the bracketed paragraph?

_____

_____

_____

◆ **Reading Check**

Underline two parts of the bracketed passage that explain why the colonists were no longer afraid.

◆ **Read Fluently**

Read the last paragraph aloud. Who or what does Smith say is responsible for the "good success of the business"?

_____

_____

_____

1. According to Smith, why were the colonists so weak and sickly?

_____

_____

2. When Powhatan was about to execute Smith, who saved him?

_____

_____

3. What agreement did Powhatan reach with Smith?

_____

_____

4. **Literary Analysis:** In a firsthand **narrative account**, the writer is personally involved in events. Give one example of the way Smith praises his own good qualities.

_____

_____

5. **Reading Strategy:** You can often find the main idea by **breaking down** a long, difficult sentence. Look back at the selection and choose two sentences that you found challenging. Write them in the chart. Locate the *who* and the *did what* in each sentence. Then, write the meaning of the sentences as you understand them.

Sentence 1	Sentence 2

Who (Subject)	Did What (Main Verb)	Who (Subject)	Did What (Main Verb)

Main Idea	Main Idea

 © Pearson Education, Inc.

Listening and Speaking

Persuasive Speech

In a **persuasive speech**, you try to convince your listeners to think or behave a certain way. Good persuasion uses many different tools. For example, a speaker may support a position with **logical appeals**:

Logical Appeals

/ | \

Facts   Examples   Reasons

Persuasive speakers also use **emotional appeals**. A speaker may appeal to the feelings of the audience, such as pride or fear. Certain words, like *love, victory, country,* or *glory*, are charged with strong emotional associations.

Put yourself in the position of Captain John Smith. As Smith, deliver a persuasive speech to the colonists in favor of remaining in Virginia and making an alliance with Powhatan. As you plan your speech, answer these questions:

- What are the hardships that the colonists have overcome so far?

_____

- In what ways has Powhatan already shown friendship?

_____

- What provisions and land does the Indian leader have under his control?

_____

- How is staying in Virginia in the best interest of the settlers themselves?

_____

- What are the likely needs of the colonists in the future?

_____

Now organize and write your speech in a way that makes sense, using both logical and emotional appeals. Then present your speech to the class and ask for their feedback.

from Sinners in the Hands of an Angry God
Jonathan Edwards

Summary

This excerpt, or section, from Edwards's sermon describes God's rising anger against the sinners in the congregation. These sinners, Edwards says, are like spiders that their angry God holds over hell. Edwards tells his listeners that they can save their souls from everlasting suffering only if they beg God for forgiveness now and experience the saving grace of conversion, which will give them a place among the elect, or those chosen by God.

Visual Summary

Purpose	Details to Achieve This Purpose
To motivate listeners to convert and save their souls	• Only the power of God holds you up. • Black clouds of God's anger hang over your heads. • Only God's pleasure keeps you from being destroyed forever. • Sinners are in great danger. • You have nothing that can persuade God to spare you. • God will not pity you. • Today the door of mercy is open.

© Pearson Education, Inc.

LITERARY ANALYSIS

Sermon

A **sermon** is usually a speech given by a preacher in a house of worship. Sermons are normally part of a religious service.

A sermon is an example of persuasion. Persuasion tries to convince listeners or readers to adopt a particular opinion or to act in a certain way. As you read, keep in mind these features of an effective sermon:

- It touches the emotions of listeners.
- It inspires listeners to take action.
- It addresses the needs and concerns of the audience.
- It uses colorful and rhythmic language.

READING STRATEGY

Using Context Clues

You can often understand the meaning of unfamiliar words by **using context clues**. A word's context is its surrounding words, phrases, and sentences. For example, suppose you want to find the meaning of the word *abominable* in this passage from Jonathan Edwards's sermon:

> You are ten thousand times more *abominable* in his [God's] eyes than the most hateful venomous serpent is in ours. . . .

The context clue here is in the form of a comparison. Edwards says that the way a sinner looks in God's eyes is like the way a hateful snake looks in our eyes. From this clue, you can guess that *abominable* must be close in meaning to horrible or *disgusting*.

Use this chart to define other difficult words by using context clues.

Word	Context Clues	Meaning

© Pearson Education, Inc.

◆ **Literary Analysis**

Underline two words in the **sermon's** title that suggest the emotional focus of Edwards's message.

◆ **Reading Strategy**

Circle the **context clues** that help you understand the meaning of *gaping*. What does *gaping* mean?

_____

_____

_____

◆ **English Language Development**

Adjectives and adverbs in English have three forms: positive (*pretty, beautiful*), comparative (*prettier, more beautiful*), and superlative (*prettiest, most beautiful*). Adjectives and adverbs form the comparative by adding *-er* to the end of the word (prettier) or *more* at the beginning of the word (more beautiful). Comparative adjectives and adverbs in the bracketed section include *longer* and *stronger*. What is the superlative form of the adjectives *long* and *strong*?

_____

from Sinners in the Hands of an Angry God
Jonathan Edwards

The author, Jonathan Edwards, directs his sermon toward those with whom God is not pleased. He talks about a world of misery for them.

◆　◆　◆

There is the dreadful pit of the glowing flames of the <u>wrath</u> of God; there is Hell's wide <u>gaping</u> mouth open; and you have nothing to <u>stand</u> upon, nor anything to take hold of; there is nothing between you and Hell but the air; it is only the power and mere pleasure of God that holds you up.

◆　◆　◆

Sinners may think they are kept out of Hell by their own life and strength, but they are wrong. Sinners are like heavy weights of lead. If God chose to let them go, they would sink straight to Hell. God's anger is like a terrible storm, held back for the moment.

God's wrath is like steam that is dammed. The longer it is dammed, the stronger the waters will be once the dam is opened.

◆　◆　◆

It is true, that judgment against your evil works has not been executed hitherto;[1] the Hoods of God's vengeance have been withheld; but your guilt in the meantime is constantly increasing, and you are every day treasuring up more wrath; the waters are constantly rising, and <u>waxing</u> more and more mighty; and

---

Vocabulary Development

wrath (RATH) *n.* great anger
waxing (WAKS ing) *v.* increasing

---

1. **hitherto** (hi thuhr TOO) *adv.* up to now.

© Pearson Education, Inc.

there is nothing but the mere pleasure of God, that holds the waters back, that are unwilling to be stopped, and press hard to go forward.

◆　◆　◆

God's hand is holding the gate that controls the dam. If he should decide to move his hand, the flood of anger would be inconceivable. No human strength, or even the strength of the devil, could stop it.

◆　◆　◆

The bow of God's wrath is bent, and the arrow made ready on the string, and justice bends the arrow at your heart, and strains the bow, and it is nothing but the mere pleasure of God, and that of an angry God, without any promise or obligation at all, that keeps the arrow one moment from being made drunk with your blood.

◆　◆　◆

Everyone who does not repent risks being destroyed. Sinners may not believe that they are in danger now. There will come a time, though, when they will be convinced.

◆　◆　◆

The God that holds you over the pit of Hell, much as one holds a spider, or some loathsome insect over the fire, abhors you, and is dreadfully provoked: his wrath towards you burns like fire; he looks upon you as worthy of nothing else, but to be cast into the fire; he is

© Pearson Education, Inc.

from Sinners in the Hands of an Angry God **29**

◆ **Vocabulary and Pronunciation**

The word *inconceivable* contains the prefix *in-* meaning "not," and also the suffix *-able*, meaning "capable of." These word parts help you to determine the meaning: "not able to be imagined or conceived." What would the word *inseparable* mean?

_____

_____

_____

◆ **Stop to Reflect**

To what does Edwards compare the wrath of God?

_____

_____

_____

◆ **Read Fluently**

Read the bracketed paragraph aloud. Then fill in the blanks below.

1. The wrath of God is like a

_____

that is bent.

2. Justice directs the

_____

to the heart of the sinner.

In this **sermon**, how does Edwards see the relationship between God and sinners?

_____

_____

_____

of purer eyes than to bear to have you in his sight; you are ten thousand times more <u>abominable</u> in his eyes, than the most hateful <u>venomous</u> serpent is in ours. . . .

◆ ◆ ◆

Edwards warns sinners that they are in great danger. God is as angry with them as he is with those already in Hell.

◆ ◆ ◆

You hang by a slender thread, with the flames of divine wrath flashing about it, and ready every moment to singe it, and burn it <u>asunder</u>; and you have no interest in any mediator, and nothing to lay hold of to save yourself, nothing to keep off the flames of wrath, nothing of your own, nothing that you ever have done, nothing that you can do, to <u>induce</u> God to spare you one moment. . . .

◆ ◆ ◆

◆ **Stop to Reflect**

Circle the word that Edwards keeps repeating in the bracketed passage. Why do you think he emphasizes this word?

_____

_____

Edwards says that God will have no mercy on sinners who do not repent. However, the punishments of sinners will be just. If sinners repent now, God will show them mercy. If they refuse to repent, they will be tormented forever. Sinners who do not repent are in daily and hourly danger. Think of those who are now suffering endless misery in Hell. They have no more chances to obtain salvation. But those who are still alive may still be saved.

Vocabulary Development

abominable (uh BAHM uh nuh buhl) *adj.* hateful, disgusting
venomous (VEN uh muhs) *adj.* poisonous
asunder (a SUN duhr) *adv.* apart
induce (in DOOS) *v.* persuade

© Pearson Education, Inc.

Sinners now have a wonderful opportunity to gain forgiveness. They can save their souls from everlasting suffering. Many other sinners are flocking to him and entering his kingdom. They are coming from everywhere. These sinners had been miserable, but now God has washed their sins away and they are rejoicing. It would be awful to be left behind and not join in this joyful celebration. Edwards says all sinners in his <u>congregation</u> should escape God's wrath and experience the saving grace of conversion.

◆ ◆ ◆

"Haste and escape for your lives, look not behind you, escape to the mountain, lest you be consumed."[2]

Reading Strategy

Circle the **context clues** that help you determine this meaning of *flocking*. What does *flocking* mean?

_____

_____

_____

English Language Development

Circle the punctuation marks on this page that show a quotation. What book is the quotation from?

_____

_____

_____

Literary Analysis

In the bracketed summary of the passage of this persuasive **sermon**, what does Edwards want the congregation to do?

_____

_____

_____

Reading Check

Underline the quotation from the Bible in the last paragraph. Why is the Biblical quotation appropriate for Edwards's sermon?

_____

_____

_____

Vocabulary Development

congregation (kahn gruh GAY shuhn) *n.* members of a place of worship

---

2. **"Haste . . . consumed"** from Genesis 19:17, the angels' warning to Lot, the only virtuous man in Sodom, to flee the city before they destroy it.

1. According to the first paragraph, what keeps sinners from falling into Hell?

_____

_____

2. On the chart below, identify two images from nature that Edwards uses to describe the anger of God.

	Image 1	Image 2
God's anger is like:	_____	_____

3. Toward the end of the sermon, what does Edwards say that sinners can obtain, and how can they obtain it?

_____

_____

4. **Literary Analysis:** In a **sermon**, the speaker wants to persuade listeners to adopt a definite point of view. What emotions in his listeners does Edwards hope to touch in this sermon?

_____

_____

5. **Reading Strategy:** You can often guess the meaning of difficult words by **using context clues**, or clues from nearby words, phrases, and sentences. Use context clues to define the italicized words:

(a) "The God that holds you over the pit of Hell, much as one holds a spider, or some loathsome insect over the fire, *abhors* you, and is dreadfully provoked. . . ."

Definition of *abhor*: _____

(b) "To see so many others feasting, while you are *pining* and perishing!"

Definition of *pining*: _____

© Pearson Education, Inc.

Writing

Evaluation of Persuasion

When you **evaluate** something, you use standards to judge its worth or effectiveness. In his sermon, Jonathan Edwards uses persuasion to convey a definite point of view. Write an **evaluation of persuasion** to judge how effective the sermon is. As you plan your evaluation, consider the following questions.

- What is Edwards's *purpose* in the sermon?

  _____

- Who is the *audience* for the sermon, and what is the occasion?

  _____

- What powerful *images* does Edwards use?

  _____

- What *emotions* in the audience does the sermon appeal to?

  _____

1. Begin your evaluation with a general statement about the sermon's effectiveness.

   _____

   _____

2. Identify specific examples.
   - Quote lines from the text that show Edwards appealing to fear and guilt.

     _____

   - Identify the specific images from nature that Edwards uses.

     _____

3. At the end of your evaluation, summarize or restate your main idea.

   _____

   _____

4. Now read over your essay as if you were seeing it for the first time. Cut out any information that is not related to the main idea.
5. Share your essay with your classmates. Find out if they agree with your evaluation.

from The Autobiography

Benjamin Franklin

Summary

In this excerpt, or section, from his autobiography, Franklin describes his plan for achieving moral perfection by listing thirteen virtues. He plans to work on one virtue at a time, recording his progress in a notebook. He makes seven columns on a page, one for each day of the week. He makes thirteen rows on the page, one for each virtue. Each day, he marks with a black spot every fault he commits. For each week, he works on one virtue and tries to keep that virtue's row free of black marks. He finds his plan helpful and instructive but not completely successful.

Visual Summary

Goal: Moral perfection		
Methods		
List of virtues	**Notebook**	**Daily schedule**
• temperance	• one page for each virtue	• Question: What good shall I do this day?
• silence	• seven columns on each page, one for each day of the week	• 5:00 A.M.–7:00 A.M.: Rise, wash, pray, plan the day, review the virtues, and eat breakfast
• order	• columns drawn in red	• 9:00 A.M.: Begin work
• resolution	• each column marked with a letter for the day	• NOON: Read, review accounts, and dine
• frugality	• thirteen rows, one for each virtue	• 3:00 P.M.: Continue work
• industry	• rows drawn in red	• Question: What good have I done today?
• sincerity	• each row marked with the first letter of a virtue	• 6:00 P.M.: Put things in their places
• justice	• black mark in proper row and column for each fault	• 8:00 P.M.: Supper, music or diversion, examine the day
• moderation	• one week's attention to one virtue at a time	• 1:00 A.M.: Sleep
• cleanliness		
• tranquillity		
• chastity		
• humility		

Result: "...though I never arrived at the perfection I had been so ambitious of obtaining, but fell far short of it, yet I was, by the endeavor, a better and happier man ..."

 © Pearson Education, Inc.

LITERARY ANALYSIS

Autobiography

What is an **autobiography**?

- An **autobiography** is the story of a person's life.
- It is told by the person.
- The pronoun *I* is used throughout.
- An autobiography can give personal views of history.

In this section of his *Autobiography,* Franklin tells about his system for forming good habits. He finds that it is not as easy as he thought. But he keeps trying. He never becomes perfect, but he finds that he is happy just to try. In the following passage, Franklin explains how difficult the task is.

> But I soon found I had undertaken a task of more difficulty than I had imagined. While my care was employed in guarding against one fault, I was often surprised by another.

READING STRATEGY

Drawing Conclusions

When you read an autobiography, look beyond just what the person is saying. Ask yourself, "What does this tell us about the person?" Then you can **draw conclusions** about what kind of person the writer is. On the chart below, list three statements that Franklin makes about himself. Then explain what each statement tells you about Franklin. When you finish reading, use this information to draw conclusions about Franklin's character.

Statement by Franklin	What It Tells About Him
EX: "I therefore contrived the following method."	He likes to use methods to get things done.

© Pearson Education, Inc.

◆ **Stop to Reflect**

Franklin makes a list to organize his plan. What does this show about his character?

_____

_____

_____

◆ **English Language Development**

Sometimes the *ee* sound in English is spelled *ie* or *ei*. How do you know when to use each spelling? There is a rule in English that goes like this: *i* before *e* except after *c*, or when sounded as *a* as in *neighbor* and *weigh*. Notice that in *deceit*, the *e* comes first. That's because a *c* is before the letters. Write *ei* or *ie* in each of the blanks in these words. Follow the rule to spell the words correctly.

1. rec_____pt

2. bel_____ve

3. _____ghteen

4. gr_____ve

5. ch___f

6. conc_____t

◆ **Reading Check**

What is Franklin's attitude about wasting time? Circle the answer.

from The Autobiography
Benjamin Franklin

Franklin decides to take up a difficult project. He will try to live a perfect life. He knows, or thinks he knows, what is right and wrong. He doesn't see why he cannot always do the one and avoid the other.

◆　◆　◆

But I soon found I had undertaken a task of more difficulty than I had imagined. While my care was employed in guarding against one fault, I was often surprised by another. . . . I therefore contrived the following method.

◆　◆　◆

Franklin has read other people's lists of virtues in the past. These lists don't seem quite right to him. He writes his own list of thirteen virtues. He adds short notes. The notes explain what the virtue means to him. Here is his list.

◆　◆　◆

1. TEMPERANCE Eat not to dullness; drink not to elevation.

2. SILENCE Speak not but what may benefit others or yourself; avoid trifling conversation.

3. ORDER Let all your things have their places; let each part of your business have its time.

4. RESOLUTION Resolve to perform what you ought; perform without fail what you resolve.

5. FRUGALITY Make no expense but to do good to others or yourself; i.e., waste nothing.

6. INDUSTRY Lose no time; be always employed in something useful; cut off all unnecessary actions.

7. SINCERITY Use no hurtful <u>deceit</u>; think innocently and justly, and, if you speak, speak accordingly.

© Pearson Education, Inc.

8. JUSTICE Wrong none by doing injuries, or omitting the benefits that are your duty.

9. MODERATION Avoid extremes; forebear resenting injuries so much as you think they deserve.

10. CLEANLINESS Tolerate no uncleanliness in body, clothes, or habitation.

11. <u>TRANQUILLITY Be not disturbed at trifles, or at accidents common or unavoidable.</u>

12. CHASTITY

13. HUMILITY Imitate Jesus and Socrates.

◆ ◆ ◆

Franklin's goal is to get into the habit of all these virtues. He tries one at a time, then goes on to the next. He thinks that some virtues might make other ones easier. That is why he lists *Temperance* first. Temperance helps you keep a clear head. A clear head helps you guard against bad habits. With the habit of temperance, *Silence* would be easier.

He also wants to gain knowledge. He knows that knowledge is obtained more by listening than by speaking. He gives *Silence* the second place. This virtue and the next, *Order,* would give him more time for his studies. *Resolution* is next. It will help Franklin stick to his plan. *Frugality* and *Industry* will help him pay all his debts. They will also help him add to his wealth. Then it will be easier to practice *Sincerity* and *Justice,* and so on. He decides to check his progress every day.

◆ ◆ ◆

I made a little book, in which I <u>allotted</u> a page for each of the virtues. I ruled each page with red ink, so as to have seven columns,

Vocabulary Development

allotted (uh LOT ted) *v.* assigned, gave a part

from The Autobiography **37**

◆ **Vocabulary and Pronunciation**

A suffix is a word part added to the end of a word. It changes the part of speech of the word. The word *frugal* is used to describe a person who does not waste things. When you add the suffix *-ity*, it means "the quality of not being wasteful." The suffix *-ity* means "quality, state, or condition of." Find two other words in Franklin's list that end in *-ity*. Write them here:

1. _____

2. _____

◆ **Reading Strategy**

What might Franklin say to someone who was very upset about a minor traffic accident? **Draw conclusions** from the underlined text.

_____

_____

◆ **Reading Strategy**

What **conclusion** can you **draw** from the bracketed text about the values of the time? Complete this sentence with your answer.

In Franklin's day, people thought virtues such as _____ and _____ were good to have.

◆ **Reading Strategy**

How does Franklin think we add to our knowledge? Circle the answer.

◆ Reading Check

Use separate paper to show what a page in Franklin's book would look like.

◆ Background

Benjamin Franklin's "business in Europe" was to represent the United States there. He spent time in both England and France as a diplomat. In fact, while he was in France, he helped arrange the terms to end the Revolutionary War between England and the United States.

◆ Literary Analysis

In this **autobiography,** Franklin mentions that he does other things besides keep a list of virtues. Underline the sentence in the bracketed passage that tells you what else Franklin is doing.

one for each day of the week, marking each column with a letter for the day. I crossed these columns with thirteen red lines, marking the beginning of each line with the first letter of one of the virtues, on which line and in its proper column I might mark, by a little black spot, every fault I found upon examination to have been committed respecting that virtue upon that day.

◆ ◆ ◆

He decides to spend a week on each virtue. In the first week, he practices Temperance. His goal the first week is to keep his first line, marked T, clear of spots. The next week, he might try the next virtue. He will try to keep both lines clear of spots. He can go through the whole list in thirteen weeks, and he repeats this process four times a year.

Franklin follows his plan for some time. One thing surprises him. He has more faults than he had imagined. But he is glad to see them become less and less. After a while, he goes through only one course in a year. Later, he goes through one in several years. At last, he stops doing it. He is too busy with trips and business in Europe. But he always carries his little book with him.

The virtue of Order gives him the most trouble. He just isn't used to putting papers and things in their places. He has a very good memory. So he can always remember where he has left something.

◆ ◆ ◆

This article, therefore, cost me so much painful attention, and my faults in it <u>vexed</u> me so much, and I made so little progress in

---

Vocabulary Development

vexed (VEKST) *v.* annoyed, bothered

© Pearson Education, Inc.

amendment, and had such frequent relapses, that I was almost ready to give up the attempt, and content myself with a faulty character in that respect, like the man who, in buying an ax of a smith,[1] my neighbor, desired to have the whole of its surface as bright as the edge. The smith consented to grind it bright for him if he would turn the wheel; he turned, while the smith pressed the broad face of the ax hard and heavily on the stone, which made the turning of it very fatiguing. The man came every now and then from the wheel to see how the work went on, and at length would take his ax as it was, without farther grinding. "No," said the smith, "turn on, turn on; we shall have it bright by and by; as yet, it is only speckled." "Yes," says the man, *"but I think I like a speckled ax best."*

◆ ◆ ◆

Franklin believes that many people are like this man. Some people find it too difficult to form good habits. They just give up the struggle. They decide that "a speckled ax is best." Franklin is the same way about the virtue of Order. He thinks that other people might envy or hate him if he becomes perfect. He thinks that a good man should keep a few faults. This way, he can keep his friends.

◆ ◆ ◆

In truth, I found myself incorrigible with respect to Order; and now I am grown old, and

◆ Reading Strategy

Here, Franklin tells a story about a man with an ax. What **conclusion** can you **draw** from this story about Franklin's sense of humor?

_____

_____

_____

◆ Reading Check

Why does Franklin think a good man should keep a few faults?

_____

_____

_____

_____

Vocabulary Development

amendment (uh MEND ment) *n.* improvement, correction
relapses (REE lap ses) *n.* slips back to a former state
fatiguing (fuh TEEG ing) *adj.* tiring
speckled (SPEK uhld) *adj.* covered with small spots
incorrigible (in KOR ij uh buhl) *adj.* not able to be corrected

---

1. **smith** (SMITH) *n.* a person who works in metals.

© Pearson Education, Inc.

◆ **Literary Analysis**

An **autobiography** uses first-person pronouns like *I, me, my, we, us, mine, our,* and *ours.* Underline the words in the bracketed section that show that Franklin is writing an autobiography.

◆ **Stop to Reflect**

Franklin tells us that he fell short of his goals. Does his attitude about this seem normal to you? Explain.

_____

_____

_____

_____

◆ **Read Fluently**

Read aloud the underlined section. Then, circle the qualities that other people liked in Franklin.

my memory bad, I feel very sensibly the want of it. But, on the whole, though I never arrived at the perfection I had been so ambitious of obtaining, but fell far short of it, yet I was, by the endeavor, a better and a happier man than I otherwise should have been if I had not attempted it.

◆ ◆ ◆

Franklin wants his descendants to know about their ancestor. His list of virtues is important to him. In fact, he says he owes the constant happiness in his life to it. He is now seventy-nine years old. He owes his good health to *Temperance*. He owes his fortune to *Industry* and *Frugality*. To *Sincerity* and *Justice*, he owes the confidence his country has in him.

◆ ◆ ◆

. . . and to the joint influence of the whole mass of the virtues, even in the imperfect state he was able to acquire them, [their ancestor ascribes] all that evenness of temper, and that cheerfulness in conversation, which makes his company still sought for, and agreeable even to his younger acquaintance. I hope, therefore, that some of my descendants may follow the example and reap the benefit.

Vocabulary Development

endeavor (en DEV er) *n.* try, attempt

descendants (dee SEN dents) *n.* people in one's family who come after

ancestor (AN ses ter) *n.* a person in one's family who came before

© Pearson Education, Inc.

1. What difficult project does Franklin start?

_____

2. Franklin makes a list of thirteen items. Each item on the list has two parts. What are those parts?

1. _____ 2. _____

3. Franklin's list has a certain order. He gives the reasons behind that order. On the organizer below, explain the reason for the order of the items.

Temperance is first on the list	because	
Silence is second on the list	because	
Order is third on the list	because	
Resolution is fourth on the list	because	

4. **Reading Strategy:** Franklin tells us that he made a little book. It helped him track his progress with the virtues. What **conclusion** can you **draw** about Franklin's personality, based on this fact?

_____

_____

5. **Literary Analysis:** Put a check in front of each of the two sentences that indicate this work is an **autobiography**.

_____ Franklin is telling the story of his own life.

_____ Franklin wrote this book when he was seventy-nine.

_____ Franklin talks about himself, using the pronoun *I*.

_____ Many people read this book.

_____ The book has lists in it.

Writing

Autobiographical Account

Write a paragraph about something that has happened in your own life. It might involve your activities, friends, family, or school. Choose an experience that made an impression on you. Tell why the experience was important to you.

1. **Prewriting** Make a list of details about the experience.

   - What happened? _____

   - How did you feel? _____

   - What did you learn? _____

2. **Drafting** Write a draft of your paragraph.

   - As you write, add details that will help your reader understand what happened.

   - Talk about sights, sounds, smells, or anything else that will make your writing more interesting.

   _____

   _____

   _____

   _____

   _____

   _____

3. **Revising** Read your paragraph out loud.

   - Does it sound smooth? If not, maybe you need to add transition words like *first, next, then, because, so,* and *therefore.*

4. **Publishing and Presenting** Write your final paragraph on a separate sheet of paper. Share it with your classmates.

  © Pearson Education, Inc.

from The Crisis, Number 1

Thomas Paine

Summary

In his essay, Paine encourages the American colonists to fight against the British. He tells his readers that God supports the American cause. Paine says that a good father will fight so that his child may live in peace, and he appeals to all Americans in all states to unite.

Visual Summary

Proposition	Support
All American colonists should fight against the British.	Britain has declared her right to tax Americans in all cases, and that is tyranny. Americans have tried to avoid war in every way. God will not help the British against the Americans because God does not support Britain's tyranny. A separation from Britain must occur at some point, and it is better to have war now so that our children will have peace. An offensive war is murder, but this war is just. The king is like a thief and must be treated the way a thief would be treated.
Conclusion	All Americans should support and participate in the war against the British.

LITERARY ANALYSIS

Persuasion

Persuasion is writing that has these qualities:
- It tries to convince readers to think in a certain way.
- It appeals to emotions or reason or both.
- It gives the writer's opinion.
- It urges action.

In "The Crisis," Thomas Paine tries to persuade the American colonists to fight for freedom from Britain's control. In this passage from the essay, he uses words that appeal to reason and to the emotions:

These are the times that try men's souls. The summer soldier and the sunshine patriot will in this crisis, shrink from the service of his country; but he that stands it now, deserves the love and thanks of man and woman. Tyranny, like hell, is not easily conquered; yet we have this consolation with us, that the harder the conflict, the more glorious the triumph.

READING STRATEGY

Recognizing Charged Words

Words that get your emotions worked up are called **charged words**. A writer who is trying to persuade is likely to use charged words. These words will get the reader to agree with the writer's point of view. Paine uses many charged words in his essay. As you read, look for some of his charged words. Write them in this chart, and then explain what they mean.

Charged Word	What It Means
EX: tyranny	strong, unfair power over another

 © Pearson Education, Inc.

from The Crisis
Thomas Paine

Paine says that these are difficult times. He says that those who fight against the British deserve thanks from everyone. He knows that the summer soldier and sunshine patriot[1] will not serve their country in this crisis.

◆　◆　◆

Tyranny, like hell, is not easily conquered; yet we have this consolation with us, that the harder the conflict, the more glorious the triumph. What we obtain too cheap, we esteem too lightly; 'tis dearness only that gives everything its value. Heaven knows how to put a proper price upon its goods.

◆　◆　◆

Paine goes on to say that Britain has a big army to stand behind her tyranny. She has said that she will keep on taxing the colonists and controlling them. Paine says this sounds like slavery. Britain has great power over America. Such power can belong only to God.

Paine believes that God Almighty will not give up on America. That is because America has tried so hard to avoid war. God would not give America up to the care of the devils. Paine says that the king of Britain is like a common murderer or robber. He has no grounds to look up to heaven for help against America.

Reading Strategy

Paine uses **charged words** and phrases in the paragraph. Circle two that are positive. Underline four that are negative.

Literary Analysis

Paine uses facts and emotion to **persuade** his reader to agree with him. List four facts in the bracketed passage.

1. _____
2. _____
3. _____
4. _____

English Language Development

The apostrophe is used in English for two reasons. One is to show possession, as in the word *men's*. The second use of the apostrophe is to show that a letter or letters are missing, as in the word *'tis* in the first paragraph. The word *'tis* is not used much in modern English. In the past, it was used to mean *it is*. The apostrophe stands for the missing letter *i*. Write the complete meaning of each of the following words on the lines.

1. wasn't _____
2. aren't _____
3. couldn't _____
4. shouldn't _____

Vocabulary Development

tyranny (TEER uh nee) *n.* oppressive or unfair power
consolation (kon suh LAY shuhn) *n.* comfort
esteem (es TEEM) *v.* value

---

1. **summer soldier and sunshine patriot** those who fight only when winning and those who are loyal only during good times.

I once felt all that kind of anger, which a man ought to feel, against the mean principles that are held by the Tories;[2] a noted one, who kept a tavern at Amboy, was standing at his door, with as pretty a child in his hand, about eight or nine years old, as I ever saw, and after speaking his mind as freely as he thought was <u>prudent</u>, finished with this unfatherly expression, *"Well! give me peace in my day."*

◆ ◆ ◆

Paine says that <u>a generous parent should have said, *"If there must be a war, let it be in my day. That way, my child can have peace."*</u> America could be the happiest place on earth. She is located far from all the <u>wrangling</u> world. All she has to do is trade with the other countries. Paine is sure that America will not be happy until she gets clear of foreign control. Wars, with no endings, will break out until that time comes. America must be the winner in the end.

Paine appeals to Americans in all states to unite. He feels that there cannot be too much strength for such an important mission. He wants those in the future to know that when danger arrived, the Americans joined together to fight.

Paine explains that British control will affect them all, no matter who they are or where they live.

◆ ◆ ◆

◆ **Stop to Reflect**

Read the underlined sentences. Do you agree with Paine's view here? Why, or why not?

_____

_____

_____

◆ **Reading Check**

What will happen until America wins her freedom? Circle the sentence that answers this question.

Vocabulary Development

prudent (PROO duhnt) *adj.* wise
wrangling (RANG ling) *n.* fighting, bickering, arguing

---

2. **Tories** colonists who were loyal to Britain.

© Pearson Education, Inc.

The heart that feels not now, is dead: the blood of his children will curse his <u>cowardice</u>, who shrinks back at a time when a little might have saved the whole, and made *them* happy. (I love the man that can smile at trouble; that can gather strength from distress, and grow brave by reflection.)

◆ ◆ ◆

Paine says that only those with little minds will shrink back. <u>The strong of heart will fight unto death.</u> He would not support an offensive war for all the treasures in the world. Such a war is murder. Paine then asks an important question.

He wonders what the difference is between a thief breaking into his house and ordering him to obey and a king who orders him to obey. He finds no difference and feels that both deserve the same treatment.

◆ ◆ ◆

◆ **Read Fluently**

Read the bracketed sentences. What kind of man does Paine love?

_____

_____

_____

◆ **Vocabulary and Pronunciation**

When you see the letters *gh* together in English, they are often silent. For example, the word *right* is pronounced rīt. In the underlined sentence, circle the word that has silent *gh*.

◆ **Culture Note**

The United States was not always free. It started out as a group of colonies under the rule of Britain. The Revolutionary War of 1775–1781 was fought to break free of Britain. Name one thing that the early colonists did not like about being under Britain's rule.

_____

_____

Vocabulary Development

cowardice (KOW uhr dis) *n.* lack of courage

© Pearson Education, Inc.

1. Check the answer that completes the sentence.

   Paine compares tyranny to _____ because it is not easily conquered.

   _____ Great Britain

   _____ summer soldiers

   _____ hell

   _____ heaven

2. On the line, write the answer that best completes the sentence. Choose from the answers in the box.

the Tories are	parents are	children are	God is

   Paine believes that America will win because _____ on America's side.

3. Paine tells of seeing a tavern-keeper in Amboy. The man had a child of eight or nine years old. The man said something that made Paine angry. What did the man say?

   _____

4. Why did Paine get angry at what the man in Amboy said?

   _____

   _____

5. **Literary Analysis:** In your own words, what is Paine trying to **persuade** his readers to do?

   _____

   _____

  © Pearson Education, Inc.

6. **Reading Strategy:** Circle the one word in each row that could best be called a **charged word**.

glorious	satisfying
control	tyranny
Britain	devils
curse	regret

Listening and Speaking

News Report

With a small group, talk about how a news reporter of the day might have commented on Paine's words. Before your group discussion, write brief answers to these questions:

Who? _____

_____

What? _____

_____

When? _____

_____

Where? _____

_____

Why? _____

_____

When it is your turn to speak, refer to your notes for ideas.

Speech in the Virginia Convention
Patrick Henry

Summary

In this speech, Patrick Henry begins by saying that, without disrespect, he must disagree with the previous speeches. Judging by their conduct, he says, the British are preparing for war. We have tried discussing the problem. We are being ignored; there is no retreat except into slavery. The time for getting along peacefully is over. The war has already begun. "Give me liberty or give me death" is Henry's strong and well-known closing.

Visual Summary

MAIN IDEA

War against the British must happen.

The previous speakers are able and patriotic.	We can only judge the future by the past.	Some say we are too weak to fight the British.
But different men see things differently.	The British have received the petition with a smile.	When will we be stronger?
The question being considered is very important.	But the British are sending fleets and armies to America.	We have three million people to be armed in a just cause.
The debate needs to be free.	We have done everything we can to avoid war.	God will find us friends to fight with us.

© Pearson Education, Inc.

SPEECHES

Speeches are often written first and then delivered orally. A good speaker does these things:
- Uses **restatement**, or restates ideas in a variety of ways
- Uses **repetition**, or repeats ideas using the same words
- Uses **parallelism**, or repeats words and grammatical structure
- Asks **rhetorical questions**, or questions that have obvious answers

In "Speech in the Virginia Convention," Patrick Henry uses all these techniques. Here is an example of his use of rhetorical questions:

> They tell us, sir, that we are weak. . . . But when shall we be stronger? Will it be the next week, or the next year? Will it be when we are totally disarmed, and when a British guard shall be stationed in every house?

READING STRATEGY

Evaluating Persuasive Appeals

When you read a persuasive speech, **evaluate** the **persuasive appeals** being made. Ask yourself if the speaker is appealing to your emotions or to your mind or reason. Use this chart to keep track of phrases and sentences that appeal to the emotions and to reason.

Appeals to Emotions	Appeals to Reason
EX: "nothing less than a question of freedom or slavery"	EX: "different men often see the same subject in different lights"

© Pearson Education, Inc.

Speech in the Virginia Convention
Patrick Henry

Mr. President: No man thinks more highly than I do of the patriotism, as well as abilities, of the very worthy gentlemen who have just addressed the house. But different men often see the same subject in different lights. . . .

◆ ◆ ◆

Patrick Henry then says that the question before the house is very important. He cannot allow fear of offending someone to stop him from saying what he thinks.

He says it is natural for people to hold on to hope. But no matter how much it hurts, it's best to know the worst and to plan for it.

◆ ◆ ◆

I have but one lamp by which my feet are guided, and that is the lamp of experience. I know of no way of judging of the future but by the past. And judging by the past, I wish to know what there has been in the conduct of the British ministry for the last ten years to justify those hopes with which gentlemen have been pleased to solace themselves and the house? Is it that insidious smile with which our petition has been lately received? Trust it not, sir; it will prove a snare to your feet. Suffer not yourselves to be betrayed with a kiss.[1]

◆ ◆ ◆

Vocabulary Development

solace (SAHL uhs) *v.* comfort
insidious (in SID ee uhs) *adj.* waiting for a chance to harm
snare (SNAIR) *n.* a trap

---

1. **betrayed with a kiss** In the Bible, Judas betrays Jesus with a kiss. This is a signal to the people who want to arrest Jesus.

© Pearson Education, Inc.

◆ **Stop to Reflect**

Do you agree that it is best to know the worst? Why, or why not?

_____

_____

_____

◆ **Read Fluently**

Read aloud the underlined sentences. Then circle the words that tell how Patrick Henry judges the future.

◆ **English Language Development**

In English, when we make words that end in *f* or *fe* plural, we change the ending to *ve* before adding *s*. For example, the word *yourself* become *yourselves* when it means more than one. Write the plural forms of these words:

shelf _____

knife _____

calf _____

elf _____

scarf _____

He then says that the British are using the tools of war. What else can the display of British force mean? Does Britain have any enemies in this area of the world? No, she has none. So the navies and armies are here for one reason only.

◆ ◆ ◆

They are meant for us: they can be meant for no other. They are sent over to bind and rivet upon us those chains which the British ministry have been so long forging.

And what have we to oppose to them? Shall we try argument? Sir, we have been trying that for the last ten years. Have we anything new to offer upon the subject? Nothing. We have held the subject up in every light of which it is capable; but it has been all in vain.

◆ ◆ ◆

Henry says that the colonists' petitions have been ignored. Their protests have met more violence. Their pleas have been set aside. They have been insulted from the foot of the throne.

◆ ◆ ◆

There is no longer any room for hope. If we wish to be free, if we mean to preserve inviolate those inestimable privileges for which we have been so long contending, if we mean not basely to abandon the noble struggle in which we have been so long engaged, and which we have pledged ourselves never to abandon until the glorious object of our contest shall be obtained—we must fight! I repeat it, sir, we must fight! An appeal to arms and the God of Hosts is all that is left us!

They tell us, sir, that we are weak—unable to cope with so formidable an adversary. But

© Pearson Education, Inc.

◆ Reading Strategy

Reread the bracketed passage. Then, to evaluate Patrick Henry's persuasive appeals, check the answer that best completes the sentence.

When Patrick Henry refers to "those chains" that the British have been "forging," he wants his listeners to think that _____.

_____ the British want the colonists to buy new chains from them

_____ the British have put a new tax on chains

_____ the British want to treat the colonists like slaves

_____ the British want the colonists to make more chains

◆ Reading Check

Underline the three sentences that tell how the colonists have been treated by Britain.

◆ Literary Analysis

Underline the three rhetorical questions in the bracketed paragraph here and on page 54. Remember that a rhetorical question is one that has an obvious answer. What are the obvious answers to these questions?

question 1: _____

question 2: _____

question 3: _____

Vocabulary Development

formidable (FOR mi duh buhl) *adj.* inspiring fear or awe

adversary (AD ver sair ee) *n.* enemy, opponent

Speech in the Virginia Convention **53**

Henry tells us that the battle is "not to the strong alone." Then he uses **parallelism** to tell us who will fight the battle.

1. What three phrases tell who will fight the battle?

_____

_____

2. Later in this paragraph Henry uses **repetition**. What phrase does Henry repeat twice?

_____

_____

◆ **Vocabulary and Pronunciation**

In English, the suffix *-ment* often means "action or process of." For example, the word *argument* means "the action or process of arguing." List two other English words that end in the suffix *-ment*, and give their meanings.

Word ending in *-ment*	Meaning

◆ **Reading Strategy**

Evaluate the **persuasive appeals** made by Patrick Henry in the last paragraph.

1. How does this paragraph make you feel?

_____

2. Which sentences or phrases make you feel this way? Underline the three sentences or phrases that seem the most powerful to you. Number them 1, 2, 3 in the order of their importance to you.

when shall we be stronger? Will it be the next week, or the next year? Will it be when we are totally disarmed, and when a British guard shall be stationed in every house?

◆ ◆ ◆

He continues by saying that the colonists are not weak. There are three million of them. They are "armed in the holy cause of liberty." They cannot be beaten by any force the enemy might send.

◆ ◆ ◆

The battle, sir, is not to the strong alone; it is to the vigilant, the active, the brave. Besides, sir, we have no election; if we were base enough to desire it, it is now too late to retire from the contest. There is no retreat but in submission and slavery! Our chains are forged! Their clanging may be heard on the plains of Boston! The war is inevitable—and let it come! I repeat it, sir, let it come!

It is vain, sir, to extenuate the matter. Gentlemen may cry "Peace, peace"—but there is no peace. The war is actually begun! The next gale that sweeps from the north will bring to our ears the clash of resounding arms! Our brethren are already in the field! Why stand we here idle? What is it that gentlemen wish? What would they have? Is life so dear, or peace so sweet, as to be purchased at the price of chains and slavery? Forbid it, Almighty God! I know not what course others may take; but as for me, give me liberty or give me death!

Vocabulary Development

vigilant (VIJ uh luhnt) *adj.* watchful, alert

extenuate (ex TEN yoo ayt) *v.* to try to lessen how serious something is

© Pearson Education, Inc.

1. What does Patrick Henry use to judge what will happen in the future? He states his answer in two ways that mean the same thing. What are they?

   1. _____   2. _____

2. Patrick Henry talks about the navies and armies that Britain has sent to the colonies. Why does he think they are here?

   _____

3. How has Britain responded to the colonists' petitions?

   _____

   _____

4. **Literary Analysis:** Give one example of each of these techniques used in Patrick Henry's speech: **restatement, repetition, parallelism,** and **rhetorical questions.**

   restatement:

   _____

   repetition:

   _____

   parallelism:

   _____

   rhetorical questions:

   _____

5. **Reading Strategy:** **Evaluate** the **persuasive appeal** of the sentences below by circling the one that is more powerful.

   | There is no retreat but in submission and slavery! |
   | It is now too late to retire from the contest. |

© Pearson Education, Inc.

Writing

Write Comments on a Speech

Find a written version of a modern speech that you like, such as the Inaugural Speech of John Fitzgerald Kennedy or the Nobel Prize Acceptance Speech of William Faulkner.

Write your comments on the speech. As you write, give your ideas on how well the speaker leads the audience to agree with his or her ideas.

Follow these steps:

1. **Prewriting** Make a bulleted list of the key points in the speech.

   * _____

   * _____

   * _____

   * _____

2. **Drafting** For each point, write a note that tells how the speaker develops that point. In your note, consider these questions:

   (a) Is the point developed through restatement, repetition, parallelism, or rhetorical question?

   _____

   (b) Is the point developed through an appeal to the emotions?

   _____

   (c) Is the point developed through an appeal to reason?

   _____

3. **Revising** Find an example from the speech to prove each point in your draft. Write the example next to your point.

4. **Publishing and Presenting** Compare your comments to the comments of your classmates about the same speech.

© Pearson Education, Inc.

Letter to Her Daughter
From the New White House
Abigail Adams

Summary

In this selection, Abigail Adams describes her journey to Washington as First Lady. Washington is a new city, with just a few public buildings. The White House is huge, but there are no bells to ring for the thirty servants and there is very little firewood. Adams tells her daughter to tell others that she finds the house and city beautiful. She closes by saying that Mrs. Washington has just invited her to visit Mount Vernon.

Visual Summary

Topic
Life in the new city of Washington

↓

Details						
woods until you reach city	river can be seen from window	grand house but no bells for servants	not enough firewood	six comfortable rooms	oval room very hand-some	invitation from Mrs. Washington

↓

Main Idea Sentence
It is a beautiful spot, capable of every improvement, and, the more I view it, the more I am delighted with it.

PRIVATE LETTERS

Private letters are—
- Spontaneous: they are written without being planned.
- Conversational: they sound like everyday speech.
- Private: they are meant to be read only by the person or persons to whom they are written.
- Primary source documents: they reveal information about the time in which they are written.

READING STRATEGY

Distinguishing Between Fact and Opinion

A **fact** is something that can be proved.

An **opinion** is a personal belief that cannot be proved.

When you are judging literary works, it is important to **distinguish between fact and opinion**. Use a chart like this to keep track of facts and opinions in this letter. If you can complete the box under "Yes," then you know the statement is a fact. If you can complete the box under "No," then you know it is an opinion.

EX: The principal stairs are not up, and will not be this winter.

↓

Is it a fact?

↓   ↓

Yes	No

↓   ↓

How it can be proved:	Words that show it is an opinion:
_____	_____
_____	_____
_____	_____

© Pearson Education, Inc.

Letter to Her Daughter from the New White House

Abigail Adams

Washington, 21 November, 1800

My Dear Child:

◆ ◆ ◆

Abigail Adams opens her letter by saying that she got to Washington on Sunday without accidents. But they did get lost outside of Baltimore. Adams says that woods are all you can see from Baltimore until you reach Washington. Here and there you see a small cottage, but you might travel miles without seeing a human being.

◆ ◆ ◆

In the city there are buildings enough, if they were <u>compact</u> and finished, to <u>accommodate</u> Congress and those attached to it; but as they are, and scattered as they are, I see no great comfort for them. <u>The river</u>,[1] which runs up to Alexandria,[2] is in full view of my window, and I see the <u>vessels</u> as they pass and repass. The house is upon a grand and superb scale, requiring about thirty servants to attend and keep the apartments in proper order, and perform the ordinary business of the house and stables; an establishment very well proportioned to the President's salary.

◆ ◆ ◆

Vocabulary Development

compact (KAHM pakt) *adj.* close together
accommodate (uh KAHM uh dayt) *v.* to provide with places to live

---

1. **river** the Potomac River, which runs through Washington, D.C.
2. **Alexandria** (al ex AN dree uh): a city in northeastern Virginia.

© Pearson Education, Inc.

◆ **Reading Check**

How would you describe the land that Adams crosses on her trip to the White House?

_____

_____

_____

◆ **Culture Note**

In the early years of the United States, it was easier for big cities to grow if they were located near rivers. The reason for this was that the rivers were used as trade routes. Ships carried goods needed by the settlers. Washington, D.C., is on the Potomac River. Name two other important rivers in the United States.

_____

_____

◆ **Vocabulary and Pronunciation**

Many English words have multiple meanings. The word *vessels*, for example, can mean either "ships" or "hollow containers, such as bottles, cups, glasses, and bowls." Other multiple-meaning words in this paragraph include *scale* and *order*. Write two meanings for each of these words. Make the first meaning the one that Abigail Adams is using in her letter. If necessary, use a dictionary and separate paper.

scale: _____ _____

order: _____ _____

◆ Literary Analysis

In this **primary source document**, Adams's **private letter** tells us about the social custom of visiting people. Remember that telephones did not exist in those days. (1) How many visits did Abigail Adams make in one day?

_____

(2) Do you think those visits were short or long?

_____

(3) Explain your reasoning.

_____

_____

◆ Read Fluently

Read this paragraph aloud. Then circle the answer to this question: Why isn't wood available for fires?

◆ Vocabulary and Pronunciation

Many words in English are spelled the same but are pronounced differently and have different meanings. When *content* is accented on the second syllable (kuhn TENT), it means "happy" or "to make oneself happy." When it is accented on the first syllable (KAHN tent), it means "something that is contained." Read the words below, along with their pronunciations. Write their meanings. If necessary, use a dictionary.
desert (dee ZERT) _____

_____

desert (DEZ ert) _____

_____

Adams goes on to say that the lighting of the apartments is a very difficult job. They also have to keep fires going to keep them from shivering. There are no bells anywhere in the building for calling the servants. <u>Many of the ladies from Georgetown[3] and the city have visited her. Yesterday she returned fifteen visits.</u> She starts to say something about Georgetown but doesn't finish her thought. Instead, she says "our Milton[4] is beautiful."

◆ ◆ ◆

But no comparisons—if they will put me up some bells and let me have wood enough to keep fires, I <u>design</u> to be pleased. I could <u>content</u> myself almost anywhere three months; but, surrounded with forests, can you believe that wood is not to be had because people cannot be found to cut and cart it?

◆ ◆ ◆

She then explains that Briesler was able to get only a few cords of wood. Most of that was used to dry the walls of the house before she and the President got there. Now they have to use coals instead, but they cannot get any grates for the coal.

◆ ◆ ◆

We have, indeed, come into a *new country*. You must keep all this to yourself, and, when

---

Vocabulary Development

design (dee ZĪN) *v.* intend, plan

---

3. **Georgetown** (JAWRJ town): a section of Washington, D.C.
4. **Milton** (MIL tuhn): a town in eastern Massachusetts, south of Boston.

© Pearson Education, Inc.

<u>asked how I like it, say that I write you the situation is beautiful, which is true</u>. The house is made <u>habitable</u>, but there is not a single apartment finished, and all withinside,[5] except the plastering, has been done since Briesler came. We have not the least fence, yard, or other convenience without[6] and the great unfinished audience room I make a drying-room of, to hang up the clothes in. The principal stairs are not up, and will not be this winter.

◆ ◆ ◆

Six rooms are comfortable. Two are used by the President and Mr. Shaw. For the past twelve years, this house has been considered as the future headquarters of government. ~~If it had been located in New England, it would have been fixed by now.~~

◆ ◆ ◆

It is a beautiful spot, capable of every improvement, and, the more I view it, the more I am delighted with it.

Since I sat down to write, I have been called down to a servant from Mount Vernon, with a <u>billet</u> from Major Custis, and a haunch of venison[7], and a kind, congratulatory letter from Mrs. Lewis, upon my arrival in the city, with Mrs. Washington's love, inviting me to Mount Vernon,[8] where, health permitting, I will go before I leave this place.

Affectionately, your mother,
Abigail Adams

Vocabulary Development

habitable (HAB it uh buhl) *adj.* able to be lived in
billet (BIL uht) *n.* a short letter, a note

---

5. **withinside** (with IN sīd): an old-fashioned way of saying "inside" or "indoors".
6. **without** (with OUT): an old-fashioned way of saying "outside".
7. **haunch of venison** (HAWNCH uv VEN uh suhn) *n.* a large piece of deer meat; half of the back side of a deer.
8. **Mount Vernon** (MOWNT VER nuhn) the estate in Virginia where George and Martha Washington lived.

◆ **Literary Analysis**

When you read the first underlined sentence, you know that this is a **private letter**. How do you know? Give two reasons.

_____

_____

_____

◆ **Reading Strategy**

Is the second underlined sentence a **fact** or an **opinion**? How do you know? Give one good reason.

_____

_____

_____

1. Check the answer that best completes the sentence.

   In 1800, the area between Baltimore and Washington, D.C., was mostly filled with ＿＿＿.

   ＿＿＿ little cottages

   ＿＿＿ woods

   ＿＿＿ rivers

   ＿＿＿ buildings with glass windows

2. Complete this sentence by writing the correct word in each blank.

   According to Adams, the two biggest problems in the White House were how to ＿＿＿＿＿ it and how to ＿＿＿＿＿ it.

3. Where does Abigail Adams dry the family's laundry?

   ＿＿＿＿＿＿＿＿＿＿＿＿＿＿＿＿＿＿＿＿＿＿＿＿＿＿＿＿＿＿＿＿＿

4. Abigail Adams tells her daughter that she has been invited for a visit. Who has invited her, and where has she been invited?

   Who: ＿＿＿＿＿＿＿＿＿＿＿＿＿＿＿＿＿＿＿＿＿＿＿＿＿＿＿＿＿

   Where: ＿＿＿＿＿＿＿＿＿＿＿＿＿＿＿＿＿＿＿＿＿＿＿＿＿＿＿＿

5. **Literary Analysis:** As a **primary source document**, this **private letter** gives Adams's view of the White House. Complete this chart listing things Adams says about the new White House. Write three good things and three bad things.

Good Things	Bad Things

© Pearson Education, Inc.

6. **Reading Strategy:** Read each phrase or sentence below. Then **distinguish between fact and opinion**. Write *fact* or *opinion* on the line.

1. They went eight or nine miles out of their way on the Frederick road. _____

2. It's a city in name only. _____

3. Wood is not to be had because people cannot be found to cut and cart it. _____

4. It is a beautiful spot, capable of every improvement. _____

Writing

Interview an New Arrival

Interview someone who recently came to this country to live. Find out why and how this person came here. Follow these steps:

- Write a list of questions to ask during the interview.

    1. _____

    2. _____

    3. _____

    4. _____

    5. _____

- Set up a tape recorder to record the interview.

- Make an appointment for your interview.

- During the interview, ask the questions that are on your list.

- Then ask more questions, depending on the person's answers to your questions.

- Take photographs of the person if he or she gives you permission.

- Play your tape recording of the interview for the class and show your photographs.

from Letters From an American Farmer

Michel-Guillaume Jean de Crèvecoeur

Summary

Crèvecoeur describes the opportunities for American immigrants. In Europe, these people are starving and unemployed, but the protective laws of the new land of America help people work and do well. Europeans from all nations come together in America, where all people can work for their own self-interest. Free from dependence and hunger, they can start a new life.

Visual Summary

Topic
Opportunities in America

Europe	America
poverty and starvation	food and opportunity
severe laws	protective laws
no citizenship	citizenship
no ownership of land	potential to own land
the frowns of the rich	rank
no attachment to the country	love of America

Main Idea Sentence
This is an American.

© Pearson Education, Inc.

LITERARY ANALYSIS

Public Letters

Public letters are—
- Essays written in letter form. They are also called **epistles**.
- Intended for a wide audience.
- **Primary source documents**. This means that they reveal information about the time in which they are written.

READING STRATEGY

Distinguishing Between Fact and Opinion

A **fact** is something that can be proved.

An **opinion** is a personal belief that cannot be proved.

When you are judging literary works, it is important to **distinguish between fact and opinion**. Use this chart to keep track of facts and opinions in this letter. Write facts in the first column. Write opinions in the second column.

Facts	Opinions
EX: The poor of Europe have come to America.	EX: Without owning land, a person can't call a place his country.

© Pearson Education, Inc.   *from* Letters from an American Farmer **65**

◆ Literary Analysis

This **epistle**, or public letter, is a **primary source document**. It tells us about the time in which it was written. What does this paragraph tell you about living conditions for the poor in England at the time? List three facts that are suggested here.

1. _____
2. _____
3. _____

◆ English Language Development

For words that end in *e*, we usually drop the *e* before adding *-ing*. Follow this rule to complete the chart below.

Base Word	+ -*ing* = New Word
live	living
leave	_____
come	_____
receive	_____
cause	_____

◆ Reading Check

In the underlined section, to what natural object does Crèvecoeur compare the people who have left Europe?

_____

_____

_____

from Letters from an American Farmer

Michel-Guillaume Jean de Crèvecoeur

Crèvecoeur opens by saying that the poor of Europe have come to America for various reasons. He says that two thirds of them had no country. He explains it in this way.

◆　◆　◆

Can a wretch who wanders about, who works and starves, whose life is a continual scene of sore <u>affliction</u> or pinching <u>penury</u>, can that man call England or any other kingdom his country? A country that had no bread for him, whose fields <u>procured</u> him no harvest, who met with nothing but the frowns of the rich, the severity of the laws, with jails and punishments; who owned not a single foot of the extensive surface of this planet? No! Urged by a variety of motives, here they came.

◆　◆　◆

He goes on to say that everything in America has been better for the poor. <u>In Europe they were like useless plants, in need of rich soil and cool rains. They dried up. They were mowed down by poverty, hunger, and war. Now they have been transplanted here. They have taken root and done well.</u> Here, they are citizens. The laws and their hard work have done it.

◆　◆　◆

What attachment can a poor European emigrant have for a country where he had

---

Vocabulary Development

affliction (uh FLIK shuhn) *n.* terrible troubles, state of distress

penury (PEN yuh ree) *n.* extreme poverty

procured (proh KYOORD) *v.* got, obtained

© Pearson Education, Inc.

nothing? The knowledge of the language, the love of a few kindred as poor as himself, were the only cords that tied him; his country is now that which gives him land, bread, protection, and <u>consequence</u>: *Ubi panis ibi patria*[1] is the motto of all emigrants. What then is the American, this new man? He is either a European, or the descendant of a European, hence that strange mixture of blood, which you find in no other country. I could point out to you a family whose grandfather was an Englishman, whose wife was Dutch, whose son married a French woman, and whose present four sons have now four wives of different nations. *He* is an American, who, leaving behind him all his ancient prejudices and manners, receives new ones from the new mode of life he has embraced, the new <u>government</u> he obeys, and the new rank he holds.

◆ ◆ ◆

Crevecoeur goes on to say that the emigrant becomes an American by being received into America's broad <u>lap</u>. Here, persons from all nations are melted into a new race of people. The Americans came from all over Europe, and now they live together under the finest system that has ever appeared.

◆ ◆ ◆

Vocabulary Development

consequence (KAHN suh kwens) *n.* social importance

1. *Ubi panis ibi patria:* (OO bee PAH nis IB ee PAH tree uh): Latin for "Where there is bread, there is one's fatherland."

◆ **Read Fluently**

Read aloud the bracketed passage. Then count to find the answer to this question. How many different countries, including America, are represented in this family? _____

◆ **Vocabulary and Pronunciation**

The suffix -*ment* changes a verb to a noun. The word *government* is an example of this. *Govern* means "to rule." *Government* means "the act of ruling." Complete this chart to learn other words that end in -*ment*.

Word	Meaning of Word
EX: allure	to tempt
entertain	
employ	
enjoy	

Word + -*ment*	Meaning of New Word
allurement	the act of tempting
entertain _____	
employ _____	
enjoy _____	

◆ **Vocabulary and Pronunciation**

Many English words have **multiple meanings**. The word *lap* is an example. It can mean "the front part of the lower trunk and thighs of a seated person." It can also mean "to make a gentle splashing sound." Write two meanings for each of these words:

race 1. _____

2. _____

long 1. _____

2. _____

vain 1. _____

2. _____

◆ **Reading Strategy**

Is the underlined sentence a **fact** or an **opinion**? _____
Circle the word that helped you figure out the answer.

◆ **Culture Note**

Crèveceour points out the role of religion in American life. The separation of church and state is an important principle in America. What does he suggest about the role of religion in some other countries?

_____

_____

_____

The American ought therefore love this country much better than that wherein either he or his forefathers were born. Here the rewards of his industry follow with equal steps the progress of his labor; his labor is founded on the basis of nature, *self-interest*; can it want a stronger <u>allurement</u>? Wives and children, who before in vain demanded of him a morsel of bread, now, fat and <u>frolicsome</u>, gladly help their father to clear those fields whence <u>exuberant</u> crops are to arise to feed and to clothe them all.

◆ ◆ ◆

In America, the farmer does not have to pay large parts of his crop to any princes, abbots,[2] or lords. Here, religion demands little from him. All he has to do is give a small salary to the minister and thanks to God.

◆ ◆ ◆

The American is a new man, who acts upon new principles; he must therefore entertain new ideas, and form new opinions. From involuntary idleness, servile dependence, penury, and useless labor, he has passed to toils of a very different nature, rewarded by ample <u>subsistence</u>—This is an American.

Vocabulary Development

allurement (uh LOOR muhnt) *n.* attraction, charm
frolicsome (FRAH lik suhm) *adj.* full of fun
exuberant (ex OO buhr uhnt) *adj.* extreme in amount
subsistence (sub SIS tuhns) *n.* the means to obtain food, shelter, and clothing

---

2. **abbots** (A buhts) heads of small religious groups.

© Pearson Education, Inc.

1. How does Crèvecoeur describe the life of the poor European? List three examples.

   1. _____

   2. _____

   3. _____

2. According to Crèvecoeur, what are the advantages of living in America? List them on this graphic organizer.

3. **Literary Analysis:** Suppose Crèvecoeur wrote a **private letter** on the same subject as this **public letter**, or **epistle**. Put a check by each of the phrases below that would appear in a private letter but not in an epistle.

   ____ the new American

   ____ you won't believe this, but

   ____ the rewards of his industry

   ____ don't tell anyone I said this, but

   ____ hope to see you soon

   ____ a new way of living

   ____ acts upon new principles

© Pearson Education, Inc.   *from* Letters from an American Farmer

4. **Reading Strategy:** Crèvecoeur says that in America, everything has been better for the people who came here from Europe. This is his **opinion**. Name at least two **facts** that he uses to support his opinion.

1. _____

2. _____

Writing

Public Letter, or Epistle

Write a **public letter,** or **epistle**, about life in modern America. Imagine that you are writing to people who live in another country. You want them to understand your world. Follow these steps:

1. Think about your audience.

   • To which country are you writing your letter? _____

   • What would be of most interest to your audience? _____

   _____

2. Before you write, limit your topic. You can't write about all aspects of life in America.

   • Pick one aspect to discuss. Write it here: _____

   _____

3. On a separate sheet of paper, write a rough draft of your epistle. Include enough details for your readers to understand your points.

4. Read your letter over to yourself. Imagine that you are a person from the other country.

   • What questions might you want to ask? Write them here: _____

   _____

5. Add any information that would answer those questions and improve your letter.

6. Share your letter with your classmates.

 © Pearson Education, Inc.

The Devil and Tom Walker
Washington Irving

Summary

Tom Walker meets the Devil ("Old Scratch") in a swamp in thick woods. The Devil offers the pirate Captain Kidd's treasure to Tom on certain conditions. Tom's wife encourages him to accept, but Tom refuses. She leaves to find the Devil and make her own bargain. After her second try, when she takes all the valuable items in the house with her, she doesn't come back. Later, Tom finds her apron with a heart and liver in it. He assumes that the Devil has killed her. Almost grateful, Tom looks for the Devil again. This time, he makes a deal. Tom will get Captain Kidd's treasure if he becomes a moneylender. Later, Tom regrets his deal and starts going to church often. But the Devil returns and sends Tom off on horseback into a storm. Tom never comes back, though his troubled spirit appears on stormy nights.

Visual Summary

Story Map		
Characters	• Tom Walker • his wife	• the Devil
Setting	**Place:** a wooded swamp in Massachusetts	**Time:** early eighteenth century (1700s)
Problem	The Devil wants Tom Walker to sell his soul to him.	

1: Tom Walker takes a shortcut through the swamp. Near an old Indian fort, he stops to rest and finds a skull.
2: When he kicks the skull, a stranger shouts at him. The stranger turns out to be the Devil.
3: The Devil offers Tom treasure buried by the pirate Captain Kidd—with conditions.
4: Tom tells his wife about the Devil's offer. His wife wants Tom to accept, but Tom refuses.
5: His wife leaves to bargain with the Devil herself, but she cannot come to terms with him.
6: The next day Tom's wife goes back to meet the Devil, carrying all the valuables from their home.
7: Tom's wife is never seen again. Tom finds only her checked apron—with a heart and liver tied up in it.
8: Now Tom decides to accept the Devil's offer. He agrees to become a moneylender.
9: Tom sets himself up in Boston and loans money at high interest rates. He becomes rich.
10: As he gets older, Tom begins to worry about his bargain with the Devil. He begins going to church and always carries his Bible with him.

Climax (turning point)
One day Tom steps outside his office—without his Bible—to answer three loud knocks on the door. The Devil has arrived to take his part of the bargain—Tom.

Resolution (conclusion)
Tom is never seen again. But sometimes on stormy nights, a figure on horseback haunts the swamp and the old Indian fort.

LITERARY ANALYSIS

Third-Person Omniscient Point of View

Every story has a narrator, or a storyteller. The narrator tells the story from a particular point of view. In the **third-person point of view**, the narrator stands outside the action and is not usually a story character. The third-person narrator is sometimes omniscient (om-NISH-uhnt), or "all knowing." An omniscient narrator. . .

- provides the thoughts and experiences of many characters.
- may tell us things that no character could possibly know.
- may make comments about story events and characters.

As you read Irving's story, use this chart to list details that show that the point of view is omniscient.

Different Characters' Thoughts & Experiences	Things No Character Could Know	Comments About Events & Characters

READING STRATEGY

Inferring Cultural Attitudes

Cultural attitudes are the opinions and values of a particular group of people at a particular time. "The Devil and Tom Walker" takes place in colonial America in the 1720s. From the story's details you can **make inferences**, or draw conclusions, about American cultural attitudes at that time. Use a chart like this one to make inferences.

Detail	Cultural Attitude
Oh, I go by various names. . . . I am the wild huntsman in some countries; the black miner in others. In this neighborhood I am known by the name of the black woodsman.	People believed in the Devil and called him by several nicknames.

  © Pearson Education, Inc.

The Devil and Tom Walker
Washington Irving

Outside Boston, Massachusetts, in about 1727, Tom Walker lives near a swampy forest. Captain Kidd supposedly buried his pirate treasure in this forest. Tom and his wife are very stingy—so stingy that they even cheat each other. One day, Tom takes a shortcut through the forest. At an old fort that Native Americans had once used in fighting the colonists, Tom meets a mysterious stranger. The stranger, who carries an ax on his shoulder, is not Native American or African American, but he is still very dark, as if covered in soot.

◆ ◆ ◆

"What are you doing on my grounds?" said the black man, with a <u>hoarse</u> growling voice.

"Your grounds!" said Tom with a sneer, "no more your grounds than mine; they belong to Deacon Peabody."

"Deacon Peabody be d____d," said the stranger, "as I flatter myself[1] he will be, if he does not look more to his own sins and less to those of his neighbors. Look <u>yonder</u>, and see how Deacon Peabody is faring."[2]

◆ ◆ ◆

Tom looks at a tree and sees carved into it the name of Deacon Peabody, a local churchman grown rich through clever land deals. Other trees bear the names of other wealthy members of the community. The trees all have ax marks, and one with the name Crowninshield is completely chopped down.

◆ ◆ ◆

◆ **Culture Note**

In 1727, there was no United States, and Massachusetts was still a British colony in North America. Circle two details here about life in colonial Massachusetts BEFORE Tom Walker's day.

◆ **Vocabulary and Pronunciation**

The word *hoarse*, which means "a raspy, unclear way of speaking," is pronounced the same as the four-legged animal called a *horse*. The /ôrs/ sound in *hoarse* and *horse* has other spellings too. Say these words aloud. Circle the letters that spell /ôrs/.

coarse	force	horse
course	forcing	porcelain
divorce	hoarse	torso

◆ **Vocabulary and Pronunciation**

Yonder was once used much more than it is in American English today, though it is still used in some regions. What do you think *yonder* means? Write your guess below.

yonder: _____

---

1. **as I flatter myself** as I am delighted to think.
2. **faring** (FAYR ing) *v.* doing.

© Pearson Education, Inc.

Firewood is a **compound word** formed by putting two smaller words together:

fire + wood = firewood

By studying the meaning of the smaller words, you can figure out that *firewood* means "wood to burn for a fire." Circle another compound word in the bracketed passage. Below, write the word and its meaning.

Compound Word:

_____

Meaning:

_____

_____

◆ Literary Analysis

An **omniscient**, or all-knowing, **narrator** tells us the thoughts and attitudes of different characters. Circle Tom's wife's thoughts or attitudes about the treasure. Write one word to describe the wife.

_____

"He's just ready for burning!" said the black man, with a growl of triumph. "You see I am likely to have a good stock of firewood for winter."

"But what right have you," said Tom, "to cut down Deacon Peabody's timber?"

"The right of a <u>prior</u> claim," said the other. "This woodland belonged to me long before one of your white-faced race put foot upon the soil."

"And pray, who are you, if I may be so bold?" said Tom.

"Oh, I go by various names. I am the wild huntsman in some countries; the black miner in others. In this neighborhood I am known by the name of the black woodsman. . . . "

"The upshot of all which is, that, if I mistake not," said Tom, sturdily, "you are he commonly called Old Scratch."

"The same, at your service," replied the black man, with a half-civil nod.

◆ ◆ ◆

The Devil offers Tom Captain Kidd's pirate treasure if Tom agrees to his terms. Tom makes no decision. Instead he asks for proof that the Devil is who he says he is. So the Devil presses his finger to Tom's forehead and then goes off. When Tom gets home, he finds a black thumbprint burned into his forehead. He also learns of the sudden death of Absalom Crowninshield. Convinced he has met the Devil, he tells his wife all about it.

◆ ◆ ◆

All her <u>avarice</u> was awakened at the mention of hidden gold, and she urged her husband to <u>comply</u> with the black man's terms and

Vocabulary Development

prior (PRĪ uh) *adj.* previous; from before
avarice (A vuh riz) *adj.* greed
comply (kum PLĪ) *v.* go along with; agree to

© Pearson Education, Inc.

<u>secure</u> what would make them wealthy for life. However Tom might have felt <u>disposed</u> to sell himself to the Devil, he was determined not to do so to <u>oblige</u> his wife; so he flatly refused out of the mere spirit of contradiction. Many and bitter were the quarrels they had on the subject. . . .

At length she determined to drive the bargain on her own account, and if she succeeded, to keep all the gain to herself. Being of the same <u>fearless</u> temper as her husband, she set off for the old Indian fort at the close of a summer's day.

◆ ◆ ◆

To bargain with the Devil, Tom's wife takes the household silverware and other valuables, tying them up in her apron. She is never heard from again. According to one story, Tom goes hunting for her and finds nothing but her apron, with a heart and liver inside! Whatever happened, Tom seems more upset about losing his property than losing his wife. In fact, he decides that the Devil might have done him a favor. Soon he is again bargaining with the Devil to obtain the pirate's treasure.

◆ ◆ ◆

There was one condition which need not be mentioned, being generally understood in all cases where the Devil grants favors; but there were others about which, though of less importance, he was <u>inflexibly</u> <u>obstinate</u>. He insisted

---

Vocabulary Development

secure (se KYOOR) *v.* to make certain about; to guarantee

disposed (dis POHZD) *adj.* inclined; prone to

oblige (u BLĪDG) *v.* do what someone else wants; please

inflexibly (in FLEHKS uh blee) *adv.* completely unwilling to move or change

obstinate (AWB sti net) *adj.* stubborn

© Pearson Education, Inc.

The Devil and Tom Walker **75**

◆ Vocabulary and Pronunciation

A **suffix** is a word part added to the end of a word to change its meaning. The suffix *-less* means "without." *Fearless* means "without fear." Think of another word that ends with *-less*. On the lines below, write the word and its meaning.

Word: _____

Meaning: _____

◆ Stop to Reflect

What "one condition which need not be mentioned" is always involved when someone makes a deal with the Devil? Circle the letter of the correct answer below.

(a) person damned in the after-life

(b) person signs name in blood

(c) person becomes rich

(d) person gets revenge on enemies

◆ **English Language Development**

In the bracketed passage, circle all the quotation marks that show when Tom and the Devil are speaking. Then show who is speaking by labeling each remark *Tom* or *Devil*. How does Irving show a change of speaker?

_____

_____

_____

◆ **Stop to Reflect**

Do you think Tom will regret his decision? Circle your answer.

      yes   no

Why, or why not?

_____

_____

_____

_____

_____

that money found through his means should be employed in his service. He proposed, therefore, that Tom should employ it in the black traffic; that is to say, that he should fit out a slave ship. This, however, Tom <u>resolutely</u> refused: he was bad enough in all conscience, but the Devil himself could not tempt him to turn slave-trader.

Finding Tom so squeamish on this point, he did not insist upon it, but proposed, instead, that he should turn usurer.[3] . . . To this no objections were made, for it was just to Tom's taste.

"You shall open a broker's shop[4] in Boston next month," said the black man.

"I'll do it tomorrow, if you wish," said Tom Walker.

"You shall lend money at two per cent a month."

"Egad, I'll charge four!" replied Tom Walker. . . .

"Done!" said the Devil.

"Done!" said Tom Walker. So they shook hands and struck a bargain.

◆ ◆ ◆

So Tom becomes a cruel moneylender, charging his highest rates to his most desperate customers. He grows rich and powerful. He builds a large, showy house, though he is too stingy to furnish it well. He buys a fancy carriage but lets the horses nearly starve. Yet as he nears old age, he begins to worry.

◆ ◆ ◆

Vocabulary Development

resolutely (re zoh LOOT lee) *adv.* firmly

---

3. **usurer** (YOO zer rer) *n.* a moneylender who charges high interest rates.
4. **a broker's shop** a moneylending business.

© Pearson Education, Inc.

Having secured the good things of this world, he began to feel anxious about those of the next. He thought with regret on the bargain he had made with his black friend, and set his wits to work to cheat him out of the conditions. He became, therefore, all of a sudden, a violent churchgoer. . . . Tom was as rigid in religious as in money matters; he was a stern supervisor and censurer[5] of his neighbors, and seemed to think every sin entered up to their account became a credit on his own side of the page.

◆ ◆ ◆

Frightened of the Devil, Tom keeps a small Bible in his coat pocket and a large one on his desk at work. One hot afternoon, while still in his bathrobe, Tom goes down to his office to demand repayment of a loan. The man who has taken the loan is a land jobber, or speculator who tried to make money by buying and selling land. In the past, Tom has acted as if this man were a good friend, but now Tom refuses to give him more time to repay his loan.

◆ ◆ ◆

"My family will be ruined and brought upon the parish," said the land jobber.

"Charity begins at home," replied Tom; "I must take care of myself in these hard times."

"You have made so much money out of me," said the speculator.

Tom lost his patience and his piety—"The Devil take me," said he, "if I have made a farthing!"[6]

Vocabulary Development

piety (PĪ e tee) *n.* religious devotion

---

5. **censurer** (SEN sher rer) *n.* someone who criticizes the behavior of others.
6. **farthing** (FAHR thing) *n.* a small coin of little value.

© Pearson Education, Inc.

◆ **English Language Development**

The **past perfect tense** uses the helping verb *had* + the past participle of the main verb:

had lived   had done

It is used to show an action that happened before another action in the past. In this underlined part of a sentence, label the verbs "1-past" and "2-past perfect" to show which action came first.

◆ **Reading Check**

As a result of worrying about his deal with the Devil, what does Tom become?

_____

_____

_____

_____

◆ **Culture Note**

"Charity begins at home" is a common proverb or saying in English. It means that a person should first help family or others in his or her own household before going on to help outsiders. What is dishonest about Tom's use of this proverb to defend his behavior?

_____

_____

_____

Do you think Tom deserves this doom?

_____

Why, or why not?

_____

_____

_____

◆ **Literary Analysis**

Circle the sentence in which the **omniscient narrator** gives advice directly to some of his readers. What does he want those readers to learn from the story?

_____

_____

_____

Just then there were three loud knocks at the street door. He stepped out to see who was there. A black man was holding a black horse, which neighed and stamped with impatience.

"Tom, you're come for," said the black fellow, <u>gruffly</u>. Tom shrunk back, but too late. He had left his little Bible at the bottom of his coat pocket, and his big Bible on the desk . . . never was a sinner taken more unawares.

◆ ◆ ◆

The Devil takes Tom up and rides off into a thunderstorm. They are said to have galloped like mad to the swamp by the old fort. Shortly afterward the forest is struck by lightning. The next day Tom's fancy new house catches fire and burns to the ground. Tom himself is never seen again. Those appointed to settle his affairs find nothing but ashes where his business papers should be and chests filled with worthless wood shavings instead of gold.

◆ ◆ ◆

Such was the end of Tom Walker and his ill-gotten wealth. Let all <u>griping</u> money brokers lay this story to heart. The truth of it is not to be doubted. The very hole under the oak trees, whence[7] he dug Kidd's money, is to be seen to this day; and the neighboring swamp and old Indian fort are often haunted in stormy nights by a figure on horseback, in morning gown and white cap, which is doubtless the troubled spirit of the usurer.

Vocabulary Development

gruffly (GRUHF lee) *adv.* abruptly
griping (GRĪP ing) *adj.* complaining

---

7. **whence** (WENS) *prep.* from where.

© Pearson Education, Inc.

1. Circle the words that best describe Tom Walker.

   greedy   loyal   loving   selfish   lazy

2. What happens to Tom's wife?

   _____

   _____

3. Complete these sentences to explain the bargain that Tom makes.

   Tom agrees to _____

   in exchange for _____.

4. What happens to Tom in the end?

   _____

   _____

5. **Literary Analysis:** Show that the story uses **third-person omniscient point of view** by finding examples for the chart below.

Different Characters' Thoughts & Experiences:	Comments About Events & Characters:

6. **Reading Strategy:** Put a check in front of each **cultural attitude** that you can **infer** from the details in the story.

____ Few people of the time believed in the Devil.

____ Many European colonists distrusted Native Americans.

____ Most colonists admired pirates and thought they were heroes.

____ Some people disliked the slave trade.

____ Some moneylenders charged high interest rates.

____ Boston was a center of colonial commerce.

____ The Bible was not an important book in colonial times.

Writing

Modern Story

Imagine that you are updating Irving's story. Your new version will take place in the United States today. Answer these questions about changes you might make in the story.

• Where would Tom meet the Devil?

_____

• How would Tom's wife disappear?

_____

• What treasure would the Devil give Tom?

_____

• What job or career would the Devil choose for Tom?

_____

• What would Tom buy or do when he is rich?

_____

• What would happen at the end?

_____

Now, write the first paragraph of your new story on separate paper. Share it with your classmates and get their reactions.

 © Pearson Education, Inc.

A Psalm of Life

Henry Wadsworth Longfellow

Summary

In this poem, the speaker refuses to accept the idea that life is only a dream with the grave as its only goal. The soul is eternal. Heroic action in life is important because life is short. The lives of heroes who have gone before us remind us that we, too, can be examples of courage and achievement for others.

Visual Summary

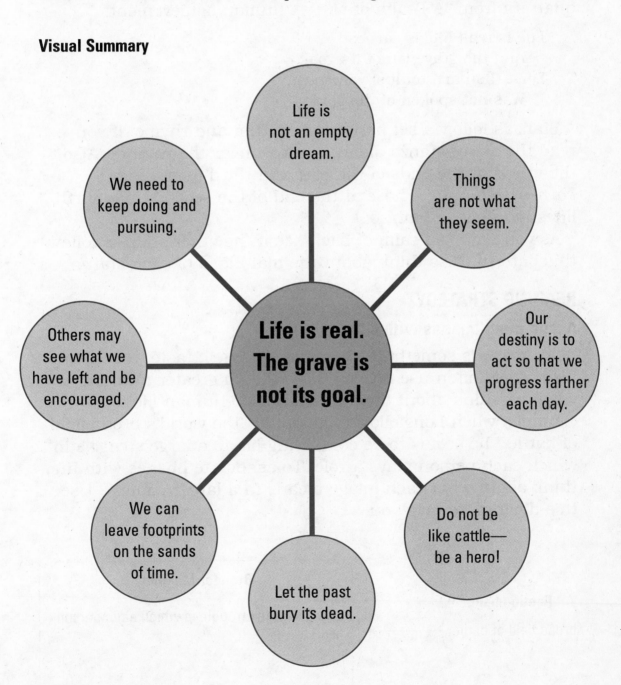

LITERARY ANALYSIS

Stanza Form

Many poems are written in groups of lines called **stanzas**. Each stanza is something like a paragraph, usually focusing on one main idea. A two-line stanza is called a couplet. A four-line stanza is called a quatrain (KWA train). The subject of this **quatrain** from "A Psalm of Life" is human achievement:

> Life is real! Life is earnest!
>   And the grave is not its goal:
> Dust thou art, to dust returnest,
>   Was not spoken of the soul.

Stanzas follow a set pattern of rhythm and rhyme. If you read the above stanza aloud, you can hear the rhythm. Also, the words at the ends of the first and third lines rhyme: *earnest/returnest*. Those at the end of the second and fourth lines rhyme too: *goal/soul*.

As you read "A Psalm of Life," see if the other stanzas follow this pattern. Also think about the main idea of each stanza.

READING STRATEGY

Associating Images with Life

An **image** is something you can see, smell, taste, touch, or hear. Poets often use images that take on greater meaning when we think about them in relation to human life. For example, when Longfellow talks about "the world's broad field of battle," he seems to be comparing life to a large struggle in which each person plays a role. To **associate images with life**, think about what each image means in a larger context. Use this diagram to help you.

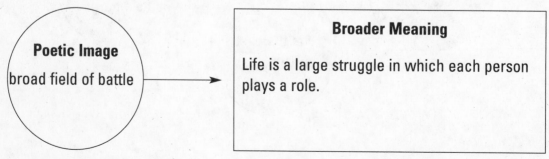

Poetic Image
broad field of battle

Broader Meaning

Life is a large struggle in which each person plays a role.

© Pearson Education, Inc.

A Psalm of Life
Henry Wadsworth Longfellow

Tell me not, in mournful numbers,
   Life is but an empty dream!–
For the soul is dead that slumbers,
   And things are not what they seem.

Life is real! Life is <u>earnest</u>!
   And the grave is not its goal:
Dust thou art, to dust returnest,[1]
   Was not spoken of the soul.

◆   ◆   ◆

   Happiness and sadness aren't our destiny.
Our destiny is to make progress every day.

◆   ◆   ◆

In the world's broad field of battle,
   In the bivouac[2] of Life,
Be not like dumb, driven cattle!
   Be a hero in the strife!

◆   ◆   ◆

   Don't worry about the past or the future.
Act in the present.

◆   ◆   ◆

<u>Lives of great men all remind us</u>
   We can make our lives <u>sublime</u>,
And, departing, leave behind us
   <u>Footprints</u> on the sands of time;

Footprints, that perhaps another,
   Sailing o'er life's solemn main,[3]
A forlorn and shipwrecked brother,
   Seeing, shall take heart again.

◆   ◆   ◆

   Let us be active and ready for any fate.

Vocabulary Development

earnest (UR nist) *adj.* Sincere; serious

sublime (suh BLĪM) *adj.* Noble; inspiring

---

1. **Dust thou art, to dust returnest** you are dust, and you return to dust; a rewording of a famous quotation from the Bible (Genesis 3:19).
2. **bivouac** (BIV wak) *n.* temporary army camp.
3. **o'er life's solemn main** over the sad open sea of life.

© Pearson Education, Inc.

◆ **Literary Analysis**

Show the sound pattern in this **stanza** by circling and connecting the rhyming words. What is the stanza's main idea? Circle the letter of the answer below.

(a) Sadness cannot be measured.

(b) Do not give up hope.

(c) The soul is dead.

(d) Everyone needs to take a rest.

◆ **English Language Development**

As a noun, *lives* rhymes with *wives*. As a verb, it rhymes with *gives*. Which is it in the underlined passage? Say the line aloud and circle the answer:

noun   verb

◆ **Reading Strategy**

Associate the image of the footprints with life. What are the footprints? Circle the letter of the best answer below.

(a) clues   (c) human achievements

(b) death   (d) walks on the beach

◆ **Vocabulary and Pronunciation**

Circle the two-word expression here that means "to become hopeful or confident."

1. Circle the word that best describes the speaker's attitude.

    bitter   positive   hopeless   humorous   shy

2. Put a check in front of those ideas with which the speaker agrees.

    ____ Life is but an empty dream!   ____ Life is real!

    ____ The grave is the goal of life.   ____ Life is earnest!

3. What does the speaker think the lives of great men can teach us?
   Circle the letter of the best answer.

    (a) how to be modest   (c) how to walk without shoes

    (b) how to make money   (d) how to be great ourselves

4. **Literary Analysis:** On the chart, list the main idea of each **stanza**.

Stanza	Main Idea
1	
2	
3	
4	
5	

5. **Reading Strategy:** Explain what each **image** below means or says
   about life in general.

Image	Broad Meaning
to dust returneth	
dumb, driven cattle	
footprints on the sands of time	
shipwrecked brother	

                                © Pearson Education, Inc.

Writing

Comparing Ideas

Choose a proverb or saying from the list below. Then, write a paragraph showing how the ideas of the proverb or saying are similar to those in the poem.

- Put a check next to the one proverb or saying you think has ideas most similar to those in the poem:

____ Make the most of life while you can.

____ It is better to give than to receive.

____ Keep hope alive.

____ We can all make a difference in life.

- In the space below, list similarities between the proverb or saying and the poem.

Proverb or Saying	Poem

- On separate paper, write a paragraph showing how the poem expresses ideas similar to those in the proverb or saying. Include the similarities you listed in the chart.
- Share the paragraph with your classmates. Ask them if they agree with your ideas.

© Pearson Education, Inc.

The Raven

Edgar Allan Poe

Summary

In this poem, the speaker is reading at night. A mysterious raven arrives. To all the speaker's questions, the raven says, "Nevermore!" The speaker demands that the raven leave, but it stays, haunting him forever.

Visual Summary

What the speaker of the poem says	What the speaker hears the raven answer
• Excuse me, I was napping.	No response
• Lenore!	No response
• Tell me your name.	"Nevermore."
• The bird will leave me tomorrow, as others have.	"Nevermore."
• I need respite from my grief over Lenore.	"Nevermore."
• "Is there balm in Gilead?"	"Nevermore."
• Will I hold Lenore again?	"Nevermore."
• Leave my door.	"Nevermore."

   © Pearson Education, Inc.

LITERARY ANALYSIS

Single Effect

Poe believed that a good poem or story should have "a certain unique and **single effect**" on the reader. He thought that all the details should work toward that effect. In most of Poe's poems and stories, the single effect he tried to achieve was horror. To achieve it in "The Raven," for instance, he writes about a large dark bird associated with bad luck. He sets the poem at night. And he uses words like *ghastly* (which means "awful") and *grim* to stress the horror:

> Ghastly grim and ancient Raven wandering from
> the Nightly shore—

As you read "The Raven," look for other details that contribute to the single effect.

READING STRATEGY

Breaking Down Long Sentences

Poems often use long sentences that continue over many lines. To understand what they are saying, it helps to **break down long sentences** into parts and see how those parts are related. To break down a sentence, identify the core of subject, verb, and direct object. Then look for clues in punctuation and connecting words. These clues help you to figure out how all the main chunks are related to the core. Use a diagram like this.

Sentence

But the Raven, sitting lonely on the placid bust, spoke only
That one word, as if his soul in that one word he did outpour.

Subject
the Raven

→

Verb
spoke

→

Object
That one word

© Pearson Education, Inc.

Adjectives in English usually come before the noun they modify. But here the adjective *dreary* comes after the noun it modifies, *midnight*. The unusual order sounds more poetic. How would you say "a midnight dreary" in usual spoken English?

_____

_____

◆ Culture Note

December is the twelfth month of the year. It is a cold winter month in many parts of the United States. On the lines below, write all twelve months in English. One is done as an example. Remember that the English names of the months each start with a capital letter.

_____ _____

_____ _____

_____ _____

_____ _____

_____ _____

_____ December

◆ Vocabulary and Pronunciation

Read this underlined line aloud and circle the four /s/ sounds. What sound do you think Poe is trying to capture?

(a) the curtains rustling
(b) the speaker's beating heart
(c) the speaker's terror
(d) a visitor knocking on the door

The Raven
Edgar Allan Poe

Once upon a midnight dreary, while I
  pondered, weak and weary,
Over many a quaint and curious volume of
  forgotten lore[1]—
While I nodded, nearly napping, suddenly there
  came a tapping,
As of some one gently rapping, rapping at my
  chamber door.
"'Tis some visitor," I muttered, "tapping at my
  chamber door—
          Only this, and nothing more."

Ah, distinctly I remember it was in the bleak
  December;
And each separate dying ember wrought its
  ghost upon the floor.
Eagerly I wished the morrow;[2]—vainly I had
  sought to borrow
From my books surcease[3] of sorrow—sorrow
  for the lost Lenore—
For the rare and radiant maiden whom the
  angels name Lenore—
          Nameless *here* for evermore.

And the silken, sad, uncertain rustling of each
  purple curtain
Thrilled me—filled me with fantastic terrors
  never felt before;
So that now, to still the beating of my heart, I
  stood repeating
"'Tis some visitor entreating entrance at my
  chamber door—

Vocabulary Development

pondered (PAHN duhrd) *v.* thought deeply
wrought (RAWT) *v.* carved

---

1. **quaint** (KWAYNT) **volume of forgotten lore** unusual book of forgotten knowledge.
2. **the morrow** the next day.
3. **surcease** (suhr SEES) **of** Relief from.

© Pearson Education, Inc.

Some late visitor entreating entrance at my
   chamber door;—
               This it is and nothing more."

Presently my soul grew stronger; hesitating
   then no longer,
"Sir," said I, "or Madam, truly your forgiveness
   I implore;
But the fact is I was napping, and so gently
   you came rapping,
And so faintly you came tapping, tapping at my
   chamber door,
That I scarce was sure I heard you"—here I
   opened wide the door;—
               Darkness there and nothing more.

                    ◆   ◆   ◆

      The speaker searches the dark for the
      source of the knocking, but he sees nothing.
      When he calls out the name "Lenore," he
      hears only an echo. Then he hears the
      knocking again. This time he thinks it is
      someone at the window.

                    ◆   ◆   ◆

Open here I flung the shutter, when, with
   many a flirt and flutter,
In there stepped a <u>stately</u> Raven of the
   saintly days of yore;[4]
<u>Not the least obeisance</u>[5] <u>made he</u>; not a
   minute stopped or stayed he;
But, with mien[6] of lord or lady, perched above
   my chamber door—
Perched upon a bust of Pallas[7] just above my
   chamber door—
               Perched, and sat, and nothing more.

Reading Check

What does the speaker
find when he opens the
door? Circle your answer.

English Language Development

The **subject** is the noun
or pronoun that performs
the action of the verb. In
English, the subject
usually comes before the
verb. But sometimes
poetry inverts the order, putting
the verb first. Circle the subject
and verb in this underlined
clause, and label them S or V.

Vocabulary Development

stately (STAYT lee) *adj.* elegant; dignified

---

4. **days of yore** (YAWR) olden days; days of long ago.
5. **obeisance** (oh BAY suhns) *n.* show of respect, such as a bow or a
curtsy.
6. **mien** (MEEN) *n.* manner; way of conducting yourself.
7. **bust of Pallas** (PAL is) sculpture of the head and shoulders of Pallas
Athena (uh THEE nuh), the ancient Greek goddess of wisdom.

© Pearson Education, Inc.

Circle the speaker's request for information in the bracketed passage. Label it *Q*. Then circle the answer the Raven seems to give and label it A.

Mark the Text

Then this ebony bird beguiling my sad fancy[8]
    into smiling,
By the grave and stern decorum[9] of the
    countenance[10] it wore,
"Though thy crest be shorn and shaven,[11]
    thou," I said, "art sure no <u>craven</u>,
Ghastly grim and ancient Raven wandering
    from the Nightly shore—
Tell me what thy lordly name is on the Night's
    Plutonian[12] shore!"
           Quoth[13] the Raven, "Nevermore."

◆ Reading Strategy

This stanza is one long sentence. Draw lines between words to **break up the long sentence** into manageable chunks. Circle the letter of the statement below that best sums up the meaning of the sentence.

(a) I was amazed by the bird and its speech, even if it made little sense.

(b) I was amazed that anything so ugly could have such a lovely voice.

(c) I chatted with the amazing bird, which sat on a bust labeled "Nevermore" over my door.

(d) I am the only human being who ever spoke with Nevermore.

Much I marveled[14] this <u>ungainly</u> fowl to hear
    discourse[15] so plainly,
Though its answer little meaning—little
    relevancy bore;[16]
For we cannot help agreeing that no living
    human being
Ever yet was blessed with seeing bird above his
    chamber door—
Bird or beast upon the sculptured bust above
    his chamber door,
          With such name as "Nevermore."

Vocabulary Development

craven (KRAYV uhn) *n.* coward
ungainly (uhn GAYN lee) *adj.* awkward; clumsy

---

8. **ebony** (EB uh nee) **bird beguiling** (bi GĪL ing) **my sad fancy** black bird charming my sad mood away.
9. **decorum** (duh KAWR uhm) *n.* act of polite behavior.
10. **countenance** (KOW tuh nuns) *n.* face.
11. **thy crest be shorn and shaven** The tuft of feathers on your head is clipped and shaved (by a previous owner).
12. **Plutonian** (ploo TOHN yuhn) *adj.* dark and evil; hellish (Pluto was the Roman god of the underworld).
13. **quoth** (KWOHTH) *v.* quoted; recited; said.
14. **marveled** found marvelous; felt awe or wonder about.
15. **discourse** (dis KAWRS) *v.* speak; talk.
16. **little relevancy** (REL uh vin see) **bore** had little meaning; did not make much sense.

© Pearson Education, Inc.

But the Raven, sitting lonely on the placid[17]
    bust, spoke only
That one word, as if his soul in that one word
    he did outpour.
Nothing farther then he uttered—not a feather
    then he fluttered—
Till I scarcely more than muttered, "Other
    friends have flown before—
On the morrow *he* will leave me, as my Hopes
    have flown before."
                <u>Then the bird said, "Nevermore."</u>

         ◆   ◆   ◆

    The speaker worries about this
"Nevermore." This time it sounds like a real
answer to the question he asked. He tells
himself that maybe the Raven knows just
this one word. Yet he still keeps trying to find
some meaning in the word. No matter what
he asks the Raven, the bird says,
"Nevermore." By now the speaker is angry.

         ◆   ◆   ◆

"Prophet!" said I, "thing of evil!—prophet still,
    if bird or devil!
By that Heaven that bends above us—by that
    God we both adore—
Tell this soul with sorrow laden[18] if, within the
    distant Aidenn,[19]
It shall clasp a sainted maiden whom the
    angels name Lenore—
Clasp a rare and radiant maiden whom the
    angels name Lenore."
             Quoth the Raven, "Nevermore."

---

17. **placid** (PLA sid) *adj.* silent.
18. **this soul with sorrow laden** (LAY duhn) the speaker's own sorrowful soul.
19. **Aidenn** (AY duhn) Eden; heaven.

© Pearson Education, Inc.

◆ **Reading Check**

What does the speaker think the Raven means when he says "Nevermore" in the underlined sentence?

_____

_____

_____

◆ **Literary Analysis**

How does repetition of "Nevermore" add to the **single effect** of horror?

_____

_____

_____

Circle two more details on this page that add to the single effect of horror.

The /ee/ sound is often spelled *e, ea, ee, ie, ei,* and *y.* Circle six examples of the /ee/ sound in this bracketed stanza.

◆ **Reading Check**

What is the situation at the end of the poem? Answer by completing this sentence: The Raven is _____

_____,

and the speaker is _____

_____.

"Be that word our sign of parting, bird or
    <u>fiend</u>!" I shrieked, upstarting[20] —
"Get thee back into the tempest and the Night's
    Plutonian shore!
Leave no black <u>plume</u> as a token of that lie thy
    soul hath spoken!
Leave my loneliness unbroken!—quit the bust
    above my door!
Take thy beak from out my heart, and take thy
    form from off my door!"
                    Quoth the Raven, "Nevermore."

And the Raven, never <u>flitting</u>, still is sitting,
    still is sitting
On the <u>pallid</u> bust of Pallas just above my
    chamber door;
And his eyes have all the seeming of a demon's
    that is dreaming;
And the lamp-light o'er him streaming throws
    his shadow on the floor;
And my soul from out that shadow that lies
    floating on the floor
                    Shall be lifted—nevermore!

Vocabulary Development

fiend (FEEND) *n.* demon; devil

plume (ploom) *n.* feather

flitting (FLIT ing) *adj.* flying rapidly

pallid (PAL uhd) *adj.* pale; white

---

20. **upstarting** starting up; standing; moving.

© Pearson Education, Inc.

1. Circle the words that best describe the speaker in this poem.

   cruel   sad   brooding   hopeless   boring   superstitious

2. On the line before each statement, write *T* if the statement seems true. Write *F* if it seems false.

   ____ The speaker misses Lenore.

   ____ Lenore is away visiting her parents for the holidays.

   ____ The speaker is reading a book about bird watching.

   ____ The Raven enters through the window.

   ____ The Raven has an extensive vocabulary.

   ____ The Raven perches on a bust of an ancient Greek goddess.

   ____ The Raven is still perched on the bust when the poem ends.

3. List three things that the speaker thinks "Nevermore" may mean.

   • _____

   • _____

   • _____

4. Many people find "The Raven" very musical. Show its music by listing at least four examples of rhyme and other repeated sounds.

   • _____

   • _____

   • _____

   • _____

© Pearson Education, Inc.

5. **Literary Analysis:** On the chart below, list details from the poem that contribute to the **single effect** of horror. Include at least two details in each part of the chart.

Setting (time or place)
Characters
Events
Word Choice

6. **Reading Strategy:** Use lines to **break this sentence** into parts. Underline and label the subject (*S*), the verb (*V*), and the object (*O*).

But the Raven, sitting lonely on the placid bust, spoke only

That one word, as if his soul in that one word he did outpour.

Listening and Speaking

Dramatic Reading

Prepare and present a dramatic reading of one stanza of "The Raven." Follow this procedure:

- Practice reading the stanza in front of a mirror, with friends or family, or on audiocassette or videotape.

- Underline any words that give you trouble, and practice until you get them right.

- Use a dramatic tone that conveys the single effect of horror.

- Use body language to help communicate ideas and feelings.

Present your dramatic reading to your class.

    © Pearson Education, Inc.

from Walden

Henry David Thoreau

Summary

In this excerpt, or section, from *Walden*, Thoreau almost buys a farm. Its attraction is that it is far from its neighbors. But the owner's wife changes her mind, and Thoreau decides it is too much of a commitment. Instead he builds a cabin in the woods, where he wants to deal only with the essentials of life. His cabin is open and airy, allowing him to live in touch with nature. He urges his readers to make their lives simple and not to spend time on useless details. He says that so-called improvements only make our lives more complicated.

Visual Summary

Topic: Living a simple life	
Thoreau's Statement	**Details**
At one time of our lives, we look for possible sites for a house.	• Thoreau looks in every direction within twelve miles of where he lives. • He discovers many good sites for a house. • He actually buys Hollowell farm, but before he can occupy it, the owner's wife changes her mind and wants to keep it.
The Hollowell farm has real attractions.	• Far from the village (two miles). • Half a mile from the nearest neighbor and separated from the highway by a field. • Situated on the river, with apple trees gnawed by rabbits.
I went to the woods because I wished to live deliberately.	• Began to spend nights there on Independence Day. • Cabin is airy and unplastered. • Wishes to live deep and to know life by experience.
Simplicity, simplicity, simplicity!	• Keep activities to two or three instead of thousands. • Have one meal a day instead of three. • Be as wise as the day you were born.
I left the woods for as good a reason as I went there.	• He had several more lives to live. • In only a week, he wore a path from his door to the side of the pond.
However mean your life is, meet it and live it.... Money is not required to buy one necessary of the soul.	• A faultfinder will find faults even in paradise. • You may have glorious hours even in a poorhouse. • Do not get new things.

Main Idea
... if one advances confidently in the direction of his dreams, and endeavors to live the life which he has imagined, he will meet with a success unexpected in common hours.

© Pearson Education, Inc.

LITERARY ANALYSIS

Style

Style is the way in which a writer puts thoughts into words. Every writer has his or her own particular style. Style includes the words the writer chooses and the way he or she joins those words together into sentences and paragraphs. Thoreau's style is known for these elements:

- simple, direct language
- images from nature and everyday life
- sentences of varied length, including occasional short sentences
- figurative language, or language not meant to be taken literally

As you read the selection from *Walden*, look for these four elements of Thoreau's style.

READING STRATEGY

Evaluating the Writer's Philosophy

A writer's **philosophy** is the body of ideas that he or she has about life and how it should be lived. When you read these ideas, you should not accept them without question. Instead, **evaluate the writer's philosophy** by asking these questions:

- Is the idea presented clearly in a way that makes sense?
- Is the idea supported with enough examples and reasons?
- Does the idea match my own knowledge and experience?

As you read this selection from *Walden*, use a diagram like this one to help you evaluate the ideas of Thoreau's philosophy.

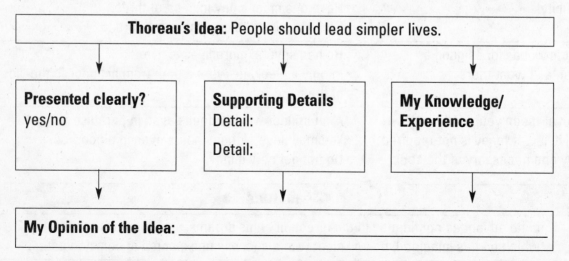

Thoreau's Idea: People should lead simpler lives.

| **Presented clearly?** yes/no | **Supporting Details** Detail: Detail: | **My Knowledge/ Experience** |

My Opinion of the Idea: _____

© Pearson Education, Inc.

from Walden
Henry David Thoreau

When he was twenty-eight, Thoreau decided to leave the village of Concord, Massachusetts. He went to live several miles from town in the woods at Walden Pond. There he built a simple cabin that was little more than a shelter from the rain. He moved in on July 4, 1845—Independence Day. In a section of *Walden* called "Where I Lived and What I Lived For," he explains why he decided to live such a simple, rugged life, close to nature.

◆　◆　◆

I went to the woods because I wished to live deliberately, to front[1] only the essential facts of life, and see if I could not learn what it had to teach, and not, when I came to die, discover that I had not lived. I did not wish to live what was not life, living is so dear; nor did I wish to practice resignation, unless it was quite necessary.

◆　◆　◆

Thoreau went to the woods because he wanted to live life fully and find out what it was all about. If it was wonderful, he wanted to enjoy it. If it was awful, he wanted to face that too. He feels that too many people don't understand the meaning of life. Instead they live in a small way, like ants.

◆　◆　◆

Vocabulary Development

deliberately (duh LIB rit lee) *adv.* with thought and care
essential (uh SEN shuhl) *adj.* vital; necessary
resignation (re zig NAY shuhn) *n.* giving in to conditions beyond your control; hopelessness

---

1. **front** confront; face.

© Pearson Education, Inc.

from Walden **97**

◆ **Culture Note**

July 4 celebrates the independence of the United States from Great Britain. It was an important holiday in Thoreau's time too. Why do you think he chose that day to go live alone in the woods?

_____

_____

_____

◆ **Reading Check**

When he went to the woods, what kind of life experiences was Thoreau hoping to face? Circle the answer in the bracketed paragraph.

◆ **Stop to Reflect**

How would living in the woods help Thoreau live life more fully?

_____

_____

_____

_____

English words change endings to change part of speech. The new word has a different but related meaning. For example, the adjective *pretty* adds *-ness* to become a noun and *-ify* to become a verb:

pretty + -ness = prettiness,

"the state of being pretty"

pretty + -ify = prettify,

"to make pretty"

In the bracketed paragraph, circle a noun and a verb formed from the adjective *simple*. Label the noun *N* and the verb *V*. On the lines below, write the words and their meanings.

noun: _____

meaning: _____

verb: _____

meaning: _____

What **statement of the writer's philosophy** does Thoreau make in the bracketed paragraph?

_____

_____

_____

_____

_____

Our life is <u>frittered away</u> by detail. An honest man has hardly need to count more than his ten fingers, or in extreme cases he may add his ten toes, and lump the rest. <u>Simplicity, simplicity, simplicity!</u> I say, let your affairs be as two or three, and not a hundred or a thousand; instead of a million count half a dozen, and keep your accounts on your thumbnail. In the midst of this chopping sea of civilized life, such are the clouds and storms and quicksands and thousand-and-one items to be allowed for, that a man has to live, if he would not founder[2] and go to the bottom and not make his port at all, by dead reckoning.[3] Simplify, simplify. Instead of three meals a day, if it be necessary eat but one; instead of a hundred dishes, five; and reduce other things in proportion.

◆ ◆ ◆

Thoreau complains that there is too much stress on business and commerce in the young American nation. To him, the focus on material things is shallow. It takes people away from the more important spiritual side of life. Instead of wasting time working on new inventions, like the telegraph and the railroad, Thoreau thinks people should work on their souls. He sees no need to travel farther and faster on the railroad. He thinks people should not be in such a hurry to get nowhere different in their lives.

◆ ◆ ◆

Vocabulary Development

frittered (FRIT uhrd) **away** wasted, bit by bit

---

2. **founder** (FOWN duhr) *v.* fill up with water and sink.
3. **dead reckoning** (REK uhn ing) sailing without using the stars to guide you.

© Pearson Education, Inc.

<u>Time is but the stream I go a-fishing in</u>. I drink at it; but while I drink I see the sandy bottom and detect how shallow it is. Its thin current slides away, but eternity remains. I would drink deeper; fish in the sky, whose bottom is pebbly with stars. I cannot count one. I know not the first letter of the alphabet. I have always been regretting that I was not as wise as the day I was born. The intellect is a <u>cleaver</u>; it <u>discerns</u> and rifts[4] its way into the secret of things. I do not wish to be any more busy with my hands than is necessary. <u>My head is hands and feet.</u> I feel all my best <u>faculties</u> concentrated in it.

◆ ◆ ◆

Thoreau explains why he leaves his cabin on Walden Pond and returns to civilization.

◆ ◆ ◆

I left the woods for as good a reason as I went there. Perhaps it seemed to me that I had several more lives to live, and could not spare any more time for that one. It is remarkable how easily and insensibly[5] we fall into a particular <u>route</u>, and make a beaten track for ourselves. I had not lived there a week before my feet wore a path from my door to the pondside; and though it is five or six years since I trod[6] it, it is still quite distinct. It is true, I fear that others may have fallen into it, and so helped to keep it open. The surface

© Pearson Education, Inc.

Vocabulary Development

cleaver (KLEE vuhr) *n.* a tool for cutting
discerns (di SERNZ) *v.* recognizes separate ideas
faculties (FAK uhl teez) *n.* powers; abilities

---

4. **rifts** cuts through; divides.
5. **insensibly** (in SEN suh blee) *adv.* without noticing.
6. **trod** walked.

◆ **English Language Development**

Using an *a-* before an *-ing* verb form is not standard English, but it occurs in nonstandard spoken English:

Standard: I'm *going* now.

Nonstandard: I'm *a-going* now.

Circle the nonstandard word in the first underlined sentence, and show how it would appear in standard English.

_____

◆ **Stop to Reflect**

What does the second underlined statement mean? Circle the letter of the best answer below.

(a) It is important to keep busy.

(b) Being disabled need not prevent someone from leading a full life.

(c) Thinking is more important than physical action.

(d) The senses of sight, smell, taste, and hearing are more important than the sense of touch.

◆ **Vocabulary and Pronunciation**

The word *route* has two pronunciations. Some people say it to rhyme with *spout*. Others say it the same as *root*. What does the word mean here?

_____

_____

_____.

◆ **Literary Analysis**

Thoreau's **style** includes lots of figurative language, or language not meant to be taken literally.

(1) Circle an example of figurative language in the bracketed paragraph.

(2) What is the paragraph literally about? Circle the answer below.

(a) a person who cares about his or her status or position in society

(b) a nonconformist who does not go along with the crowd

(c) a soldier who bravely marches off to battle

(d) a musician who shows great talent and creativity

◆ **English Language Development**

Poorest is the **superlative form** of the adjective *poor*. You use the superlative to compare more than two people, groups, or things:

• They are *poor*.

• They are *poorer* than she is.

• Of all the people in town, they are the *poorest*.

Short adjectives, like *poor*, usually add *-est* to form the superlative. Longer ones usually use *most*:

• Of all the people in Concord, Thoreau was the *most unusual*.

Circle two more superlative adjectives in this selection.

of the earth is soft and impressible by the feet of men; and so with the paths which the mind travels. How worn and dusty, then, must be the highways of the world, how deep the ruts of tradition and conformity!

◆ ◆ ◆

Thoreau explains the things he learned from living in the woods. First, if a person follows his or her dreams, he or she will be rewarded in unexpected ways. Second, the more simply a person lives, the more rewarding his or her life will be. And last, there is no need to try to be like everyone else.

◆ ◆ ◆

Why should we be in such desperate <u>haste</u> to succeed, and in such desperate <u>enterprises</u>? If a man does not keep <u>pace</u> with his companions, perhaps it is because he hears a different drummer. Let him step to the music which he hears, however measured[7] or far away.

◆ ◆ ◆

To Thoreau, being alone is not the same as being lonely. And being poor does not stop you from enjoying the important things in life.

◆ ◆ ◆

However <u>mean</u> your life is, meet it and live it; do not <u>shun</u> it and call it hard names. It is not so bad as you are. It looks poorest when you are richest. The faultfinder will find faults even in paradise. Love your life, poor as it is. You may perhaps have some pleasant, thrilling,

---

Vocabulary Development

haste (HAYST) *n.* speed

enterprises (EN tuhr prī ziz) *n.* projects; undertakings

pace (PAYS) *n.* step

mean (MEEN) *adj.* low; petty

shun (SHUN) *v.* avoid

---

7. **measured** slow and steady.

© Pearson Education, Inc.

glorious hours, even in a poorhouse. <u>The setting sun is reflected from the windows of the almshouse[8] as brightly as from the rich man's abode;[9] the snow melts before its door as early in the spring.</u> I do not see but a quiet mind may live as <u>contentedly</u> there, and have as cheering thoughts, as in a palace. The town's poor seem to me often to live the most independent lives of any. Maybe they are simply great enough to receive without <u>misgiving</u>. Most think that they are above being supported by the town; but it oftener happens that they are not above supporting themselves by dishonest means, which should be more <u>disreputable</u>. <u>Cultivate poverty like a garden herb, like sage. Do not trouble yourself much to get new things, whether clothes or friends. Turn the old;[10] return to them. Things do not change; we change. Sell your clothes and keep your thoughts.</u>

◆ ◆ ◆

Thoreau concludes with a story about a local farm family. They have a sixty-year-old kitchen table made from the wood of an apple tree. One day the family hears odd sounds from deep inside the table. Then, after several weeks, out comes a strong, beautiful bug. It hatched from an egg that

---

Vocabulary Development

contentedly (kuhn TEN tid lee) *adv.* with happy satisfaction
misgiving (mis GIV ing) *n.* regret
disreputable (dis REP yuh tuh buhl) *adj.* having a bad reputation; considered bad by society
cultivate (KUL tuh vayt) *v.* grow; encourage

---

8. **almshouse** (AHMZ HOWS) *n.* a homeless shelter for the poor.
9. **abode** (uh BOHD) *n.* home; residence.
10. **Turn the old** turn worn old clothes inside out so that you can keep wearing them.

© Pearson Education, Inc.

What does the underlined statement literally mean? Circle the letter of the best answer.

(a) Rich and poor alike can enjoy love and friendship in life.

(b) Rich and poor alike can enjoy the wonders of nature.

(c) It is better to be rich than poor.

(d) The people who deserve to be rich are rich, and the people who deserve to be poor are poor.

◆ Reading Check

What does Thoreau think is more important than clothes? Answer by circling a word in the underlined passage.

◆ Reading Strategy

Below, **evaluate the writer's philosophy** about the poor by circling whether you agree or disagree. Then, use your own knowledge or experiences to support your opinion.

(1) I agree/disagree that the poor are more independent.

(2) Support: _____

_____

_____

_____

_____

had apparently been laid in the apple tree when it was still alive, sixty years before.

♦ ♦ ♦

Who knows what beautiful and winged life, whose egg has been buried for ages under many <u>concentric</u> layers of woodenness in the dead dry life of society, deposited at first in the alburnum[11] of the green and living tree, which has been gradually <u>converted</u> into the semblance of its well-seasoned tomb[12]—heard perchance[13] <u>gnawing</u> out now for years by the astonished family of man, as they sat round the festive board[14]—may unexpectedly come forth from amidst society's most trivial and handselled[15] furniture, to enjoy its perfect summer life at last!

I do not say that John or Jonathan[16] will realize all this; but such is the character of that morrow[17] which mere lapse of time can never make to dawn. The light which puts out our eyes is darkness to us. <u>Only that day dawns to which we are awake.</u> There is more day to dawn. The sun is but a morning star.

♦ **Literary Analysis**

Which elements of Thoreau's **style** are most clearly illustrated in the last two paragraphs? Check two.

_____ simple language

_____ images from nature

_____ occasional short sentences

_____ figurative language

♦ **Stop to Reflect**

What does the underlined sentence mean?

_____

_____

_____

_____

_____

_____

Vocabulary Development

concentric (kuhn SEN trik) *adj.* with one circle inside another

converted (kuhn VER tid) *v.* changed

gnawing (NAW ing) *adj.* chewing

---

11. **alburnum** (al BUR nuhm) *n.* the soft wood between the bark and the core of the tree.
12. **the semblance** (SEM bluhns) **of its well-seasoned tomb**: what seems like an aged tomb, or burial place.
13. **perchance** (puhr CHANS) *adv.* perhaps.
14. **festive** (FES tiv) **board** table.
15. **handselled** (HAN suhld) *adj.* handmade.
16. **John or Jonathan** average person.
17. **the morrow** (MAHR oh) the next day.

     © Pearson Education, Inc.

1. Complete these sentences about Thoreau by giving the main reasons for his actions.

   Thoreau went to live in the woods because _____.

   Thoreau left the woods because _____.

2. Thoreau's remark about the different drummer is now very famous. What do you think "to hear a different drummer" now means? Circle the letter of the best answer.

   (a) to give in to peer pressure

   (b) not to go along with the crowd

   (c) to join the army or navy

   (d) to compose classical music

3. Circle the attitudes or aspects of life that seem important to Thoreau.

   wealth   independence   competition   nature   simplicity   technology

4. **Literary Analysis:** On the chart below, list two examples of each element of Thoreau's **style**.

	Example 1	Example 2
Simple Language		
Images from Nature and Everyday Life		
Short Sentences		
Figurative Language		

© Pearson Education, Inc.

5. **Reading Strategy:** Each sentence below expresses part of Thoreau's philosophy. Circle one sentence. Then, on the lines, **evaluate the philosophy** it expresses. Say whether Thoreau presents the idea clearly and supports it with enough examples and reasons. Compare the idea to your own knowledge and experience.

- Our life is frittered away by detail. . . Simplicity, simplicity, simplicity!
- However mean your life is, meet it and live it.
- Cultivate poverty like a garden herb, like sage.

_____

_____

Writing

Writing an Editorial

Would Thoreau's ideas about living simply work in today's world? Express your opinion in a one- or two-paragraph editorial.

- First, state your opinion about whether Thoreau's ideas on living simply would work today. State your opinion in a single sentence.

_____

_____

_____

- Next, on separate paper, sum up Thoreau's ideas on living simply. Include at least one quotation from *Walden* to support your summary.
- Finally, explain why you think Thoreau's ideas would or would not work in today's world. To support your opinion, include at least two reasons or examples from life today.
- Publish your editorial in the class or school newspaper.

© Pearson Education, Inc.

An Episode of War
Stephen Crane

Summary

In this short story, a young Civil War lieutenant is dividing his company's supply of coffee when he is shot in the arm. Treatment of the wounded is very poor, but the lieutenant makes his way to the field hospital. Before he gets to the hospital, another officer ties a handkerchief over the wound. When the lieutenant sees a doctor, the doctor assures him that he will not amputate the arm. When the lieutenant gets home, his mother, sisters, and wife are sad that his arm has been amputated.

Visual Summary

Story Map

Characters:	The lieutenant	Other soldiers	The doctor

Setting:	**Place:** a battlefield during a lull in the fighting **Time:** the Civil War

Problem:	The lieutenant is wounded by a stray bullet.

Event 1: The lieutenant is using his sword to divide coffee when he is unexpectedly shot in the arm.

Event 2: Because of his wound, the lieutenant has trouble getting his sword back into the scabbard.

Event 3: Another soldier helps him with the sword without touching him.

Event 4: The lieutenant leaves to find a field hospital.

Event 5: On his way to the field hospital, the lieutenant meets an officer who ties a handkerchief over the lieutenant's wound.

Event 6: The lieutenant finds the field hospital, where conditions are terrible.

Climax:	**(Turning Point):**

The lieutenant tells the doctor that he does not want his arm to be amputated.

Resolution:	**(Conclusion):**

The lieutenant goes home with a flat sleeve—he has lost his arm in spite of the doctor's promise.

© Pearson Education, Inc.

LITERARY ANALYSIS

Realism and Naturalism

Two literary movements became popular during the mid- to late-1800s: Realism and Naturalism. Both reacted against Romanticism, a style that emphasized emotion, imagination, and nature.

- **Realism** aimed to portray life faithfully and accurately. Realistic writers focused on ordinary people in everyday life.
- The goal of **Naturalism** was also to present ordinary people's lives. However, the Naturalist writers also suggested that people's fate was shaped by forces they could not control. Among these powerful forces were environment, heredity, and chance.

As you read "An Episode of War," look for elements related to these two literary movements.

READING STRATEGY

Recognizing Historical Details

Stories often reflect the time and place in which they were written. When you **recognize historical details**, you identify how the attitudes of the characters and the events of a story reflect the ideas of their time. "An Episode of War" takes place during the Civil War (1861-1865). You can therefore expect that many of the details in the story will reflect the conditions of life during that period.

As you read, use this chart to record details that are connected to the historical context.

Event	Historical Context
Battles	
Medical Practices	
Social Attitudes	

   © Pearson Education, Inc.

An Episode of War
Stephen Crane

The lieutenant's rubber blanket lay on the ground, and upon it he had poured the company's supply of coffee. Corporals and other representatives of the grimy and hot-throated men who lined the breast-work[1] had come for each squad's portion.

The lieutenant was frowning and serious at this task of division. His lips pursed as he drew with his sword various crevices in the heap, until brown squares of coffee, <u>astoundingly</u> equal in size, appeared on the blanket. He was on the verge of a great triumph in mathematics, and the corporals were thronging forward, each to reap a little square, when suddenly the lieutenant cried out and looked quickly at a man near him as if he suspected it was a case of personal assault. The others cried out also when they saw blood upon the lieutenant's sleeve.

◆　◆　◆

The lieutenant stares at the forest in the distance. He sees little puffs of smoke from the gunfire. The lieutenant holds his sword in his left hand. He struggles to put it in its scabbard, or holder. An orderly-sergeant helps him. The men stare thoughtfully at the wounded lieutenant.

◆　◆　◆

There were others who <u>proffered</u> assistance. One timidly presented his shoulder and asked the lieutenant if he cared to lean upon it, but the latter[2] waved him away mournfully.

Vocabulary Development

astoundingly (uh STOWN ding lee) *adv.* amazingly
proffered (PRAH ferd) *v.* offered

---

1. **breast-work** low wall put up quickly as a defense in battle.
2. **the latter** the second in a list of two people or things; here, "the latter" refers to the lieutenant.

© Pearson Education, Inc.

◆ **Reading Strategy**

Circle two details in the first paragraph that reflect the **historical context** of the story.

◆ **Culture Note**

During the Civil War, conditions in the army were very different from what they are today. In today's military, who would be responsible for handling food supplies?

_____

_____

_____

◆ **Stop to Reflect**

What do you think has happened to the lieutenant?

_____

_____

_____

◆ **Literary Analysis**

Circle the word in the underlined sentence that best expresses the **Naturalists'** view that human beings are shaped by forces that they cannot control.

◆ **English Language Development**

Sometimes a writer deliberately repeats a word, a phrase, or even a whole sentence. What is the effect of the repetition of the word *then* in the bracketed sentence?

_____

_____

◆ **Literary Analysis**

How is the third paragraph an example of **Realistic** writing, or writing that tries to portray life accurately?

_____

_____

_____

◆ **Reading Check**

What building serves as the center of the army field hospital? Circle the correct word in this sentence.

He wore the look of one who knows he is the victim of a terrible disease and understands his helplessness. He again stared over the breast-work at the forest, and then, turning, went slowly rearward. He held his right wrist tenderly in his left hand as if the wounded arm was made of very brittle glass.

And the men in silence stared at the wood, then at the departing lieutenant: then at the wood, then at the lieutenant.

As the wounded officer passed from the line of battle, he was enabled to see many things which as a participant in the fight were unknown to him. He saw a general on a black horse gazing over the lines of blue infantry at the green woods which veiled his problems. An aide galloped furiously, dragged his horse suddenly to a halt, saluted, and presented a paper. It was, for a wonder, precisely like a historical painting.

◆ ◆ ◆

The lieutenant observes the swirling movement of a crew of men with heavy guns. The shooting crackles like brush-fires. The lieutenant comes across some stragglers. They tell him how to find the field hospital. At the roadside, an officer uses his handkerchief to bandage the lieutenant's wound.

◆ ◆ ◆

The low white tents of the hospital were grouped around an old schoolhouse. There was here a singular[3] commotion.

Vocabulary Development

brittle (BRIT tuhl) *adj.* stiff and easily broken

---

3. **singular** (SING yoo luhr) *adj.* remarkable, noticeable.

© Pearson Education, Inc.

In the foreground two ambulances interlocked wheels in the deep mud. The drivers were tossing the blame of it back and forth, gesticulating[4] and berating,[5] while from the ambulances, both crammed with wounded, there came an occasional groan. An interminable crowd of bandaged men were coming and going. Great numbers sat under the trees nursing heads or arms or legs. There was a dispute of some kind raging on the steps of the schoolhouse. Sitting with his back against a tree a man with a face as grey as a new army blanket was serenely smoking a corncob pipe. The lieutenant wished to rush forward and inform him that he was dying.

♦ ♦ ♦

A doctor greets the lieutenant and notices his wounded arm. The doctor looks at the wound.

♦ ♦ ♦

The doctor cried out impatiently, "What mutton-head had tied it up that way anyhow?" The lieutenant answered, "Oh, a man."

When the wound was disclosed the doctor fingered it disdainfully. "Humph," he said. "You come along with me and I'll 'tend to you." His voice contained the same scorn as if he were saying: "You will have to go to jail."

Vocabulary Development

interminable (in TERM uh nuh buhl) *adj.* endless
dispute (dis PYOOT) *n.* disagreement
serenely (suh REEN lee) *adv.* calmly
disdainfully (dis DAYN fuh lee) *adv.* scornfully

---

4. **gesticulating** (jes TIK yoo layt ing) *v.* making vigorous gestures.
5. **berating** (bee RAYT ing) *v.* criticizing harshly.

© Pearson Education, Inc.

An Episode of War **109**

◆ **Read Fluently**

Read the bracketed passage aloud. What impression does the passage give you of conditions at the field hospital?

_____

_____

◆ **Vocabulary and Pronunciation**

Notice that the verb *gesticulate* has the same root as the noun *gesture*. What verb that has the same root as the adjective *interminable*? Hint: Say the word to yourself without its prefix, *-in.*

_____

◆ **Vocabulary and Pronunciation**

The word *mutton-head,* meaning "stupid person" or "fool," is an example of slang or informal English. Give two examples of slang expressions in your native language.

1._____

2._____

◆ **Stop to Reflect**

What does the doctor's attitude toward the lieutenant show about the doctor?

_____

_____

_____

◆ **Reading Strategy**

How is the end of the story an example of **Naturalistic** writing, or writing that assumes that people are influenced by forces they cannot control?

_____

_____

_____

The lieutenant had been very <u>meek</u>, but now his face was flushed, and he looked into the doctor's eyes. "I guess I won't have it <u>amputated</u>," he said.

"Nonsense, man! Nonsense! Nonsense!" cried the doctor. "Come along, now. I won't amputate it. Come along. Don't be a baby."

"Let go of me," said the lieutenant, holding back <u>wrathfully</u>, his glance fixed upon the door of the old schoolhouse, as sinister to him as the portals[6] of death.

And this is the story of how the lieutenant lost his arm. When he reached home, his sisters, his mother, his wife, sobbed for a long time at the sight of the flat sleeve. "Oh, well," he said, standing shamefaced in the midst of these tears, "I don't suppose it matters so much as all that."

Vocabulary Development

meek (MEEK) *adj.* humble, mild-mannered
amputated (AMP yoo tay tuhd) *v.* cut off
wrathfully (RATH fuh lee) *adv.* angrily

---

6. **portals** (PORT uhlz) *n.* doors.

© Pearson Education, Inc.

1. What happens to the lieutenant when he is dividing the portions of coffee?

_____

_____

2. Identify three people in the story who offer help to the lieutenant.

(a) _____

(b) _____

(c) _____

3. When the lieutenant arrives at the schoolhouse, what has happened to cause a commotion?

_____

_____

4. **Reading Strategy:** What **historical details** of Civil War medical practices do you learn in this story? List at least two.

_____

_____

5. **Literary Analysis:** According to the **Naturalists**, human beings are weak and at the mercy of powerful forces. In what way might this statement apply to "An Episode of War"?

_____

_____

Writing

A Field Report on Hospital Conditions

Assume that a colonel in the Civil War wants to know why so many of his soldiers are dying from minor wounds. Imagine that you are the lieutenant in "An Episode of War." Write a report to the colonel on the medical treatment you received at the field hospital. In your report, describe the problems you observed at the hospital.

As you plan your report, consider the following conditions of Civil War medical care:

- Barns, warehouses, and schools often served as makeshift hospitals.
- Hospitals were understaffed and underequipped. There were few nurses.
- Medicines were in short supply.
- Amputation was the routine treatment for injured limbs.
- Twice as many soldiers died of infections as died of combat wounds.

In your report, support your main ideas with **precise details**. You can take some of these details from the story. For example, you might want to refer to the shouting match between the ambulance drivers, the endless crowds of bandaged men, or the doctor's promise that he would not amputate.

You can also use items drawn from the list of conditions shown above. Add specific details as appropriate. For example, you could describe the understaffing of hospitals vividly as follows:

We must have more medical staff immediately, or more men will die. The wounded are often neglected and forced to lie on filthy beds, or even on the floor, for hours and even days at a time. No one feeds, bathes, or treats them.

When you have finished a first draft of your report, check it for logical order and precise supporting details. Improve your organization if necessary. If you need to, add or rearrange details to strengthen or clarify your writing.

Share your report with your classmates.

© Pearson Education, Inc.

from My Bondage and My Freedom
Frederick Douglass

Summary

While he is a slave, Frederick Douglass learns to read and write in spite of great difficulties. Mrs. Auld, his owner's wife and a kind woman, begins to teach him, but her husband stops her. He convinces her that it is not a good idea to educate slaves, and Mrs. Auld becomes a different person. She keeps young Frederick from reading whenever she can. He continues to learn from white boys, paying them with bread. At the age of thirteen, he buys a copy of a schoolbook, the *Columbian Orator*. As he reads about liberty, he learns to hate slavery and realizes that he, as well as Mrs. Auld, has changed. They are both victims of slavery, he says. It is because of slavery that they are enemies rather than friends.

Visual Summary

Main Idea
Both slaves and slave owners are victims of slavery.

Mrs. Auld begins to teach young Frederick Douglass to read.	Mr. Auld advises his wife to stop teaching Douglass to read.	Douglass becomes more and more upset that he is a slave.
↓	↓	↓
She is kind, tenderhearted.	Mrs. Auld loses excellent qualities in agreeing with her husband.	He learns to read from white friends.
↓	↓	↓
She treats Douglass as one human being should treat another.	She violently stops Douglass from reading.	He reads about liberty in the *Columbian Orator*.
↓	↓	↓
She needs to be taught to treat slaves as things.	She begins to believe that slavery and education are not compatible.	The more he learns, the more miserable he becomes.

LITERARY ANALYSIS

Autobiography

An **autobiography** is a person's written account of his or her own life. The author of an autobiography tells about the events that he or she considers most important.

In an autobiography, the writer's life is presented as he or she views it. Therefore, the portrayal of people and events is influenced by the author's feelings and beliefs.

Usually, writers of autobiographies believe that their lives can help others in some way. Frederick Douglass, for example, wrote his autobiography because he believed that his life could serve as an example to others.

As you read the experiences that shaped Douglass's life, notice how the events and feelings he describes might serve as examples for others.

READING STRATEGY

Establishing a Purpose

You can improve your understanding of what you read by **establishing a purpose** for your reading. As you read from Douglass's autobiography, for example, you might establish this two-part purpose:

* To learn about Douglass's special qualities of character.
* To expand your understanding of what it was like to be a slave.

Use this chart to record details reflecting your purpose.

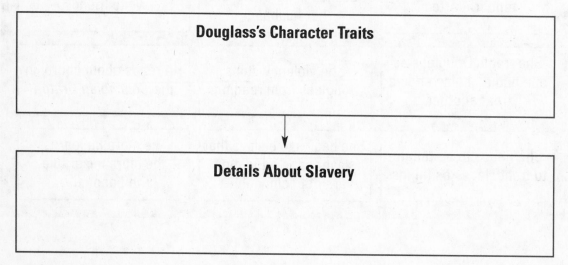

Douglass's Character Traits

Details About Slavery

© Pearson Education, Inc.

from My Bondage and My Freedom
Frederick Douglass

I lived in the family of Master Hugh, at Baltimore, seven years, during which time— as the almanac makers say of the weather— my condition was variable. The most interesting feature of my history here, was my learning to read and write, under somewhat marked disadvantages. In attaining this knowledge, I was compelled to resort to indirections by no means <u>congenial</u> to my nature, and which were really humiliating to me. My mistress—who had begun to teach me—was suddenly checked[1] in her <u>benevolent</u> design, by the strong advice of her husband. In faithful compliance with this advice, the good lady had not only ceased to instruct me, herself, but had set her face as a <u>flint</u> against my learning to read by any means.

◆ ◆ ◆

Douglass says that nature does not prepare people to be either slaves or slaveholders. At first, Mrs. Auld treats Douglass well. It takes a struggle inside her own soul to make her treat him as less than human.

◆ ◆ ◆

When I went into their family, it was the <u>abode</u> of happiness and contentment. The mistress of the house was a model of affection and tenderness. Her fervent <u>piety</u> and watchful

◆ **Reading Check**

Did Douglass have an easy or a hard time learning to read? Circle the phrase that serves as a clue to the answer.

◆ **English Language Development**

A *flint* is a piece of hard, firm stone. What does this comparison suggest about Mrs. Auld's attitude?

_____

_____

_____

_____

Vocabulary Development

congenial (kuhn JEEN yuhl) *adj.* agreeable
benevolent (buh NEV uh luhnt) *adj.* kindly, charitable
abode (uh BOHD) *n.* home
piety (PĪ uh tee) *n.* devotion to religious beliefs or practices

---

1. **checked** stopped, prevented.

© Pearson Education, Inc.

In English, two negative words cancel each other out, producing a positive. Try rewriting the underlined sentence without using the words "no," "nor," or "not." Be sure that your sentence has the same meaning as the original sentence.

_____

_____

According to Douglass in this **autobiography,** why were his owners suspicious of him?

_____

_____

_____

uprightness made it impossible to see her without thinking and feeling—"that woman is a Christian." <u>There was no sorrow nor suffering for which she had not a tear, and there was no innocent joy for which she did not [have] a smile.</u> She had bread for the hungry, clothes for the naked, and comfort for every mourner that came within her reach. Slavery soon proved its ability to divest[2] her of these excellent qualities, and her home of its early happiness.

◆ ◆ ◆

Mrs. Auld stops teaching Douglass. Then she becomes even more opposed than her husband to his learning to read. She angrily snatches a book or a newspaper from his hand.

◆ ◆ ◆

Mrs. Auld was an apt[3] woman, and the advice of her husband, and her own experience, soon demonstrated, to her entire satisfaction, that education and slavery are <u>incompatible</u> with each other. When this conviction was thoroughly established, I was most narrowly watched in all my movements. If I remained in a separate room from the family for any considerable length of time, I was sure to be suspected of having a book, and was at once called upon to give an account of myself.

◆ ◆ ◆

However, these efforts come too late to stop Douglass from learning to read.

◆ ◆ ◆

Vocabulary Development

incompatible (in kuhm PAT uh buhl) *adj.* not able to exist together with

---

2. **divest** (duh VEST) *v.* strip, remove from.
3. **apt** (APT) *adj.* quick to learn.

© Pearson Education, Inc.

Seized with a determination to learn to read, at any cost, I hit upon many expedients[4] to accomplish the desired end. The plea which I mainly adopted, and the one by which I was most successful, was that of using my young white playmates, with whom I met in the street, as teachers. I used to carry, almost constantly, a copy of Webster's spelling book in my pocket; and, when sent on errands, or when play time was allowed me, I would step, with my young friends, aside, and take a lesson in spelling. I generally paid my *tuition fee* to the boys, with bread, which I also carried in my pocket.

◆　◆　◆

Douglass feels grateful to the boys, but he does not want to identify his teachers by name. They might get into trouble for helping him.

◆　◆　◆

Although slavery was a delicate subject, and very cautiously talked about among grownup people in Maryland, I frequently talked about it—and that very freely—with the white boys. I would, sometimes, say to them, while seated on a curbstone or a cellar door, "I wish I could be free, as you will be when you get to be men." "You will be free, you know, as soon as you are twenty-one, and can go where you like, but I am a slave for life. Have I not as good a right to be free as you have?" Words like these, I observed, always troubled them; and I had no small satisfaction in wringing from the boys, occasionally, that fresh and bitter condemnation of slavery, that springs from nature, unseared and unperverted.[5]

◆　◆　◆

◆ **Read Fluently**

Read the bracketed passage aloud. How did Douglass accomplish his goal of learning to read?

_____

_____

_____

◆ **Reading Strategy**

One **purpose** for reading Douglass's account is to understand what it was like to be a slave. How does Douglass think his future will be different from the future of his white playmates?

_____

_____

_____

◆ **Reading Check**

How do human beings react by nature to slavery? Underline the phrase that gives Douglass's opinion.

---

4. **expedients** (ek SPEE dee uhnts) *n.* ways of getting things done.
5. **unperverted** (un puhr VERT id) *adj.* uncorrupted, pure.

© Pearson Education, Inc.

A word or expression is archaic, or old-fashioned, if it is no longer in current use. What is the modern equivalent of the word *trump*?

_____

_____

_____

One **purpose for reading** Douglass's account is to understand his character. From the evidence of the bracketed passage, how does Douglass feel about being a slave?

_____

_____

_____

In the underlined passage, Douglass uses parallelism by repeating a word in the same grammatical structure four times. What is that repeated word?

_____

Douglass never meets a boy who defends slavery. His love of liberty grows steadily. By age thirteen, he has learned to read. He buys a schoolbook. But the praise of liberty in what he reads makes him feel unhappy and depressed. He cannot bear the idea that he will be a slave all his life.

◆ ◆ ◆

Once awakened by the silver trump[6] of knowledge, my spirit was roused to eternal wakefulness. Liberty! the inestimable[7] birthright of every man, had, for me, converted every object into an asserter of this great right. It was heard in every sound, and beheld in every object. It was ever present, to torment me with a sense of my wretched condition. The more beautiful and charming were the smiles of nature, the more horrible and desolate was my condition. I saw nothing without seeing it, and I heard nothing without hearing it. <u>I do not exaggerate, when I say, that it looked from every star, smiled in every calm, breathed in every wind, and moved in every storm.</u>

◆ ◆ ◆

Douglass has no doubt that Mrs. Auld notices his attitude. While nature has made them friends, slavery has made them enemies. Douglass is not cruelly treated, but he still hates the condition of slavery.

◆ ◆ ◆

I had been cheated. I saw through the attempt to keep me in ignorance . . . The feeding and clothing me well, could not <u>atone</u> for taking my liberty from me. The smiles of my mistress could not remove the deep sorrow

---

Vocabulary Development

atone (uh TOHN) *v.* make up for

---

6. **trump** trumpet.
7. **inestimable** (in ES tuh muh buhl) *adj.* priceless.

© Pearson Education, Inc.

that dwelt in my young bosom. Indeed, these, in time, came only to deepen my sorrow. She had changed; and the reader will see that I had changed, too. We were both victims of the same overshadowing evil—*she*, as mistress, *I*, as slave. I will not <u>censure</u> her harshly; she cannot censure me, for she knows I speak but the truth, and have acted in my opposition to slavery, just as she herself would have acted, in a reverse of circumstances.

◆ ◆ ◆

◆ **Stop to Reflect**

How was Douglass's mistress a "victim," in your opinion?

_____

_____

_____

◆ **Vocabulary and Pronunciation**

The word *but* in the last sentence means "no more than." What does the word *but* usually mean when it joins two ideas?

_____

_____

_____

Vocabulary Development

censure (SEN shuhr) *v.* condemn as wrong

1. Why does Mrs. Auld stop teaching Douglass how to read?

_____

_____

2. How does Douglass finally learn to read?

_____

_____

3. What attitude do the white boys have about slavery?

_____

_____

4. What event transforms Douglass, making him feel unhappy and depressed?

_____

_____

5. **Reading Strategy:** By **establishing a purpose** for reading, you can focus on an idea or concept in a passage. Use this chart to identify what you learned about the effects of slavery from Douglass's account.

Douglass's Account	Effects of Slavery
_____	_____
_____	_____
_____	_____

© Pearson Education, Inc.

6. **Literary Analysis:** In an **autobiography,** the author presents people and events from his or her personal point of view. In what ways would this account be different if it had been written by Mrs. Auld?

_____

_____

Listening and Speaking

An Oral Presentation

Frederick Douglass was a gifted public speaker, as well as a powerful writer. Assume that you are making a speech to an audience of abolitionists, or those opposed to slavery. In your speech, you will use parts of Douglass's autobiography, together with statements of your own for emphasis.

Choose passages from the selection that you think are especially strong in opposing slavery. Here is a list of passages you might consider:

- THE PASSAGE BEGINNING "When I went into their family, it was the abode of happiness and contentment . . ." AND ENDING " . . . and her home of its early happiness." (pages 115–116)
- THE PASSAGE BEGINNING "Although slavery was a delicate subject . . ." AND ENDING " . . . that springs from nature, unseared and unperverted." (page 117)
- THE PASSAGE BEGINNING "Once awakened by the silver trump of knowledge . . ." AND ENDING " . . . breathed in every wind, and moved in every storm." (page 118)

Add statements of your own for emphasis. Make your statements consistent with Douglass's intent and purpose. Here are some guidelines for preparing your speech:

- When you are reading Douglass's exact words, make sure you identify the passage as a quotation from him.
- Use punctuation marks to guide your reading. Pause slightly for a comma. Make a full stop at a period.
- Note where Douglass uses parallel structure and repetition. Bring out these devices in your reading.
- Add strong emotion to convey Douglass's tone.
- When you use your own words, choose persuasive language to compel your audience.

After you have rehearsed your oral presentation, deliver it to the class.

© Pearson Education, Inc.

The Notorious Jumping Frog of Calaveras County

Mark Twain

Summary

In this short story, the narrator asks a talkative old man, Simon Wheeler, about a man named Leonidas W. Smiley. Instead of talking about Leonidas W. Smiley, Wheeler tells a tall tale about a man named Jim Smiley. Jim loves to gamble and will bet on anything. He bets a stranger that his frog can outjump any frog in Calaveras County. The stranger accepts the bet, but he needs a frog. Jim goes to find one, and the stranger fills Jim's frog with lead pellets. The pellets make the frog too heavy to jump, so the stranger wins the bet. Jim discovers the trick, but he can't catch up with the stranger. Wheeler has more to tell, but the narrator leaves.

Visual Summary

The narrator	• Calls on a talkative old man named Simon Wheeler. • Asks after a friend of a friend—a man called Leonidas W. Smiley. • Says he suspects Leonidas W. Smiley is a myth.					
Simon Wheeler	• Tells a monotonous story, never changing the tone of his voice or his expression. • The story is about Jim Smiley, who is always betting on something and usually wins.					
1. → Smiley will bet on a horse race, a cat or dog fight, a chicken fight— anything.	**2.** → Once Smiley bet on the life of Parson Walker's wife.	**3.** → Smiley owned a horse who won races at the last minute and a dog who won fights by grabbing the other dog's leg— until he was up against a dog with no hind legs.	**4.** → Once Smiley had a frog—he named him Daniel Webster and taught him to jump.	**5.** → A stranger offers to bet against Daniel Webster, but he has no frog. Smiley goes to find the stranger a frog.	**6.** → While Smiley is gone, the stranger fills Smiley's frog's mouth with quailshot.	**7.** → Smiley's frog loses. By the time Smiley dis- covers the quailshot, the stranger is long gone.
Simon Wheeler	Is called from the front yard—says he'll only be gone a second.					
The narrator	Takes the opportunity to leave, saying he's not going to get any information about Leonidas W. Smiley.					

© Pearson Education, Inc.

LITERARY ANALYSIS

Humor

Humor is writing intended to make you laugh. Humorists use many techniques to make their work funny. Many western humorists of the 1800s, like Mark Twain, use these techniques:

- They exaggerate or overstate events out of all proportion to their importance.
- They add many imaginative or ridiculous details.
- They use a narrator or a storyteller who speaks in a serious tone.
- They suggest that the teller of the story doesn't realize that the story is ridiculous.

As you read Mark Twain's story about a jumping frog, take note of the details that make the tale a classic of humor.

READING STRATEGY

Understanding Regional Dialect

Twain uses language colorfully, often with humorous results. He was a master at including regional dialect in his stories. **Regional dialect** is language specific to a particular area of the country.

At first sight, some of the words and phrases in dialect may seem like words you have never seen or heard before. If you read those unfamiliar words aloud, however, you will usually find that they are regional pronunciations of words you already know.

Use a chart like this one to translate dialect into modern Standard English.

Regional Dialect

... he was the curiousest man about always betting on anything that turned up you ever see, if he could get anybody to bet on the other side.

↓

Standard English

He was determined to bet on anything he could, if he could get someone to bet on the other side.

The Notorious Jumping Frog of Calaveras County

Mark Twain

A friend of the narrator's asks him to call on talkative old Simon Wheeler. The friend says he wants news of his friend Reverend Leonidas W. Smiley. Instead, Wheeler tells the narrator a long-drawn-out story about Jim Smiley. As he tells the story, Wheeler never smiles, and he never frowns.

◆ ◆ ◆

"Rev. Leonidas W. H'm, Reverend Le—well, there was a feller here once by the name of Jim Smiley, in the winter of '49—or maybe it was the spring of '50—I don't <u>recollect</u> exactly, somehow, though what makes me think it was one or the other is because I remember the big flume[1] warn't finished when he first come to the camp; but anyway, he was the curiousest man about always betting on anything that turned up you ever see, if he could get anybody to bet on the other side; and if he couldn't he'd change sides.

◆ ◆ ◆

Wheeler says Smiley was lucky. He almost always won his bets. He'd bet on horse races, dog fights, cat fights, and chicken fights. If he saw two birds sitting on a fence, he'd bet on which bird would fly first. He had several animals he'd bet on: a mare, a small bull-pup named Andrew Jackson, and lots of others. One day he caught a frog, taught him to catch flies, and named him Dan'l Webster.

◆ ◆ ◆

Vocabulary Development

recollect (rek uh LEKT) v. remember

1. **flume** (FLOOM) n. artificial channel for carrying water to provide power and transport objects.

According to Wheeler, what was Jim Smiley's outstanding personality trait? Underline the part of the bracketed passage that gives the answer.

◆ **Literary Analysis**

Humor often involves exaggeration, or overstatement. Identify two ways that Wheeler exaggerates.

1. _____

_____

2. _____

_____

© Pearson Education, Inc.

Well, Smiley kep' the beast in a little lattice box, and he used to fetch him downtown sometimes and lay for a bet. One day a feller—a stranger in the camp, he was—come acrost him with his box, and says:

"What might it be that you've got in the box?"

And Smiley says, sorter indifferent-like, "It might be a parrot, or it might be a canary, maybe, but it ain't—it's only just a frog."

And the feller took it, and looked at it careful, and turned it round this way and that, and says, "H'm—so 'tis. Well, what's *he* good for?"

"Well," Smiley says, easy and careless, "he's good enough for *one* thing, I should judge—he can outjump any frog in Calaveras county."

The feller took the box again, and took another long, particular look, and gave it back to Smiley, and says, very deliberate, "Well," he says, "I don't see no p'ints[2] about that frog that's any better'n any other frog."

"Maybe you don't," Smiley says. "Maybe you understand frogs and maybe you don't understand 'em; maybe you've had experience, and maybe you ain't only a amature,[3] as it were. Anyways, I've got *my* opinion, and I'll resk forty dollars that he can outjump any frog in Calaveras county."

And the feller studied a minute, and then says, kinder sad like, "Well, I'm only a stranger here, and I ain't got no frog; but if I had a frog, I'd bet you."

◆ ◆ ◆

◆ **Reading Strategy**

Rewrite the underlined passage of **regional dialect** in standard English.

_____

_____

_____

◆ **English Language Development**

In English, adverbs modify verbs. Twain uses the adjective form *careful* for the sake of the regional dialect. What adverb can you form from *careful?*

_____

◆ **Read Fluently**

Read the bracketed paragraph aloud. What does this description of the stranger suggest about his personality?

_____

_____

_____

◆ **Literary Analysis**

Smiley's long-drawn-out answer adds to the **humor**. Underline the word he repeats several times in order to spin out his answer to the stranger.

Vocabulary Development

deliberate (di LIB rit) *adj.* carefully thought out

2. **p'ints** dialect for *points,* meaning fine points or advantages.
3. **amature** dialect for *amateur* (AM uh chuhr) *n.* unskillful person.

Smiley offers to get the stranger a frog. Smiley leaves his own frog with the stranger while he looks for another frog. The stranger waits.

◆ ◆ ◆

So he set there a good while thinking and thinking to hisself, and then he got the frog out and prized his mouth open and took a teaspoon and filled him full of quailshot[4]—filled him pretty near up to his chin—and set him on the floor. Smiley he went to the swamp and slopped around in the mud for a long time, and finally he ketched a frog, and fetched him in, and give him to this feller, and says:

"Now, if you're ready, set him alongside of Dan'l, with his forepaws just even with Dan'l's, and I'll give the word." Then he says, "One—two—three—*git!*" and him and the feller touched up the frogs from behind, and the new frog hopped off lively, but Dan'l give a heave, and hysted[5] up his shoulders—so—like a Frenchman, but it warn't no use—he couldn't budge; he was planted as solid as a church, and he couldn't no more stir than if he was anchored out. Smiley was a good deal surprised, and he was disgusted too, but he didn't have no idea what the matter was, of course.

The feller took the money and started away, and when he was going out at the door, he sorter jerked his thumb over his shoulder—so—at Dan'l, and says again, very deliberate, "Well," he says, "I don't see no p'ints about that frog that's any better'n any other frog."

Smiley he stood scratching his head and looking down at Dan'l a long time, and at last he says, "I do wonder what in the nation that frog throw'd off for—I wonder if there ain't something the matter with him—he 'pears to

---

4. **quailshot** small lead pellets used for shooting quail.
5. **hysted** dialect for *hoisted,* meaning raised.

Circle two words in the bracketed passage that are examples of **regional dialect**.

How do these details about what the stranger does to Smiley's frog add to the story's **humor**?

_____

_____

_____

Because of the regional dialect, Twain uses a double negative: "I don't see no p'ints about that frog that's any better'n any other frog." Rewrite this sentence in standard English.

_____

_____

_____

_____

© Pearson Education, Inc.

look mighty baggy, somehow." And he ketched Dan'l by the nap of the neck, and hefted him, and says, "Why blame my cats if he don't weigh five pound!" and turned him upside down and he belched out a double handful of shot. And then he see how it was, and he was the maddest man—he set the frog down and took out after that feller, but he never ketched him. And—

♦ ♦ ♦

At this point someone calls Wheeler from the front yard. The narrator knows that Wheeler has no information about the Rev. Leonidas W. Smiley, so he starts to leave. He meets Wheeler at the door, and Wheeler says:

♦ ♦ ♦

"Well, thish-yer Smiley had a yaller one-eyed cow that didn't have no tail, only just a short stump like a bannanner, and—"

However, lacking both time and <u>inclination</u>, I did not wait to hear about the afflicted cow, but took my leave.

◆ **English Language Development**

The phrase "what in the nation" on page 126 has more familiar equivalents: "what on earth" and "what in the world." These phrases are *idioms,* or informal expressions that are not intended literally. What would be another way of saying, "How on earth did you get here"?

_____

_____

_____

◆ **Culture Note**

A **tall tale** is an exaggerated story told for entertainment. Telling tall tales like this one was a common form of entertainment on the western frontier. What does such a tale suggest about the character of the developing West?

_____

_____

_____

_____

◆ **Literary Analysis**

What do you think Wheeler is about to do at the end of this story? How does that contribute to the **humor** of the story?

_____

_____

_____

Vocabulary Development

inclination (in kluh NAY shuhn) *n.* liking or preference

© Pearson Education, Inc.

1. What was Jim Smiley's response to any event?

_____

_____

2. Why was Smiley so proud of his frog?

_____

_____

3. What caused Smiley to lose his bet to the stranger?

_____

_____

4. How does this story reveal the character of Simon Wheeler as well as it shows the character of Jim Smiley? Explain your answer.

_____

_____

5. **Literary Analysis:** One technique Twain uses to create **humor** is exaggeration, or overstatement. On the chart below, identify two examples of exaggeration. Then explain why each is amusing.

Exaggeration	
Example 1: _____	Example 2: _____
_____	_____
Why It Is Amusing: _____	Why It Is Amusing: _____
_____	_____

© Pearson Education, Inc.

6. **Reading Strategy:** The language specific to a particular area of the country is called **regional dialect**. Rewrite the following passage in your own words:

"Well, thish-yer Smiley had a yaller one-eyed cow that didn't have no tail, only just a short stump like a bannanner . . ."

_____

_____

Writing

Analytic Essay

Mark Twain once described the techniques a writer uses to create humor this way:

"The humorous story may be spun out to great length, and may wander around as much as it pleases, and arrive at nowhere in particular . . . [It] is told gravely; the teller does his best to conceal the fact that he even dimly suspects there is anything funny about it."

Write an essay discussing Twain's use of these humorous techniques in "The Notorious Jumping Frog of Calaveras County."

1. Start by choosing passages from the story that serve as examples of Twain's main ideas as quoted in the passage above. Use this chart to organize your thoughts:

Idea	spins out at length	arrives nowhere	is told gravely	conceals humor
Example				

2. As you continue work on your essay, keep these guidelines in mind.
   - Organize your paper point by point, connecting each of Twain's ideas to passages from the story.
   - Make sure you clearly explain the connection in each case.

3. Review your first draft to find places you could improve. For example, you might add examples, details, or quotations to support your ideas.

4. Share your essay with a small group of classmates. Use their suggestions to make additional revisions.

The Story of an Hour

Kate Chopin

Summary

When Mrs. Mallard hears that her husband has been killed in a train accident, she cries and goes to her room. Alone there, she realizes that she is free from the control of her husband. As she leaves her room, she is very happy. Just then, her husband, who had not been on the train after all, comes in the door. Mrs. Mallard dies of a heart attack.

Visual Summary

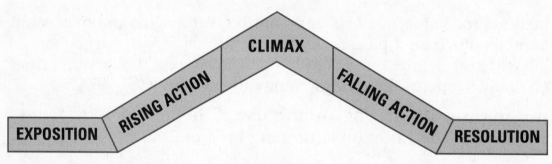

EXPOSITION	RISING ACTION	CLIMAX	FALLING ACTION	RESOLUTION
Mrs. Mallard has a weak heart. Her sister and Richards, a close family friend, tell her carefully of the death of her husband in a train accident.	Mrs. Mallard weeps immediately. Then she goes to her room and gradually begins to feel the freedom of being able to live for herself.	Mrs. Mallard leaves her room in a sort of triumph. As she goes downstairs, she sees her husband coming in the door.	Mrs. Mallard's sister cries out, Richards tries to shield Mrs. Mallard from the sight of her husband, and Mr. Mallard is amazed.	Mrs. Mallard dies of a heart attack. The doctors say it was caused by joy, but the reader knows the real cause.

© Pearson Education, Inc.

LITERARY ANALYSIS

Irony

Irony is a literary technique involving a contradiction or a sharp difference. Sometimes, an irony exists between what a speaker says and what he or she really means. Other times, irony may result from a difference between what is expected and what actually happens. Irony can be surprising, interesting, or amusing.

When you read literature, you will frequently meet three types of irony:

Type of Irony	Nature of Contrast
Verbal irony	Words suggest the opposite of their usual meaning.
Dramatic irony	Readers are aware of something that a character does not know.
Situational irony	The outcome of an action or situation is very different from what we expect.

As you read "The Story of an Hour," decide which type of irony best fits the story.

READING STRATEGY

Recognizing Ironic Details

When you read a story, the details in it often lead you to expect certain events. When events do not turn out the way you expect, you experience a sense of irony. Looking back, you can **recognize ironic details**.

While you read "The Story of an Hour," use this chart to note ironic details. On the chart, write events or feelings that do not turn out to be what they appear to be at first.

Detail →	Expected outcome →	Actual outcome
Care is taken to reveal bad news to Mrs. Mallard.	She would be upset.	

© Pearson Education, Inc.

◆ Vocabulary and Pronunciation

The word *intelligence* can mean "mental ability" or "news." Which meaning is used in the underlined sentence?

_____

_____

◆ Stop to Reflect

Why is Richards careful to be sure that the message is true?

_____

_____

_____

◆ Reading Strategy

Mrs. Mallard has just received news of her husband's death. Circle three **details** in the bracketed passage that you recognize as **ironic** under the circumstances.

The Story of an Hour
Kate Chopin

Knowing that Mrs. Mallard was afflicted[1] with a heart trouble, great care was taken to break to her as gently as possible the news of her husband's death.

It was her sister Josephine who told her, in broken sentences; veiled hints that revealed in half concealing. Her husband's friend Richards was there too, near her. <u>It was he who had been in the newspaper office when intelligence[2] of the railroad disaster was received, with Brently Mallard's name leading the list of "killed."</u> He had only taken the time to assure himself of its truth by a second telegram, and had hastened to <u>forestall</u> any less careful, less tender friend in bearing the sad message.

◆ ◆ ◆

Mrs. Mallard bursts out weeping in her sister's arms. She goes to her room alone. There she sits in a chair facing the open window.

◆ ◆ ◆

She could see in the open square before her house the tops of trees that were all aquiver with the new spring life. The delicious breath of rain was in the air. In the street below a peddler was crying his wares.[3] The notes of a distant song which someone was singing reached her faintly, and countless sparrows were twittering in the eaves.

Vocabulary Development

forestall (fawr STAWL) *v.* prevent by acting ahead of time

---

1. **afflicted** (uh FLIK ted) *adj.* suffering from.
2. **intelligence** (in TEL i juhnts) *n.* news.
3. **wares** (wayrz) *n.* merchandise.

© Pearson Education, Inc.

<u>There were patches of blue sky showing here and there through the clouds that had met and piled one above the other in the west facing her window.</u>

♦ ♦ ♦

Mrs. Mallard still sobs occasionally. She stares dully at the sky. Then she senses a new emotion coming over her. She tries to fight her new feelings, but her effort is not successful.

♦ ♦ ♦

When she abandoned herself,[4] a little whispered word escaped her slightly parted lips. She said it over and over under her breath: "free, free, free!" The vacant stare and the look of terror that had followed it went from her eyes. They stayed keen and bright. Her pulses beat fast, and the coursing blood warmed and relaxed every inch of her body.

She did not stop to ask if it were or were not a monstrous joy that held her. A clear and exalted perception enabled her to dismiss the suggestion as <u>trivial</u>.

She knew that she would weep again when she saw the kind, tender hands folded in death; the face that had never looked save with love upon her, fixed and gray and dead. But she saw beyond that bitter moment a long procession of years to come that would belong to her absolutely. And she opened and spread her arms out to them in welcome.

There would be no one to live for her during those coming years; she would live for herself. There would be no powerful will bending hers in that blind persistence with which men and women believe they have a right to impose a private will upon a fellow creature.

♦ ♦ ♦

Vocabulary Development

trivial (TRIV i uhl) *adj.* unimportant

---

4. **abandoned herself** surrendered or gave herself up.

© Pearson Education, Inc.

◆ **Read Fluently**

Read the underlined paragraph aloud. What might the "patches of blue sky" showing through the clouds suggest about a change in Mrs. Mallard's mood?

_____

_____

_____

◆ **English Language Development**

In English, the most common way to form a plural noun is to add –s to the singular form. A noun adds –es to form the plural if it ends in *s, x, ch,* or *sh,* like *patches.* What are two other nouns in English that have –es in the plural?

1. _____

2. _____

◆ **Literary Analysis**

What **irony**, or contrast, does the bracketed passage reveal between what was expected and what actually happens?

_____

_____

_____

Mrs. Mallard reflects on her new-found freedom. Compared to the future, the past matters little. Suddenly she hears her sister Josephine begging her to open the door. Mrs. Mallard dreams of her future life a little longer. She prays for a long life. Then she opens the door and puts her arm around her sister. They go down the stairs together. At the bottom, Richards stands waiting for them.

◆ ◆ ◆

Someone was opening the front door with a latchkey. It was Brently Mallard who entered, a little travel-stained, composedly[5] carrying his gripsack[6] and umbrella. He had been far from the scene of the accident, and did not know there had been one. He stood amazed at Josephine's piercing cry; at Richards's quick motion to screen him from the view of his wife.

But Richards was too late.

When the doctors came they said she had died of heart disease—of joy that kills.

5. **composedly** (kum POHZ uhd le) *adj.* calmly.
6. **gripsack** (GRIP sak) *n.* small bag for holding clothes.

© **Pearson Education**, Inc.

◆ **Reading Check**

How is it possible for Brently Mallard to be alive and well?

_____

_____

_____

◆ **Literary Analysis**

In **verbal irony**, words suggest the opposite of their usual meaning. Underline the phrase in this sentence that is an example of verbal irony.

Mark the Text

1. At the beginning of the story, the narrator says that Mrs. Mallard suffers from a "heart trouble." What, in addition to a medical condition, might the narrator mean by this phrase?

_____

_____

2. On the chart below, list four details that Mrs. Mallard sees, hears, or senses outside her window.

Detail 1	Detail 3
Detail 2	Detail 4

3. In what way do these sights, smells, and sounds outside foreshadow, or predict, the feelings that sweep over Mrs. Mallard?

_____

_____

4. Mrs. Mallard repeatedly whispers the word "free" to herself. What has she apparently resented about her marriage?

_____

_____

5. **Literary Analysis:** When events turn out contrary to what we expect, the result is **situational irony**. In what ways are Brently Mallard's return and Mrs. Mallard's death examples of situational irony?

_____

_____

© Pearson Education, Inc.

6. **Reading Strategy:** When you **recognize ironic details**, you realize that the actual outcome of an event or situation is very different from the expected outcome. What detail in the story's second paragraph makes Mr. Mallard's arrival at the end all the more ironic?

_____

_____

Listening and Speaking

A Soliloquy

A **soliloquy** is a long speech made by a character who is alone. The character reveals private feelings to the reader or the audience.

Imagine that Brently Mallard had never returned. Present a soliloquy in which Mrs. Mallard reflects on her life ten years later. Consider the following questions:

- Has Mrs. Mallard's heart trouble improved, or not?

_____

- Where is she living now?

_____

- Has she remarried? If so, what is her new husband like? If Mrs. Mallard has not remarried, why not?

_____

_____

- Has she traveled? If so, what memorable sights has she seen?

_____

_____

As you plan your soliloquy, keep in mind these guidelines:

- Use the thoughts and feelings in the story to create a real voice for Mrs. Mallard. For example, from the story you know that Mrs. Mallard values freedom and independence. She also notices details, like the sights and sounds outside her window.
- A soliloquy shares inner thoughts and feelings.

Present your soliloquy to your classmates.

 © Pearson Education, Inc.

The Turtle *from* The Grapes of Wrath

John Steinbeck

Summary

Near a highway is a mass of tangled, dry grass full of seeds of every kind. The seeds are waiting for a way to travel. It might be the hem of a woman's skirt or the paw of a passing animal. A land turtle crawls over the grass toward the highway. A head of wild oats attaches itself to the turtle's front legs. With great effort, the turtle gets onto the highway. A car driven by a woman swerves to avoid the turtle. A light truck driven by a man swerves to hit it. The front wheel of the truck hits the turtle's shell. The turtle spins and rolls off the highway on its shell. After a long time, the turtle rolls itself over. The head of oats falls off and the seeds spill out. As the turtle pulls itself along, its shell drags dirt over the seeds.

Visual Summary

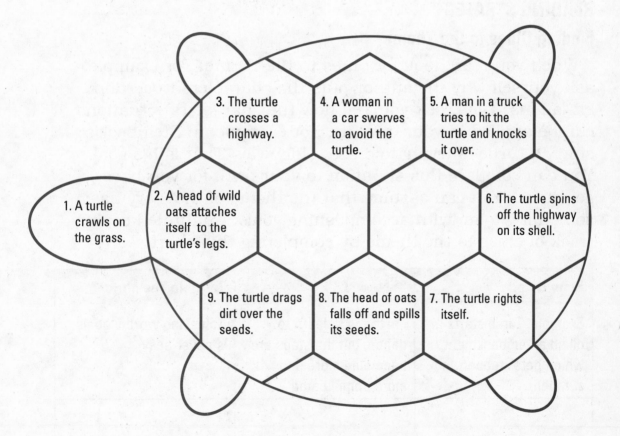

LITERARY ANALYSIS
Theme

A story's **theme** is its message about life. Authors reveal themes in these ways:

- Through what the characters say and do
- By what happens in the plot
- By using symbols, or details that stand for something else

In "The Turtle," John Steinbeck uses a turtle as a symbol for people. To figure out the theme of the story, consider these questions:

1. What is the turtle's goal?
2. What obstacles does the turtle face?
3. How does the turtle overcome the obstacles?

READING STRATEGY
Finding Clues to the Theme

When you read, look for **clues to the theme.** For example, ask yourself why the author puts the characters in certain situations. Then, ask yourself how the characters' situations can be applied to your own life. For example, in Steinbeck's story, a turtle is trying to cross a highway. That is his goal. You can compare this situation to your own, for you have goals, too. You can assume that the theme of the story has something to do with accomplishing goals. Continue keeping track of clues to the theme by completing this chart.

Story Detail	My Own Life	Possible Theme
Example: Turtle starts to climb an embankment, which gets steeper and steeper.	I'm trying to learn to dance, but the steps are becoming more and more complicated.	Achieving worthy goals is never easy.

    © Pearson Education, Inc.

The Turtle
John Steinbeck

Steinbeck opens by describing the land at the edge of a concrete highway. It is covered with a mat of dry grass full of various kinds of seeds. The seeds are waiting to be picked up by passing animals or to be carried by the wind.

Steinbeck continues by saying that the sun warms the grass. In the shade of the grass, many insects live.

◆ ◆ ◆

And over the grass at the roadside a land turtle crawled, <u>turning aside for nothing, dragging his high-domed shell over the grass.</u> His hard legs and yellow-nailed feet <u>threshed slowly through the grass, not really walking, but boosting and dragging his shell along.</u>

◆ ◆ ◆

The turtle does not notice seeds and burrs in his way. He moves ahead with his beak slightly open. His eyes stare straight ahead.

Steinbeck describes how the turtle moves across the grass. He leaves a trail behind him. The turtle sees a hill, which is really the highway <u>embankment</u>, ahead of him. Climbing the hill is a very difficult job for the turtle. Very slowly, he manages to get up the embankment. But then he gets to the shoulder of the highway. He faces what looks like a concrete wall. It is the concrete of the highway, four inches thick.

◆ ◆ ◆

Vocabulary Development

threshed (THRESHT) *v.* struck over and over again
embankment (em BANGK ment) *n.* a long mound of earth or stone that keeps water back or supports a road

---

© Pearson Education, Inc.

◆ **Literary Analysis**

Read the underlined sections in this paragraph. Then complete this sentence based on the **theme** of the story.

We can tell that the turtle is determined to get across the road because he does the following things:

he _____,

_____

and he _____

_____.

◆ **Vocabulary and Pronunciation**

In English, the letter *c* has two pronunciations. It can sound like a *k,* as in *concrete.* It can also sound like an *s,* as in *cement.* What sound does *c* have in each of these words? Write *k* or *s.*

clover ___ insect ___ climb ___

fierce ___ faces ___ braced ___

◆ **Vocabulary and Pronunciation**

In English, the past tense is usually shown by adding -d or -ed to
a verb. Sometimes this ending
sounds like d, as in covered.
Sometimes this ending sounds
like ed, as in lifted. And sometimes it sounds like t, as in
picked. Write d, ed, or t to tell
how the ending sounds in each
of these words:

pushed _____   upraised _____

peered _____   braced _____

◆ **English Language Development**

When the ending -ly is added to
an adjective, it changes the
word to an adverb. The ending
means "in a _____ manner."
Thus, slowly means "in a slow
manner." Write the meaning of
each of these words:

suddenly _____

finally _____

◆ **Reading Strategy**

To **find clues to the theme,**
underline the part that
tells how the woman
acted when she saw
the turtle. Circle the
part on the next page
that tells how the man
acted.
Then answer these questions:

(1) What do you think the woman
symbolizes?

_____

(2) What do you think the man
symbolizes?

_____

As though they worked independently the
<u>hind</u> legs pushed the shell against the wall.
The head upraised and peered over the wall to
the broad smooth plain of cement.

◆   ◆   ◆

After much straining, the turtle lifts itself
on the edge of the wall. As the turtle rests, a
red ant runs into the turtle's shell. The turtle
crushes it between its body and legs.

Steinbeck describes how some wild
oat seeds are brought into the shell by the
turtle's front leg. The turtle lies still for a
moment. Then his head, legs, and tail come
out of the shell. The turtle begins straining to
reach the top of the cement. The hind legs
slowly boost the rest of the turtle's body up.
At last he gets to the top. The wild oat seeds
are still attached around the turtle's front
legs.

Movement is easy for the turtle now.
The turtle begins to cross the highway.

◆   ◆   ◆

A <u>sedan</u> driven by a forty-year-old woman
approached. She saw the turtle and swung to
the right, off the highway, the wheels screamed
and a cloud of dust boiled up.

◆   ◆   ◆

The car tips with the sudden swerve.
After regaining control, the woman drives on
slowly. The turtle had hidden in its shell in
fear, but now the turtle hurries across the
road.

◆   ◆   ◆

Vocabulary Development

hind (HĪND) adj. back

sedan (si DAN) n. a hard-top car big enough for four to
seven people

© Pearson Education, Inc.

And now a light truck approached, and as it came near, the driver saw the turtle and <u>swerved</u> to hit it.

♦ ♦ ♦

The front wheel of the truck hits the turtle. The turtle flips over and rolls off the highway.

Steinbeck describes how the turtle lies on its back. Its body is drawn into its shell. Finally, the legs come out and start waving around in the air. The turtle is looking for something to grab onto. At last its front foot gets hold of a piece of quartz. Very slowly, the turtle manages to pull itself over. At this point, the wild oat seeds fall out and get stuck in the ground.

As the turtle moves along, its shell buries the seeds with dirt.

♦ ♦ ♦

The turtle entered a dust road and jerked itself along, drawing a wavy shallow <u>trench</u> with its shell. The old humorous eyes looked ahead, and the horny beak opened a little. His yellow toe nails slipped a fraction in the dust.

Vocabulary Development

swerved (SWERVD) *v.* turned aside from a straight course
trench (TRENCH) *n.* a deep ditch dug in the ground

© Pearson Education, Inc.

The Turtle **141**

◆ **English Language Development**

Sometimes a noun is described by two or more words that work together as a single adjective that comes before the noun. When this happens, the words are connected by hyphens. Rewrite these phrases, changing the underlined words to a hyphenated adjective before the noun. Example: a woman who is forty years old = a forty-year-old woman

concrete that is four inches thick =

_____

a turtle with a hard shell =

_____

◆ **Culture Note**

More cars are on the road in the United States than in any other country. What forms of transportation are commonly used in your native country?

_____

_____

◆ **Stop to Reflect**

(1) How does the turtle help the wild oat seeds?

_____

_____

_____

(2) What do you think Steinbeck is saying about how different forms of life relate to one another?

_____

_____

_____

1. The dry, tangled grass by the highway is full of signs of life. Name three things that show this.

   1. _____ 2. _____ 3. _____

2. The turtle wants to cross the highway. But he runs into three problems that make it difficult for him to do so. Complete this chart by writing the three problems and then telling how the turtle deals with them.

Problems	How the Turtle Deals with Them

3. What does the turtle do to help the oat seeds?

   _____

   _____

4. The man in the light truck tries to hurt the turtle. How does his action actually help the turtle instead?

   _____

   _____

5. **Literary Analysis:** In the end, the turtle's shell drags dirt over the oat seeds. What **theme** is Steinbeck expressing here?

   _____

   _____

© Pearson Education, Inc.

6. **Reading Strategy:** Put a check in front of the three details that you think are the best **clues to the theme.**

____ The turtle turned aside for nothing.

____ The turtle stared straight ahead.

____ The sedan was driven by a woman.

____ The light truck's driver was a man.

____ The turtle grabs onto a piece of quartz and pulls itself over.

Listening and Speaking

Conduct an Interview

Interview someone who lived during the Great Depression of the 1930s.

1. Choose the person you will interview.

_____

_____

2. Write three questions to ask during the interview.

1. _____

_____

2. _____

_____

3. _____

_____

3. Schedule your interview.

4. Ask your questions. You may follow either one of these methods:
   • Ask the person for permission to tape-record the interview, and then do so.
   • Take notes as the person answers your questions.

5. After you conduct the interview, get together with a small group and share the information you received.

The Far and the Near

Thomas Wolfe

Summary

For twenty years, the engineer of a train blows the whistle every day as he approaches a certain pleasant little cottage near the tracks. A woman and her daughter, both otherwise strangers to him, come out and wave to him as he passes. He has increasingly more tender feelings about them and the little house, which become symbols of happiness for him. At last, when he retires, he goes to visit the spot, to be near what he has only seen from the train for so long. At close range, though, the town is strange to him, the house is unattractive, and the women are unfriendly. He leaves, feeling disappointed, old, and sad.

Visual Summary

Sequence of Events					
1.	2.	3.	4.	5.	6.
For twenty years, a train engineer blows his whistle at a white cottage with green blinds.	A woman always comes out to wave. At first she has her baby in her arms. The engineer watches as the baby grows up.	The engineer experiences tragedy and grief, but the women and the house are symbols of beauty and endurance for him.	When the engineer retires, he decides to visit the women.	The town is different and the women are not attractive—in fact they are barely friendly.	The engineer leaves, feeling old and discouraged.

© Pearson Education, Inc.

LITERARY ANALYSIS

Climax and Anticlimax

A **climax** is the high point of a story. Sometimes that point is a letdown. It might be a disappointment to the characters. It might even be a disappointment to the reader. When this happens, it is called an **anticlimax**.

In "The Far and the Near," Thomas Wolfe tells the story of a train conductor. For twenty years, he drives through various towns across the United States. He sees these towns "from the high windows of his cab." In other words, he sees them from afar, like an outsider. One place in particular seems very attractive to him.

What do you think might happen when he has the chance to visit that place? Will it look the same when it becomes "the near" rather than "the far"?

READING STRATEGY

Predicting

When you **predict,** you tell what you think will happen next. Your prediction should be based on your knowledge of real life. Use your own experience and knowledge to help you make predictions.

As you read, practice making predictions by filling in this chart.

Story Detail	My Experience or Knowledge About This Detail	My Prediction
Example: Every day for more than twenty years	Many changes take place in twenty years.	The characters in the story will change.

© Pearson Education, Inc.

The Far and the Near
Thomas Wolfe

The story opens with a description of a tidy little cottage. It is white with green blinds. It has a vegetable garden, a grape arbor, and flower beds. In front of the house are three big oak trees. The house looks neat and comfortable. Every afternoon, just after two o'clock, an express train passes by the house.

◆ ◆ ◆

Every day for more than twenty years, as the train had approached this house, the engineer had blown on the whistle, and every day, as soon as she heard this signal, a woman had appeared on the back porch of the little house and waved to him.

◆ ◆ ◆

The woman brings her young daughter to the porch. The girl also waves to the engineer each day. As the years pass, the girl grows up.

The engineer grows old and gray during these twenty years. His own children have also grown up.

He has seen terrible tragedies on the tracks. One time, his train hit a wagon full of children. Another time a cheap car stalls on the tracks. The people inside are so frightened that they cannot move. Once an old, deaf hobo is walking along the tracks. He does not hear the warning whistle.

◆ ◆ ◆

But no matter what peril or tragedy he had known, the vision of the little house and the women waving to him with a brave free motion of the arm had become fixed in the mind of the engineer as something beautiful and enduring, something beyond all change and ruin, and something that would always be the same, no

◆ **Read Fluently**

Read the bracketed paragraph aloud. Then underline the part that tells what the engineer did every day.

◆ **English Language Development**

The word *tragedies* is the plural of *tragedy*. In English, when you add an *s* to a word that ends in *y*, you sometimes have to change the *y* to *i* and add *es* instead. This is true if a consonant comes before the *y*. If a vowel comes before the *y*, you don't change the *y* to *i*. Here are some examples: *story—stories, toy—toys.*

Write the plurals of these words:

day _____

country _____

◆ **Culture Note**

Hobo is a word that is not used very much anymore. The word refers to a person who wanders from place to place, usually by sneaking rides on freight trains. The words *hobo, tramp,* and *bum* have similar meanings. The only difference is that a hobo will work from time to time, if work is available. What is the word for someone like this in your native language?

_____

© Pearson Education, Inc.

matter what <u>mishap</u>, grief or error might break the iron schedule of his days.

◆ ◆ ◆

Wolfe goes on to say that the engineer has tender feelings toward the women and their house. He makes up his mind that someday he will go and visit them.

At last that day comes. The engineer is retired. He has no more work to do. He rides the train to the town where the women live. He walks through the station and out into the town. As he does this, he begins to feel strange. It doesn't seem like the same town he saw from the train. He becomes more and more puzzled as he walks on. The engineer walks down the hot and dusty road until he gets to the house. The experience seems more and more like a bad dream. He knocks at the door. Then he hears the steps from inside. Finally, the door opens. The woman stands before him.

◆ ◆ ◆

And instantly, with a sense of bitter loss and grief, he was sorry he had come. He knew at once that the woman who stood there looking at him with a mistrustful eye was the same woman who had waved to him so many thousand times. But her face was harsh and pinched and <u>meager</u>; the flesh sagged wearily in <u>sallow</u> folds, and the small eyes peered at him with timid suspicion and uneasy doubt. All the brave freedom, the warmth and the affection that he had read into her gesture, vanished in the moment that he saw her and heard her unfriendly tongue.

◆ ◆ ◆

Vocabulary Development

mishap (MIS hap) *n.* accident
meager (MEE ger) *adj.* having little flesh, thin
sallow (SAL loh) *adj.* sickly, pale yellow

◆ **Reading Strategy**

How does the engineer feel about the woman and the house? Based on his feelings, **predict** what will happen next.

_____

_____

_____

_____

_____

◆ **Vocabulary and Pronunciation**

In English, the letter *g* has two sounds. It has its own sound, as in *garden*. It also borrows the sound of *j*, as in *engineer*. For each of the following words, write *g* or *j* to tell how the letter *g* is pronounced.

_____ green   _____ grape
_____ signal   _____ change
_____ sagged   _____ gesture
_____ strange   _____ visage
_____ magic   _____ imagined
_____ gone   _____ again

◆ **Reading Check**

How does the man feel as he walks toward the house?

_____

_____

_____

_____

_____

How does the man feel when he meets the woman? Complete these sentences about the moment of **anticlimax**.

The man is disappointed when he meets the woman because she looks at him

_____.

Her face is

_____.

Her eyes are filled with

_____.

He had thought she was warm and friendly, but

_____.

Imagine that you are the mother or the daughter. Do you think their reaction to the man is normal? Explain why you feel as you do.

_____

_____

_____

The word *parlor* comes from a root word that means "to speak." That was what was done in the old-fashioned parlor. People gathered there for conversation. The room was usually not used for anything but entertaining company. It usually had the best furniture in the house. If you have a room like this in your house, what do you call it? _____

Wolfe describes how the man explains why he came. The woman finally invites him in, but she seems unwilling to do so. She calls to her daughter in a harsh, shrill voice. They have a short visit in the women's ugly little parlor. As the man tries to talk, the women stare at him in a dull way. They seem hostile and afraid.

The engineer feels disappointed and leaves the cottage. He suddenly feels old and sad. The things that he thought he knew were not the way he expected them to be.

◆ ◆ ◆

And he knew that all the magic of that bright lost way, the vista of that shining line, the imagined corner of that small good universe of hope's desire, was gone forever, could never be got back again.

© Pearson Education, Inc.

1. Describe the cottage that the engineer sees from the train. Include the names of four kinds of plants that grow by the cottage.

_____

_____

2. What happened every day just after two o'clock for twenty years? Complete this sequence chart for your answer.

First,

↓

Then,

↓

Then,

↓

After that,

3. Before he retired, the engineer thought of the women as something special. Put a check by each of the four words he might have used to describe them.

___ beautiful   ___ tragic

___ enduring   ___ warm

___ mistrustful   ___ affectionate

___ harsh   ___ unfriendly

4. In the beginning of the story, the engineer has a certain attitude toward the women. This attitude tells something about his own character. How would you describe the character of the engineer?

_____

_____

5. **Literary Analysis:** How do you know that the engineer's meeting with the women is the **anticlimax** of the story?

_____

_____

6. **Reading Strategy:** Thomas Wolfe includes details that help you **predict** the ending. Put a check in front of the three details that prepare you for the ending.

____ The house was white with green blinds.

____ The engineer blew the train's whistle every day at the same time.

____ A woman and her daughter waved as the train passed.

____ The engineer thought that the women would always stay the same.

____ The engineer begins to think that he knows the women well.

____ The woman has an unfriendly tone when she answers the door.

Writing

Comparison-and-Contrast Sentences

The engineer thought the women were one way, but they turned out to be another way. On separate paper, write three sentences in which you compare and contrast the two views of the women. Your sentences may have the following topics:
- What the women look like
- How friendly the women are
- How the women's attitude makes the engineer feel

You may write your own sentences, or you may complete these sentences.

1. The engineer thought the women would look _____, but they turned out to look _____.

2. The engineer thought the women would be _____, but they turned out to be _____.

3. The engineer thought his visit would make him feel _____, but it made him feel _____.

© Pearson Education, Inc.

In Another Country
Ernest Hemingway

Summary

In this short story, an American officer who is recovering from a war injury meets four other wounded men: three young Italian officers and an older major. The major helps the American with his Italian grammar, advises him not to marry, and mourns the death of his own wife.

Visual Summary

Characters
Narrator
Doctor
Major
Three boys
Another boy with no nose

Setting
Place: a hospital in Milan
Time: World War I

Problem
The characters have been wounded in the war.

1: The doctor tells the narrator that the narrator will play football again in spite of his wound.

2: The doctor shows the wounded major a picture of a withered hand. Then he shows the major the same hand after a machine course. It looks a little bigger.

3: The major, who was a great fencer before the war, says he is not confident that his hand will get better.

4: The narrator and the boys have the same medals.

5: The narrator says he is afraid to die. He worries about how things will be when he goes back to the front.

6: The major and the narrator work on Italian grammar together.

7: One day the major tells the narrator that he must not marry.

8: It turns out that the major's wife has just died unexpectedly. The major cries and says he cannot resign himself to it.

9: The major returns to the hospital after three days. In that time, the doctor has put up pictures of completely restored hands. But the major only looks out the window.

© **Pearson Education, Inc.**

LITERARY ANALYSIS
Point of View

The **point of view** is the "eyes" through which a story is told.

Stories can be told from the **first-person point of view.** In such a story, the narrator uses the pronouns *I, me, we,* and the like. The narrator can be the main character or a minor character in the story.

Stories can be told from the **limited third-person point of view.** In such a story, the speaker telling the story does not use the pronoun *I.* The speaker tells the events of the story and also gets into the mind of one of the characters.

As you read, look for answers to these questions:
- What is the point of view of the story?
- Is the narrator the main character or a minor character in the story?

READING STRATEGY
Identifying with Characters

Characters in stories might have experiences that are different from yours. However, you will find that you share many of their feelings and emotions. When you **identify with characters,** you see what you have in common with them.

As you read, compare your own experiences and feelings with the characters in the story. Keep track in this chart.

Sentence from Story	My Own Feelings
Example: The narrator has been injured in the war.	It would be very scary to be injured in a war, but it would be a relief to get away from the fighting.

© Pearson Education, Inc.

In Another Country
Ernest Hemingway

The story opens in Milan, Italy, during World War I. The narrator has been injured in the war. He and the other wounded men do not go to the front anymore. Instead, they go to a hospital for treatment every afternoon. There, they are treated with new machines that are supposed to help them heal.

The doctor approaches the narrator and asks him what he did before the war.

◆ ◆ ◆

"Did you practice a sport?"
I said: "Yes, football."
"Good," he said. "You will be able to play football again better than ever."

◆ ◆ ◆

The narrator tells about another patient, a major. The major's hand is being treated in a machine. Before the war, the man had been the greatest fencer in Italy. The doctor shows the major a picture of a hand that had been almost as small as the major's. He also shows him a picture of the same hand after treatment. In the second picture, the hand is a little larger.

The major asks if the hand in the picture had been wounded.

◆ ◆ ◆

"An industrial accident," the doctor said.
"Very interesting, very interesting," the major said, and handed it back to the doctor.
"You have confidence?"
"No," said the major.

◆ ◆ ◆

© Pearson Education, Inc.

The *ou* in English can sound like the *oo* in *food*. Or it can sound like *ow* as in *cow*. Write *oo* or *ow* to tell how the *ou* is pronounced in each of these words:

_____ wounded   _____ about
_____ bounce   _____ shouted

Identify with the narrator, or put yourself in his place. How would you feel about what the doctor says in the underlined sentence?

_____

_____

_____

In English, quotation marks are used to show the exact words of a speaker. Circle the quotation marks that are around the major's words in the bracketed paragraph.

Vocabulary Development

confidence (KAHN fuh duhns) *n.*   being sure, being certain

In English, the letter combination _ea_ can sound like the _e_ in _bed_. Or it can sound like the _ee_ in _deep_. For each of these words, write _e_ or _ee_ to show how the _ea_ is pronounced.

_____ instead _____ treatment

_____ leather _____ death

_____ speaks

In English, the ending _n_ or _an_ added to the name of a country can tell where a person is from. For example, an American is from America, and an Italian is from Italy. Sometimes different endings are used. For example, a Spaniard is from Spain, an Iraqi is from Iraq, and a Chinese person is from China. What is the English word for people from your native country?

_____

_____

Other patients include three boys from Milan. Sometimes, when they are done with the machines, they walk to a nearby café. They are sometimes joined by another boy. He wears a black silk handkerchief across his face because he has no nose. He was injured within an hour of going to the front line for the first time.

He didn't have any medals since he hadn't been in service long enough. One boy has three medals because he had a dangerous job. The other boys and the narrator each have one medal. They are all dealing with death.

◆ ◆ ◆

We were all a little detached, and there was nothing that held us together except that we met every afternoon at the hospital.

◆ ◆ ◆

The narrator says that the boys once asked him what he had done to get his medals. He shows them the papers, which were full of pretty words. But all they really say was that he had gotten the medals because he was an American. After that, the boys act differently toward the narrator. He is still their friend, especially against outsiders. But he is never really one of them after that. It was different with the three Italian boys. They had really earned their medals.

© Pearson Education, Inc.

The narrator had been wounded but agrees that it was an accident.

◆ ◆ ◆

I was never ashamed of the ribbons, though, and sometimes, after the cocktail hour, I would imagine myself having done all the things they had done to get their medals; but walking home at night through the empty streets with the cold wind and all the shops closed, trying to keep near the street lights, I knew that I would never have done such things, and I was very much afraid to die, and often lay in bed at night by myself, afraid to die and wondering how I would be when I went back to the front again.

◆ ◆ ◆

The major, the former fencer, does not believe in bravery. He spends a lot of time correcting the narrator's Italian grammar as they sit in the machines. The narrator had once said that Italian seemed like such an easy language. But then the major starts helping him with the grammar. Soon Italian seems so hard that the narrator is afraid to speak until he has the grammar straight in his mind.

The major comes to the hospital every day. He doesn't believe in the machines but feels that they must be tested.

◆ ◆ ◆

It was an idiotic idea, he said, "a theory, like another." I had not learned my grammar, and he said I was a stupid impossible disgrace, and he was a fool to have bothered with me.

◆ ◆ ◆

© Pearson Education, Inc.

In Another Country 155

◆ **Literary Analysis**

A story in the first-person **point of view** gives the thoughts of the narrator. What are the narrator's thoughts about death?

_____

_____

_____

_____

◆ **Literary Analysis**

Circle all the words in the bracketed paragraph that tell you the story is written from the first-person **point of view**.

Mark the Text

The narrator and the major then start talking. The major asks if the narrator is married. The narrator says no, but he hopes to be. The major says that a man must not marry. When asked to explain, he says that a man should not place himself in a position to lose. Instead, he should find things he cannot lose. He speaks with anger and bitterness. The narrator speaks up.

◆ ◆ ◆

"But why should he necessarily lose it?"

"He'll lose it," the major said. He was looking at the wall. Then he looked down at the machine and jerked his little hand out from between the straps and slapped it hard against his thigh. "He'll lose it," he almost shouted. "Don't argue with me!"

◆ ◆ ◆

The major then asks the attendant to turn off the machine. He goes to the other room for more treatment. Then he asks the doctor if he can use the phone. When he returns, he comes toward the narrator and puts his arm on his shoulder.

◆ ◆ ◆

"I am so sorry," he said, and patted me on the shoulder with his good hand. "I would not be rude. My wife has just died. You must forgive me."

"Oh—" I said, feeling sick for him. "I am so sorry."

He stood there biting his lower lip. "It is very difficult," he said. "I cannot <u>resign</u> myself."

Vocabulary Development

resign (ree ZĪN) *v.* to accept one's fate

© Pearson Education, Inc.

He looked straight past me and out through the window. Then he began to cry. "I am utterly unable to resign myself," he said and choked. And then crying, his head up looking at nothing, carrying himself straight and soldierly, with tears on both his cheeks and biting his lips, he walked past the machines and out the door.

◆ ◆ ◆

The doctor tells the narrator that the major's young wife had died of pneumonia. She had been sick for only a few days. No one thought she would die. The major stays away from the hospital for three days. When he comes back, he is wearing a black band on his sleeve.[2] Now there are large photographs on the wall of before-and-after pictures of wounds cured by the machines. There are three photographs of hands like the major's, completely cured.

◆ ◆ ◆

I do not know where the doctor got them. I always understood we were the first to use the machines. The photographs did not make much difference to the major because he only looked out of the window.

Vocabulary Development

utterly (UT er lee) *adv.* completely

2. **a black band on his sleeve** a sign of mourning.

© Pearson Education, Inc.

◆ **Read Fluently**

Read aloud the bracketed paragraph. Then describe how the major walked out of the hospital.

_____

_____

_____

◆ **Culture Note**

In the United States, black is traditionally used as a symbol of mourning. In some other countries, white or yellow might be used. What color symbolizes mourning in your native country?

_____

◆ **Reading Check**

How long had the major's wife been sick?

_____

_____

_____

◆ **Reading Strategy**

Identify with the character of the major. What do you think he is thinking about as he looks out the window?

1. _____

2. _____

1. Why do the narrator and the other men go to the hospital every day?

_____

_____

2. Write the kind of injury each of these characters has:

the narrator _____

the major _____

the boy with the black handkerchief _____

3. How are the characters being treated for their injuries?

_____

_____

4. **Literary Analysis:** Put a check in front of each sentence or passage that tells you the story is written from the first-person **point of view.**

_____ The major's hand had been injured.

_____ We all had the same medals . . .

_____ I had been wounded, it was true . . .

_____ The major came very regularly to the hospital.

_____ "Oh—" I said, feeling sick for him.

5. **Reading Strategy:** The narrator says he is afraid to die. He often lies in bed thinking about it and wondering how he will act when he goes back to the front. **Identify with** the narrator. If you were in his place, how would you feel about being on the front?

_____

_____

   © Pearson Education, Inc.

Speaking and Listening

Continue the Story

Write a paragraph that tells what happens next. Before you write, answer these questions:

- Do the major and the narrator stay in touch with each other?

_____

_____

_____

- Does the major's hand get better?

_____

_____

_____

- How does the major deal with his grief?

_____

_____

_____

- Does the narrator go back to the front?

_____

_____

_____

- What happens to the boy whose face was injured?

_____

_____

_____

In one paragraph, you can probably not answer all these questions. Choose one or more ideas, and develop a paragraph. Then, share your paragraph with the class.

© Pearson Education, Inc.

A Worn Path

Eudora Welty

Summary

In this short story, an old woman makes her way from her home to Natchez. She walks through woods and fields, along a country path and along a road. When she gets to town, she goes to a doctor's office to get medicine for her grandson. She has been taking care of him since he swallowed lye several years before.

Visual Summary

Sequence of Events			
1.	**2.**	**3.**	**4.**
In December, Phoenix Jackson walks through the pine woods.	She speaks to the wild animals and tells them to keep out of her path.	She walks up and down hills, and at one point she catches her dress in a thorny bush.	She crosses a creek, crawls through a barbed-wire fence, and sees a scarecrow.
5.	**6.**		**7.**
On the road, a dog surprises her and she falls. A hunter helps her up, and a nickel falls out of his pocket. She picks it up.	Phoenix reaches Natchez. She finds the medicine for her grandson, who had swallowed lye several years before. The attendant gives her another nickel.		She plans to buy her grandson a paper windmill before she walks back home.

© Pearson Education, Inc.

LITERARY ANALYSIS
Point of View and Narrator

Every story is told by a **narrator**. Some stories are told from the **first-person point of view**. In these stories, the narrator refers to himself or herself as *I*. The narrator also has a role in the events. The narrator's role can be major or minor.

Other stories are told from the **limited third-person point of view.** In these stories, the narrator stands outside the action. The narrator is an outside observer who does not use the pronoun *I*. The narrator might tell the thoughts of one or more characters.

As you read, look for answers to these questions:
- From what point of view is the story told?
- Which character's thoughts does the narrator reveal?

READING STRATEGY
Identifying with Characters

Many stories tell about characters you might never meet. Still, you might see that you have feelings and emotions that are the same as those of the characters. When you notice what you have in common with story characters, you are **identifying with the characters.**

As you read, ask yourself how you would feel if you were in the character's place.

Sentence from Story	My Own Feelings
Example: Far out in the country there was an old Negro woman with her head tied in a red rag, coming along a path through the pinewoods.	I enjoy walking along woodland paths. I like to hear the birds chirping, and I enjoy the fresh smells of the trees.

© Pearson Education, Inc.

_____

_____

_____

The letter combination _gh_ is sometimes silent in English. Other times, it has the same sound as the letter _f_. Write _silent_ or _f_ to tell how the _gh_ is pronounced in each of these words.

_____ bright   _____ through

_____ straight   _____ thought

_____ laughter   _____ high

_____ laughed   _____ enough

_____ lights

English has many **compound words.** These are two words that are put together to make one. _Shoelaces_ is an example. It means "laces that tie a shoe." _Pinewoods_ is another example. It means "woods with pine trees." What do you think each of these compound words means?

scarecrow

_____

overhead

_____

windmill

_____

A Worn Path
Eudora Welty

An old Negro woman named Phoenix Jackson leaves home on a cold December morning. She walks along a country path.

◆ ◆ ◆

She was very old and small and she walked slowly in the dark pine shadows, moving a little from side to side in her steps, with the balanced heaviness and lightness of a <u>pendulum</u> in a grandfather clock.

◆ ◆ ◆

The woman carries a cane that she taps as she walks.

Welty tells us that Phoenix's eyes are blue with age. Her skin is quite wrinkled. Her hair comes down in ringlets from under the red rag.

The woman notices some movement in the bushes.

◆ ◆ ◆

Old Phoenix said, "Out of my way, all you foxes, owls, beetles, jack rabbits, coons and wild animals! . . . Keep out from under these feet, little bobwhites. . . . Keep the big wild hogs out of my path. Don't let none of those come running my direction. I got a long way."

◆ ◆ ◆

Phoenix comes to a hill. She climbs up one side of the hill and down the other. On the way, a bush catches her dress. It takes her a long time to get her dress free. She crosses a creek by walking across a log with her eyes closed.

Vocabulary Development

pendulum (PEN dyoo luhm) _n._ a weight hanging from a fixed point so as to swing freely under the action of gravity

---

  © Pearson Education, Inc.

Phoenix is pleased with herself. She sits down to get comfortable and rest.

◆ ◆ ◆

Up above her was a tree in a pearly cloud of mistletoe. She did not dare to close her eyes, and when a little boy brought her a plate with a slice of marble cake on it she spoke to him. "That would be acceptable," she said. But when she went to take it there was just her own hand in the air.

◆ ◆ ◆

Phoenix keeps on walking. She has to go through a barbed-wire fence. She is very careful. She finally gets through the barbed-wire fence safely. Then she sees a buzzard.[1] She asks him who he's watching. She comes to an old cotton field and then to a field of dead corn. There is no path here. Then she sees something in front of her. It is tall, black, and thin. It is moving.

She sees what she thinks is a man but is then confused by the figure's silence.

◆ ◆ ◆

"Ghost," she said sharply, "who be you the ghost of? For I have heard of nary death close by."

◆ ◆ ◆

The figure moves in the wind but does not answer. She touches its clothes and realizes there is nothing underneath.

◆ ◆ ◆

◆ Literary Analysis

In the bracketed paragraph, what information about Phoenix does the **limited third-person narrator** suggest?

_____

_____

_____

◆ Background

Barbed-wire fences are common on farms and ranches. They are made of wire that has sharp points sticking out. The sharp points are designed to keep farm animals from getting out and to keep wild animals from getting in.

◆ Reading Check

Phoenix sees something in front of her. What does she think it is?

_____

_____

_____

_____

Vocabulary Development

mistletoe (MIS uhl toh) *n.* a green plant that lives on other plants

nary (NAIR ee) *adj.* not one

---

1. **sees a buzzard** (BUZ erd) A buzzard is a bird that waits for its prey to die, rather than killing it. Buzzards commonly circle dying prey, so they are seen as a sign of death.

© Pearson Education, Inc.

Scarecrows are like big, stuffed, life-size dolls. They are placed in fields where crops are growing. Their purpose is to scare crows and other birds who might eat the crops. The hope is that the birds will think a human being is in the field.

Read the bracketed paragraph. Then underline what Phoenix says.

How does Phoenix end up stuck in a ditch?

_____

_____

_____

"You scarecrow," she said. Her face lighted. "I ought to be shut up for good," she said with laughter. "My senses is gone. I too old. I the oldest people I ever know. Dance, old scarecrow," she said, "while I dancing with you."

◆ ◆ ◆

Phoenix keeps walking through the corn field. She gets to a wagon track. This is the easy part of the walk. She follows the track. She goes past bare fields, past some trees, past some old cabins. The doors and windows are all boarded. They remind Phoenix of old women who are under a spell, just sitting there.

◆ ◆ ◆

In a <u>ravine</u> she went where a spring was silently flowing through a hollow log. Old Phoenix bent and drank. "Sweet gum[2] makes the water sweet," she said, and drank more. "Nobody know who made this well, for it was here when I was born."

◆ ◆ ◆

As she walks along the path near a swamp, Phoenix speaks to the alligators. Then, she crosses a road that is shaded by oak trees.

A black dog comes up to Phoenix. He knocks her down, and she falls into a ditch. She cannot get out of it. A young white hunter comes along. He has a dog with him.

Vocabulary Development

ravine (ruh VEEN) *n.* a small narrow valley with steep sides

---

2. **sweet gum** *n.* a tree that has a sweet-smelling juice.

© Pearson Education, Inc.

He asks Phoenix what she is doing. She jokes that she is pretending to be an upside-down bug. She needs his help to get up.

◆ ◆ ◆

He lifted her up, gave her a swing in the air, and set her down. "Anything broken, Granny?" "No sir, them old dead weeds is springy enough," said Phoenix, when she had got her breath. "I thank you for your trouble."

◆ ◆ ◆

The man asks Phoenix where she lives and where she's going. She tells him she's on her way to town. He tells her that's too far. He says she should just go back home.

Phoenix doesn't move.

◆ ◆ ◆

The deep lines in her face went into a fierce and different <u>radiation</u>. Without warning, she had seen with her own eyes a flashing nickel fall out of the man's pocket onto the ground.

◆ ◆ ◆

Phoenix distracts the man. She cries and claps her hands. She tells the black dog to get away. She whispers, "Sic him!"[3] The man tells Phoenix to watch how he gets rid of the dog. He tells his own dog, "Sic him!" The man runs and throws sticks at the black dog. Phoenix uses this time to pick up the nickel. She slowly bends down.

◆ ◆ ◆

◆ English Language Development

Granny is one English word that is used for a *grandmother.* Other words include *Grandma, Gran,* and *Nana.* What words are used in your native language for *grandmother?*

_____

_____

_____

◆ Literary Analysis

What detail in the bracketed paragraph tells you that the **narrator** is getting into Phoenix's mind? Underline the sentence that gives the answer.

Mark the Text

Vocabulary Development

radiation (ray dee AY shuhn) *n.* arrangement from the center to the sides

---

3. **"Sic him!"** a command given to a dog to attack.

© Pearson Education, Inc.

In the bracketed paragraph, do you think Phoenix did something wrong? Write *yes* or *no*. _____

Identify with Phoenix. What would you have done?

_____

_____

_____

Her chin was lowered almost to her knees. The yellow palm of her hand came out from the fold of her apron. Her fingers slid down and along the ground under the piece of money with the grace and care they would have in lifting an egg from under a setting hen. Then she slowly straightened up, she stood erect, and the nickel was in her apron pocket. A bird flew by. Her lips moved. "God watching me the whole time. I come to stealing."

◆ ◆ ◆

The man comes back. He tells Phoenix that he scared the dog off. Then he points the gun at Phoenix. She just stands straight, facing him. He asks her if the gun scares her.

◆ ◆ ◆

"No, sir, I seen plenty go off closer by, in my day, and for less than what I done," she said, holding utterly still.

◆ ◆ ◆

The man admires her bravery. He says he would give her some money if he had any. He advises her to stay home to be safe. She tells him she has to continue her journey.

The man and Phoenix go in different directions. Phoenix keeps walking. At last she gets to Natchez.[4] The city is decorated for Christmas. Phoenix sees a lady who is carrying an armful of wrapped gifts. Phoenix asks the woman to tie her shoelaces. She says that

---

Vocabulary Development

utterly (UT er lee) *adv.* completely

---

4. **Natchez** (NACH iz) a town in southern Mississippi.

© Pearson Education, Inc.

untied shoes are fine for the country. But they don't look right in a big building. Phoenix goes into a big building. She says "Here I be" to the woman at the counter. The woman asks Phoenix for her name, but Phoenix does not answer. The woman asks if Phoenix is deaf. Then the nurse comes in.

◆ ◆ ◆

<u>"Oh, that's just old Aunt Phoenix," she said. "She doesn't come for herself—she has a little grandson. She makes these trips just as regular as clockwork. She lives away back off the Old Natchez Trace."⁵ She bent down. "Well, Aunt Phoenix, why don't you just take a seat? We won't keep you standing after your long trip."</u>

◆ ◆ ◆

Phoenix sits down. The nurse asks her about her grandson. She wants to know if his throat is any better. At first, Phoenix does not answer. The nurse asks if the boy is dead. At last, Phoenix answers. She tells the nurse that her memory had left her. She had forgotten why she had come. The nurse wonders how she could forget, after coming so far.

◆ ◆ ◆

"Throat never heals, does it?" said the nurse, speaking in a loud, sure voice to old Phoenix. By now she had a card with something written on it, a little list. "Yes. Swallowed <u>lye</u>. When was it?—January—two-three years ago—"

Phoenix spoke unasked now. "No, missy, he not dead, he just the same. Every little while his throat begin to close up again, and he not able to swallow. He not get his breath. He not able to

Vocabulary Development

lye (Lī) *n.* a strong chemical used in making soap

---

5. **the Old Natchez Trace** a trace is an old path or trail left by people, animals, or vehicles.

© Pearson Education, Inc.

Sidebar

◆ **English Language Development**

Phoenix is not using Standard English when she says "Here I be." The verb *to be* is one of the most irregular verbs in English as well as in other languages. Complete each sentence with the correct present-tense form of the verb *to be.*

Here I _____.

Here you _____.

Here he _____.

Here we _____.

Here they _____.

◆ **Read Fluently**

Read the underlined paragraph aloud. Write two words to describe the tone of voice you used.

1. _____

2. _____

◆ **Reading Check**

What is wrong with Phoenix's grandson? Circle the passages in the bracketed section that answer the question.

◆ Stop to Reflect

The narrator has waited until now to tell the reason for Phoenix's journey. Would you rather have known earlier? Write *yes* or *no,* and then explain your opinion.

_____

_____

_____

◆ Reading Strategy

Identify with the nurse. Why does she give Phoenix a nickel? Give two reasons.

1.

_____

2.

_____

◆ Reading Check

What does Phoenix plan to buy for her grandson? Circle the answer to the question.

help himself. So the time come around, and I go on another trip for the <u>soothing</u> medicine."

"All right. The doctor said as long as you came to get it, you could have it," said the nurse. "But it's an <u>obstinate</u> case."

◆ ◆ ◆

Phoenix talks about her grandson. She says that they are the only two left in the world. The boy suffers, but he is going to last. He is a sweet boy. The nurse then gives Phoenix the medicine. She says "Charity" as she makes a mark in a book. The nurse gives Phoenix a nickel out of her purse for Christmas. Phoenix takes the other nickel out of her pocket and looks at both of them.

She taps her cane to announce her plan. She is going to buy a paper windmill for her grandson. He has never seen one.

◆ ◆ ◆

She lifted her free hand, gave a little nod, turned around, and walked out of the doctor's office. Then her slow step began on the stairs, going down.

Vocabulary Development

soothing (SOO thing) *adj.* comforting

obstinate (AHB stuh nuht) *adj.* stubborn, not easily changed

© Pearson Education, Inc.

1. What time of year is it when Phoenix takes her journey?

_____

2. Put a check by four words that tell what Phoenix Jackson looks like.

   ____ small   ____ blue-eyed

   ____ tall   ____ dark-eyed

   ____ young   ____ wrinkled

   ____ old   ____ gray-haired

3. What is the purpose of Phoenix's journey?

_____

_____

_____

4. **Literary Analysis:** Put a check in front of each sentence or passage that tells you the story is written from the **limited third-person point of view.**

   ____ Far out in the country there was an old Negro woman with her head tied in a red rag, coming along a path through the pinewoods.

   ____ But when she went to take it there was just her own hand in the air.

   ____ I ought to be shut up for good.

   ____ I come to stealing.

   ____ "The doctor said as long as you came to get it, you could have it," said the nurse.

© Pearson Education, Inc.

5. **Reading Strategy:** Identify with Phoenix. How important is her grandson to her? Explain how you know.

_____

_____

_____

Writing

Memorial Speech

Imagine that Phoenix Jackson has died. On separate paper, write the speech you might give at her memorial service. In your speech, talk about the good things she did in her life. Also include information about her character.

Prewriting Reread the story and take notice of details about Phoenix. Look for evidence that she is strong, determined, and brave. Find clues that she has a good sense of humor. Look for proof that she is generous and unselfish.

Drafting To begin, identify Phoenix Jackson. Explain the sad occasion for the speech. Organize your ideas in order of importance.

Revising Reread your speech to make sure it shows what kind of person Phoenix was. Change words that are too vague. Add details that will make your audience feel emotional about Phoenix. Write your final speech on a separate sheet of paper.

 © Pearson Education, Inc.

The First Seven Years

Bernard Malamud

Summary

In this short story, Feld, a shoemaker, wants his nineteen-year-old daughter, Miriam, to go out with a local college boy named Max. One day Max brings in some shoes for repair. Feld persuades him to ask Miriam out. When Max leaves, Sobel, Feld's helper, breaks the last, or the block for repairing shoes, with his heavy pounding. Then he runs out of the shop. Feld hires a new helper who is less trustworthy. After their second date, Miriam reports that Max is a bore without a soul. When Feld finds out that his new helper has been stealing from him, he has a heart attack. When he recovers, he goes to see Sobel. He finds out that Sobel has worked for him for five years only because he is in love with Miriam. Feld asks Sobel to wait two more years before asking Miriam to marry him. The next morning, Sobel is back at work.

Visual Summary

TIMELINE			
Feld, a shoemaker, wants his daughter, Miriam, to go to college, but she isn't interested.	Max, a local college student, comes in with shoes to be repaired. Feld asks him to call Miriam.	Feld's assistant, Sobel, breaks the last and rushes out of the store.	Miriam goes out with Max twice. She says he has no soul and she will not see him again.
Feld's new assistant steals from him. Feld is so upset he has a mild heart attack.	Feld goes to see Sobel and asks him to come back to work. He discovers that Sobel has been working for Feld only because of Miriam.	Feld sadly realizes that Miriam will have to make her own choice. He asks Sobel to wait two years before asking Miriam to marry him.	

LITERARY ANALYSIS

Epiphany

An **epiphany** (ee PIF uh nee) is a moment when a character has a sudden insight.

- This insight changes how characters view themselves, other characters, or story events.
- It forms the story's climax, or the high point of interest or suspense.
- It may or may not resolve the conflict in the story.

In "The First Seven Years," the events in the story lead up to the main character's epiphany.

<u>Feld had a sudden insight</u>. In some devious way, with his books and commentary, Sobel had given Miriam to understand that he loved her.

READING STRATEGY

Identifying with Characters

When you **identify with characters** in a story, you connect what they think, feel, say, and do to your own experience. Identifying with characters helps you understand who the characters are and why they act as they do.

As you read, complete this chart. Connect the thoughts, feelings, and actions of a character in the story with your own experience.

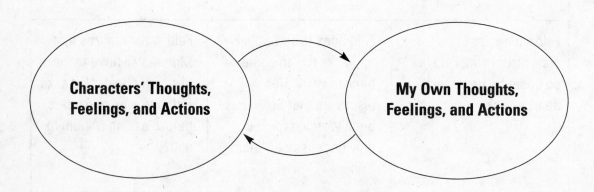

Characters' Thoughts, Feelings, and Actions

My Own Thoughts, Feelings, and Actions

© Pearson Education, Inc.

The First Seven Years
Bernard Malamud

Feld is a shoemaker who came to America from Poland. He has a helper named Sobel. Feld wishes that his daughter, Miriam, would go to college. Miriam enjoys reading books that Sobel lends her, but she would rather work than go to school. Feld admires a college student named Max because he has worked hard to get an education.

◆ ◆ ◆

A figure emerged from the snow and the door opened. At the counter the man withdrew from a wet paper bag a pair of battered shoes for repair. Who he was the shoemaker for a moment had no idea, then his heart trembled as he realized, before he had thoroughly <u>discerned</u> the face, that Max himself was standing there, embarrassedly explaining what he wanted done to his old shoes. Though Feld listened eagerly, he couldn't hear a word, for the opportunity that had burst upon him was deafening.

◆ ◆ ◆

Feld would like Max to date his daughter. He is afraid to suggest the idea. He does not know whether Max would agree or whether Miriam would be angry with him. Feld decides that there is no harm in bringing the idea up. If his daughter will not think about going to college herself, Feld wants her to marry an educated man. He wants her to have a better life.

◆ **Culture Note**

This story takes place in the 1950s in the United States. It was a time of peace and prosperity. Many parents had worked hard so that their children would have easier lives. Look at a library book, a social studies textbook, or the Internet —or talk to your grandparents or an older person you know— to find out more about the 1950s in the United States.

• What key events hurt the economy in the years before the 1950s?

_____

_____

_____

• What common values did many Americans hold in the 1950s?

_____

_____

_____

• What advances in technology, business, or popular culture took place?

_____

_____

_____

Vocabulary Development

discerned (di SERND) *v.* perceived or recognized; made out clearly

---

© Pearson Education, Inc.

Max describes to Feld what he wants done to his shoes. Then he asks about the price. Before answering, Feld asks Max to step into the hall for a conversation.

◆　◆　◆

"Ever since you went to high school," he said, in the dimly-lit hallway, "I watched you in the morning go to the subway to school, and I said always to myself, this is a fine boy that he wants so much an education."

"Thanks," Max said, nervously alert. He was tall and <u>grotesquely</u> thin, with sharply cut features, particularly a beak-like nose. He was wearing a loose, long <u>slushy</u> overcoat that hung down to his ankles, looking like a rug draped over his bony shoulders, and a soggy, old brown hat, as battered as the shoes he had brought in.

"I am a business man," the shoemaker abruptly said to conceal his embarrassment, "so I will explain you right away why I talk to you. I have a girl, my daughter Miriam—she is nineteen—a very nice girl and also so pretty that everybody looks on her when she passes by in the street. She is smart, always with a book, and I thought to myself that a boy like you, an educated boy—I thought maybe you will be interested sometime to meet a girl like this." He laughed a bit when he had finished and was tempted to say more but had the good sense not to.

◆ **Reading Strategy**

Identify with Max, or put yourself in his place. Circle one word or phrase in this paragraph that shows how Max feels during his conversation with Feld.

◆ **Reading Check**

What hope does Feld hold for Miriam and the college boy Max?

_____

_____

_____

Vocabulary Development

grotesquely (groh TESK lee) *adv.* absurdly; strikingly
slushy (SLUHSH ee) *adj.* covered with partly melted snow or ice

© Pearson Education, Inc.

Max stared down like a hawk. For an uncomfortable second he was silent, then he asked, "Did you say nineteen?"

"Yes."

"Would it be all right to inquire if you have a picture of her?"

"Just a minute." The shoemaker went into the store and hastily returned with a snapshot that Max held up to the light.

"She's all right," he said.

Feld waited.

"And is she sensible—not the flighty kind?"

"She is very sensible."

After another short pause, Max said it was okay with him if he met her.

◆ ◆ ◆

Feld gives Max his telephone number. Max puts it away and asks again about the price of the shoes. Feld gives him a price of "a dollar fifty," which is less than he usually charges. Then Feld goes back into the store.

◆ ◆ ◆

Later, as he entered the store, he was startled by a violent clanging and looked up to see Sobel pounding with all his might upon the naked last.[1] It broke, the iron striking the floor and jumping with a thump against the wall, but before the enraged shoemaker could cry out, the assistant had torn his hat and coat from the hook and rushed out into the snow.

◆ ◆ ◆

Feld is upset that Sobel has left. He depends on Sobel because he has a heart condition. Sobel, a thirty-year-old Polish refugee, had come looking for work five years before. Now Feld trusts Sobel to run his business but feels guilty because he pays him so poorly. While Sobel does not seem to care about money, he is interested in books.

---

1. **last** *n.:* a block shaped like a person's foot, on which shoes are made or repaired.

© Pearson Education, Inc.

◆ Reading Strategy

Identify with Max. Why does he ask Feld for a picture of Miriam?

_____

_____

_____

_____

◆ Read Fluently

Read this paragraph aloud. Circle three words that reveal how Sobel feels.

How does Feld run his business when Sobel refuses to return to work?

_____

_____

_____

_____

The word *received* has several different meanings. For example, it can mean "gotten," "contained," "caught a kicked football," "welcomed," or "supported." Which meaning of *received* does Malamud use in this paragraph?

_____

_____

_____

He has loaned books to Miriam and shared his written comments about them with her.

After working alone for a week, Feld goes to Sobel's rooming house to ask him to return. Sobel's landlady tells him that Sobel is not there. Feld is forced to hire a new assistant who is neither as trustworthy nor as skilled as Sobel is. Feld keeps his mind off his problems by thinking about Max and Miriam's first date. He hopes they will like each other.

◆ ◆ ◆

At last Friday came. Feld was not feeling particularly well so he stayed in bed, and Mrs. Feld thought it better to remain in the bedroom with him when Max called. Miriam <u>received</u> the boy, and her parents could hear their voices, his throaty one, as they talked. Just before leaving, Miriam brought Max to the bedroom door and he stood there a minute, a tall, slightly <u>hunched</u> figure wearing a thick, droopy suit, and apparently at ease as he greeted the shoemaker and his wife, which was surely a good sign. And Miriam, although she had worked all day, looked fresh and pretty. She was a large-framed girl with a well-shaped body, and she had a fine open face and soft hair. They made, Feld thought, a first-class couple.

Miriam returned after 11:30. Her mother was already asleep, but the shoemaker got out of bed and after locating his bathrobe went into the kitchen, where Miriam, to his surprise, sat at the table, reading.

"So where did you go?" Feld asked pleasantly.

"For a walk," she said, not looking up.

"I advised him," Feld said, clearing his throat, "he shouldn't spend so much money."

"I didn't care."

Vocabulary Development

hunched (HUNCHT) *adj.* humped over

© Pearson Education, Inc.

The shoemaker boiled up some water for tea and sat down at the table with a cupful and a thick slice of lemon.

"So how," he sighed after a sip, "did you enjoy?"

"It was all right."

He was silent. She must have sensed his disappointment, for she added, "You can't really tell much the first time."

"You will see him again?"

Turning a page, she said that Max had asked for another date.

"For when?"

"Saturday."

"So what did you say?"

"What did I say?" she asked, delaying for a moment—"I said yes."

◆ ◆ ◆

Miriam asks her father about Sobel. Feld tells her Sobel has another job. Throughout the week, Feld asks Miriam about Max. He is disappointed when he finds out that Max is taking business classes to become an accountant. Max and Miriam have a second date on Saturday. When Miriam comes home, she tells her father that Max bores her because he is only interested in things. Miriam says Max did not ask her on another date, but she has no interest in going out with him anyway. Feld still hopes that Max will call his daughter again. Instead, Max avoids the shoemaker's shop on his way to school.

One afternoon Max comes to the shop. He pays for his shoes and leaves without saying a word about Miriam. Later that night, Feld has a heart attack after finding out that his new assistant has been stealing from him. Feld stays in bed for three weeks. When Miriam offers to get Sobel, Feld reacts angrily. Once he returns to work, he feels tired. He

◆ Reading Check

Underline two sentences in the bracketed paragraphs that reveal Miriam's reaction to her first date with Max.

◆ Reading Strategy

Identify with Miriam, or put yourself in her position. Why do you think she delays before answering her father's question about a second date with Max?

_____

_____

_____

_____

◆ Reading Strategy

How does Miriam feel about Max after their second date?

_____

_____

_____

_____

realizes he needs Sobel's help. Feld visits Sobel at his rooming house. He notices stacks of books and wonders why Sobel reads so much.

◆ ◆ ◆

"So when you will come back to work?" Feld asked him.

To his surprise, Sobel burst out, "Never."

Jumping up, he strode over to the window that looked out upon the miserable street. "Why should I come back?" he cried.

"I will raise your wages."

"Who cares for your wages!"

The shoemaker, knowing he didn't care, was at a loss what else to say.

"What do you want from me, Sobel?"

"Nothing."

"I always treated you like you was my son."

Sobel vehemently denied it. "So why you look for strange boys in the street they should go out with Miriam? Why you don't think of me?"

The shoemaker's hands and feet turned freezing cold. His voice became so hoarse he couldn't speak. At last he cleared his throat and croaked, "So what has my daughter got to do with a shoemaker thirty-five years old who works for me?"

"Why do you think I worked so long for you?" Sobel cried out. "For the stingy wages I sacrificed five years of my life so you could have to eat and drink and where to sleep?"

"Then for what?" shouted the shoemaker.

"For Miriam," he blurted—"for her."

The shoemaker, after a time, managed to say, "I pay wages in cash, Sobel," and lapsed into silence. Though he was seething with

◆ **English Language Development**

In a question in English, the subject follows the verb or comes in the middle of a verb phrase. For example, the subject *I* comes in the middle of the verb phrase *should come* in this question from the story: Why <u>should</u> I <u>come</u> back? Which question in this paragraph does not have correct subject-verb order?

_____

_____

_____

◆ **Reading Strategy**

Put yourself in Sobel's position, or **identify with** him. Why is he so angry with Feld?

_____

_____

_____

Vocabulary Development

vehemently (VEE huh ment lee) *adv.* forcefully; intensely
lapsed (LAPST) *v.* passed gradually
seething (SEETH ing) *adj.* boiling

© Pearson Education, Inc.

excitement, his mind was coldly clear, and he had to admit to himself he had sensed all along that Sobel felt this way. He had never so much as thought it consciously, but he had felt it and was afraid.

"Miriam knows?" he muttered hoarsely.

"She knows."

"You told her?"

"No."

"Then how does she know?"

"How does she know?" Sobel said, "because she knows. She knows who I am and what is in my heart."

Feld had a sudden insight. In some devious way, with his books and commentary, Sobel had given Miriam to understand that he loved her. The shoemaker felt a terrible anger at him for his <u>deceit</u>.

"Sobel, you are crazy," he said bitterly. "She will never marry a man so old and ugly like you."

◆ ◆ ◆

Sobel becomes very angry and then begins to cry. Feld feels sorry for Sobel. He realizes that Sobel barely escaped being killed by the Nazis during World War II and has patiently waited for five years for the girl he loves to grow up. Feld apologizes for calling Sobel ugly. He feels sad when he thinks about the kind of life his daughter will have if she marries Sobel. Feld believes his dreams for a better life for Miriam are dead.

◆ ◆ ◆

"She is only nineteen," Feld said <u>brokenly</u>. "This is too young yet to get married. Don't ask her for two years more, till she is twenty-one, then you can talk to her."

Vocabulary Development

deceit (duh SEET) *n.* deception; misrepresentation

brokenly (BROH kuhn lee) *adv.* as if crushed by grief

© Pearson Education, Inc.

◆ **Reading Check**

How does Sobel feel about Miriam?

_____

_____

_____

◆ **Literary Analysis**

Underline a sentence in this paragraph that tells you Feld is having an **epiphany**.

◆ **Literary Analysis**

How does Feld's **epiphany** change his plans for Miriam?

_____

_____

_____

◆ **Stop to Reflect**

Identify the ambitions that Feld, Miriam, and Sobel have for Miriam's future.

1. _____

_____

_____

2. _____

_____

_____

3. _____

_____

_____

Sobel didn't answer. Feld rose and left. He went slowly down the stairs but once outside, though it was an icy night and the crisp falling snow whitened the street, he walked with a stronger stride.

But the next morning, when the shoemaker arrived, heavy-hearted, to open the store, he saw he needn't have come, for his assistant was already seated at the last, pounding leather for his love.

© Pearson Education, Inc.

1. Why is Max so appealing to Feld?

    _____

    _____

2. How does Miriam feel about Max?

    _____

    _____

3. Why does Sobel become angry with Feld?

    _____

    _____

4. How does Miriam feel about Sobel, and why do you think so?

    _____

    _____

5. **Reading Strategy:** Complete this chart to show the ways in which you **identify with a character** in this story. First, write the name of one character—Feld, Sobel, Max, or Miriam. Next, jot down examples of this character's actions, thoughts, feelings, and situation in the first column. Then list the connections you have to this character in the second column.

Character_____	My Own Experience

6. Literary Analysis: What are two changes that take place as a result of Feld's **epiphany?**

1. _____

2. _____

Writing

Personality Profile

What kind of character is Feld, the shoemaker? Refer to the story to find answers to the following questions:

- How does he feel about his daughter?
- How does he act towards his assistant, Sobel?
- What skills does he have?
- What does he value in life?

Use a cluster diagram like the one shown to record details you observe in Feld for a **personality profile.**

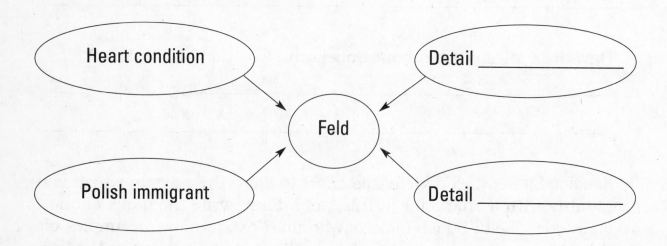

When you finish, share your cluster diagram with a classmate to compare details.

© Pearson Education, Inc.

Everyday Use

Alice Walker

Summary

In this short story, a mother and her daughter Maggie are waiting for a visit from the older daughter, Dee. The mother is a hard-working, undereducated woman who lives in a modest rural home. Maggie is shy and badly scarred from a fire that burned down their previous house. As they wait, the mother remembers how Dee had hated their poverty. Dee arrives with a long-haired male companion. She says she has changed her name to Wangero. She asks for some of the family belongings, including two handmade quilts. She wants to display them as pieces of art. But her mother has planned to give them to Maggie when she marries. The mother snatches the quilts and gives them to Maggie. Dee is angry and leaves with her companion. The story ends with Maggie and her mother sitting happily in the yard.

Visual Summary

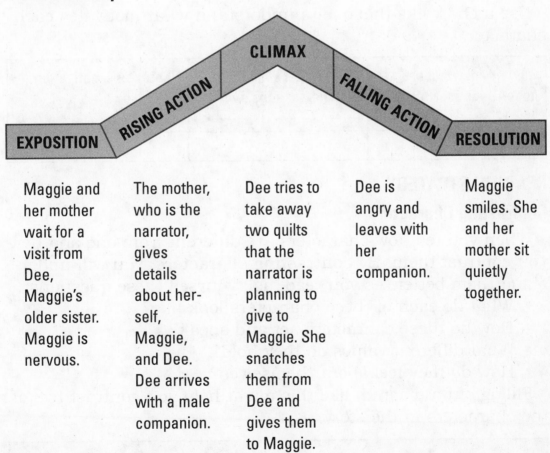

EXPOSITION	RISING ACTION	CLIMAX	FALLING ACTION	RESOLUTION
Maggie and her mother wait for a visit from Dee, Maggie's older sister. Maggie is nervous.	The mother, who is the narrator, gives details about herself, Maggie, and Dee. Dee arrives with a male companion.	Dee tries to take away two quilts that the narrator is planning to give to Maggie. She snatches them from Dee and gives them to Maggie.	Dee is angry and leaves with her companion.	Maggie smiles. She and her mother sit quietly together.

© Pearson Education, Inc.

LITERARY ANALYSIS

Character's Motivation

Think of a star athlete. What motivates, or drives, an athlete to play well? Is it pride, a need to win, money, or something else? In a story, a **character's motivation** is the reason behind his or her thoughts, actions, feelings, and words. The reasons that motivate characters might be their values, experiences, needs, or dreams.

In "Everyday Use," Walker gives clues about what motivates characters. In this sentence from the story, Walker hints at why Maggie is embarrassed about the way she looks.

> She has been like this, chin on chest, eyes on ground, feet in shuffle, ever since the fire that burned the other house to the ground.

Use a chart like this one to understand what motivates each character.

Goal or need a character hopes to satisfy ⟶	A character's thoughts, actions, feelings, words ⟶	Character's motivation

READING STRATEGY

Contrasting Characters

When you tell how characters are different from one another, you contrast them. By **contrasting characters**, you will understand them better. As you read, ask yourself these questions:
- What do each of these characters look like?
- How do these characters act and speak?
- What different values do they hold?
- How do they feel about themselves?

Filling out a diagram like this might help you contrast two of the characters in the story.

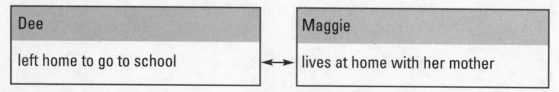

Dee		Maggie
left home to go to school	⟷	lives at home with her mother

   © Pearson Education, Inc.

Everyday Use
Alice Walker

The narrator, or storyteller, waits anxiously for her daughter, Dee, to arrive. She knows that her other daughter, Maggie, will be nervous during Dee's visit. Maggie is embarrassed about the burn scars she has on her arms and legs. As she waits, the narrator dreams what it would be like if she and Dee were brought together for a surprise reunion on television. She imagines that Dee hugs her tearfully and pins a beautiful flower on her dress. In this dream, the narrator sees herself as elegant and witty. In reality, she is big, heavy, and strong with rough hands from hard work. She believes Dee would rather have a mother who is thin and has nice skin and hair.

◆ ◆ ◆

"How do I look, Mama?" Maggie says, showing just enough of her thin body <u>enveloped</u> in pink skirt and red blouse for me to know she's there, almost hidden by the door.

"Come out into the yard," I say.

Have you ever seen a lame animal, perhaps a dog run over by some careless person rich enough to own a car, <u>sidle</u> up to someone who is ignorant enough to be kind to him? That is the way my Maggie walks. She has been like this, chin on chest, eyes on ground, feet in shuffle, ever since the fire that burned the other house to the ground.

◆ **Reading Check**

How is Maggie related to Dee?

_____

_____

◆ **Literary Analysis**

Mark the Text!

Circle words and phrases in the bracketed paragraph that tell how Maggie feels about herself. Then underline words and phrases that reveal what **motivates** her to feel this way.

Vocabulary Development

enveloped (en VEL ohpt) *v.* surrounded
sidle (SĪD ul) *v.* to move sideways in a shy way

© Pearson Education, Inc.

Dee is lighter than Maggie, with nicer hair and a fuller figure. She's a woman now, though sometimes I forget. How long ago was it that the other house burned? Ten, twelve years?

◆ ◆ ◆

The narrator can still remember the horror of the fire. Maggie was burned terribly.

◆ ◆ ◆

And Dee. I see her standing off under the sweet gum tree she used to dig gum out of; a look of <u>concentration</u> on her face as she watched the last dingy gray board of the house fall in toward the red-hot brick chimney.

◆ ◆ ◆

The narrator knows that Dee had hated the house. She wonders why Dee doesn't celebrate as the house burns down.

The narrator remembers how the church helped her raise enough money to send Dee to school in Augusta. The narrator says that Dee always got what she wanted. For example, she got a nice graduation dress and a pair of black shoes to match a suit. In the narrator's opinion, Dee was a stubborn teenager with a mind of her own.

The narrator was not educated. Her school was closed after second grade, but she doesn't know why. Maggie reads to her, although she struggles because she can't see well.

◆ ◆ ◆

She knows she is not <u>bright</u>. Like good looks and money, quickness passed her by. She will marry John Thomas (who has mossy teeth in an earnest face) and then I'll be free to sit here and I guess just sing church songs to myself.

◆ ◆ ◆

◆ **Stop to Reflect**

How is Dee's life different from Maggie's?

_____

_____

_____

_____

◆ **Vocabulary and Pronunciation**

The word *bright* has several meanings. For example, it can mean "shining" or "intelligent." Which meaning of *bright* is used in this paragraph?

_____

Vocabulary Development

concentration (kahn sen TRAY shun) *n.* close, undivided attention

© Pearson Education, Inc.

The narrator describes her house. It has three rooms, a tin roof, and holes for windows. The narrator believes Dee will hate this house. She says Dee never brought friends to visit. Maggie asks her mother if Dee ever had friends. The narrator remembers a few boys and girls who liked Dee because she was smart.

◆ ◆ ◆

When she comes I will meet—but there they are!

◆ ◆ ◆

Dee and a male friend arrive. Dee wears a flowing yellow and orange dress, long gold earrings, and bracelets. Her friend is short with long hair and a beard. Dee's friend tries to hug Maggie, but she nervously falls back against her mother's chair. While Dee snaps photographs, her mother sits with Maggie behind her. Finally, Dee puts the camera away and kisses her mother on the forehead. Dee's friend tries to shake Maggie's hand, but she doesn't want to.

Dee explains to her mother that her name is now Wangero Leewanika Kemanjo. Her mother wonders what happened to her real name, Dee.

◆ ◆ ◆

"She's dead," Wangero said. "I couldn't bear it any longer, being named after the people who oppress me."

"You know as well as me you was named after your aunt Dicie," I said. Dicie is my sister. She named Dee. We called her "Big Dee" after Dee was born.

"But who was *she* named after?" asked Wangero.

Vocabulary Development

oppress (oh PRES) *v.* keep down by cruel or unjust use of power or authority

© Pearson Education, Inc.

◆ **Literary Analysis**

Why do you think Dee is not **motivated** to bring her friends home?

_____

_____

_____

◆ **Reading Strategy**

In the bracketed passage circle the information about Dee. Underline the information about Maggie. **Contrast** the two **characters**. How do they seem different?

Mark the Text

_____

_____

_____

◆ **Reading Check**

Why has Dee changed her name?

_____

_____

_____

This story takes place in the
South in the 1960s. At this time,
many African Americans began
to take pride in their history.
In this story, Dee shows her
interest in African American folk
art. For example, she admires
benches carved by her father.
She also wants a butter churn
once used to make butter from
milk. In addition she wants two
quilts made by her mother and
grandmother.

• Why do you think Dee is so
interested in folk art?

_____

_____

_____

_____

_____

Over dinner, Dee "talked a blue
streak over the sweet potatoes."
The expression "blue streak"
means "a fast stream of words."
This expression probably comes
from the way a bolt of lightning
looks when it strikes. Lightning
strikes quickly and creates a
blue streak in the sky. How do
you picture Dee as she talks?

_____

_____

_____

_____

_____

"I guess after Grandma Dee," I said.

"And who was she named after?" asked Wangero.

"Her mother," I said, and saw Wangero was getting tired.

◆　◆　◆

To prevent further discussion, the narrator tells Dee (Wangero) that she doesn't know any more history. She actually does.

The narrator talks more about her daughter's new name. Dee (Wangero) tells her mother she does not have to use this name, but the narrator tries to learn how to say it. The narrator also tries to say the name of Dee's friend. She has trouble, so he tells her to call him Hakim-a-barber.

◆　◆　◆

We sat down to eat and right away he said he didn't eat collards[1] and pork was unclean. Wangero, though, went on through the chitlins[2] and corn bread, the greens and everything else.

◆　◆　◆

Dee (Wangero) loves everything on the table. She even loves the handmade benches they are sitting on. Her daddy had made them because they didn't have money to buy chairs.

Dee (Wangero) tells Hakim-a-barber that she hadn't appreciated the benches until now. She carefully feels the wood.

◆　◆　◆

Then she gave a sigh and her hand closed over Grandma Dee's butter dish. "That's it!" she said. "I knew there was something I wanted to ask you if I could have."

◆　◆　◆

---

1. **collards** (KAHL erdz) *n.* leaves of the collard plant, often referred to as "collard greens".
2. **chitlins** (CHIT linz) *n.* chitterlings, a pork dish popular among southern African Americans.

© Pearson Education, Inc.

Dee (Wangero) asks her mother if she can have the top and handle to an old butter churn. She wants to use the top as a center-piece. Dee (Wangero) asks who made it. Maggie says that their aunt's first husband, Stash, made it. Dee (Wangero) wraps up the pieces to the churn. After dinner, Maggie washes the dishes. Dee (Wangero) looks through a trunk in her mother's room and finds two quilts. Dee's grandmother, mother, and aunt made the quilts from scraps of old dresses and shirts. One quilt pattern is Lone Star. The other is Walk Around the Mountain.

◆ ◆ ◆

"Mama," Wangero said sweet as a bird. "Can I have these old quilts?"

<u>I heard something fall in the kitchen, and a minute later the kitchen door slammed.</u>

◆ ◆ ◆

The narrator offers some other quilts instead. She explains that she made them but that Grandma had started them.

◆ ◆ ◆

"No," said Wangero. "I don't want those. They are stitched around the borders by machine."

"That'll make them last better," I said.

"That's not the point," said Wangero. "These are all pieces of dresses Grandma used to wear. She did all this stitching by hand. Imagine!" She held the quilts securely in her arms, stroking them.

◆ ◆ ◆

Dee (Wangero) is still admiring the quilts, but the narrator explains that she has promised them to Maggie as a wedding present.

◆ ◆ ◆

© Pearson Education, Inc.

◆ **Stop to Reflect**

Why do you think Dee wants the pieces to the churn?

_____

_____

_____

◆ **Read Fluently**

Read the underlined sentence aloud. How does Maggie feel about Dee's asking for the quilts?

_____

_____

_____

◆ **English Language Development**

In English, verbs must agree in number with their subject. A singular subject names one thing. A plural subject names more than one thing. List a singular subject and verb and a plural subject and verb in the bracketed passage.

_____

_____

_____

◆ **Literary Analysis**

Underline two reasons that show why Dee values the quilts and is **motivated** to ask for them.

◆ Stop to Reflect

Dee seems to think that using the quilts for "everyday use" is the wrong way to use them. Do you agree? Why or why not?

_____

_____

_____

_____

◆ Reading Strategy

Contrast the two **characters** of Maggie and Dee. How do they differ in their views of the quilts?

_____

_____

_____

_____

◆ Stop to Reflect

Do you think Maggie or Dee would better appreciate the quilts? Circle your answer.

Maggie   Dee

Explain your answer.

_____

_____

_____

She gasped like a bee had stung her. "Maggie can't appreciate these quilts!" she said. "She'd probably be backward enough to put them to everyday use."

◆ ◆ ◆

The narrator exclaims that she hopes Maggie will use the quilts. No one has used them all this time that she has saved them. She also remembers that Dee (Wangero) had once told her that the quilts were old-fashioned and that she didn't want to take one to college with her.

◆ ◆ ◆

"But they're *priceless!*" she was saying now, furiously; for she has a temper. "Maggie would put them on the bed and in five years they'd be in rags. Less than that!"

◆ ◆ ◆

Dee (Wangero) becomes angry at the thought of Maggie having the quilts. The narrator asks Dee (Wangero) what she would do with them. Dee (Wangero) replies that she would hang them on the wall. Maggie listens nearby.

◆ ◆ ◆

"She can have them, Mama," she said, like somebody used to never winning anything, or having anything <u>reserved</u> for her. "I can 'member Grandma Dee without the quilts."

◆ ◆ ◆

The narrator looks at Maggie. She remembers that Maggie learned how to quilt from her grandmother and aunt. She sees that Maggie is slightly afraid of Dee (Wangero) but is not angry.

◆ ◆ ◆

Vocabulary Development

reserved (ree ZERVD) *v.* kept back or set apart for later use

---

© Pearson Education, Inc.

When I looked at her like that something hit me in the top of my head and ran down to the soles of my feet. Just like when I'm in church and the spirit of God touches me and I get happy and shout. I did something I never had done before: hugged Maggie to me, then dragged her on into the room, snatched the quilts out of Miss Wangero's hands and dumped them into Maggie's lap. Maggie just sat there on my bed with her mouth open.

◆ ◆ ◆

The narrator tells Dee (Wangero) to choose other quilts, but Dee (Wangero) leaves and joins her friend, who is waiting in the car. Dee (Wangero) tells the narrator and Maggie that they do not understand their heritage. She also says they are living in the past. She puts on large, modern sunglasses.

◆ ◆ ◆

She put on some sunglasses that hid everything above the tip of her nose and her chin. Maggie smiled; maybe at the sunglasses. But a real smile, not scared. After we watched the car dust settle I asked Maggie to bring me a dip of snuff.[3] And then the two of us sat there just enjoying, until it was time to go in the house and go to bed.

◆ **Literary Analysis**

What do you think **motivates** Mama to give Maggie the quilts?

_____

_____

_____

◆ **English Language Development**

Mark the Text

The past tense of a regular English-language verb ends in -ed. For example, snatched is the past tense of snatch. Many common verbs are irregular, however. For example, said is the past tense of say. Find and circle the irregular past tense of sit in the bracketed passage.

◆ **Stop to Reflect**

How does Maggie feel after her sister's visit?

_____

_____

_____

---

3. **snuff** (SNUHF) _n._ powdered tobacco.

© Pearson Education, Inc.

1. What tragic event happened to Maggie, Dee, and their mother in the past before the story begins?

   _____

2. Who comes to visit the narrator and Maggie?

   _____

3. A person's heritage includes customs, beliefs, and traditions from the past. List two statements from this story that show Dee's interest in her heritage.

   1. _____

   2. _____

4. Which character knows more about her heritage? Why do you think so?

   _____

5. **Reading Strategy:** Complete this chart to **contrast the characters** of Maggie and Dee.

	Appearance	Attitude	Behavior	Speech
Maggie				
Dee				

6. **Literary Analysis:** What do you think **motivates** the narrator to give the quilts to Maggie? List two reasons.

   1. _____

   2. _____

© Pearson Education, Inc.

Writing

Critical Review

Do you think "Everyday Use" works well as a story? Why, or why not? A **critical review** tells what you think about a short story, poem, or novel. Write down your reactions for a critical review of "Everyday Use."

1. First, write one positive reaction, or something you liked about the story. Think about the characters, the events, and the message the author wants to convey.

   _____

   _____

   Explain why you feel this way.

   _____

   _____

2. Write one negative reaction, or something you did not like about the story.

   _____

   _____

   Tell why you feel this way.

   _____

   _____

3. Now, write a sentence to tell your opinion of the entire story. Tell whether you liked the story or whether you did not like it.

   [Sentence starter] I _____ "Everyday Use."

   Tell why you feel this way. Give reasons to support your opinion.

   [Sentence starter] I _____ the story because _____

   _____

   _____

4. On a separate sheet of paper, finish your critical review. Then read it aloud to share it with your classmates.

Mother Tongue
Amy Tan

Summary

In this essay, Amy Tan talks about "all the good Englishes" she uses as a Chinese American. She begins to think about them one day when her mother attends one of her talks. Tan realizes that she is using a different English in her talk from what she uses when she speaks with her mother. Then she describes a number of times when her mother was treated less politely because of her limited and original English. Even as a child, Tan—whose English is perfect—sometimes had to make phone calls for her mother. Tan wonders whether more Asian Americans become engineers because their parents speak limited English at home. Then Tan explains that when she begins to think of her mother as her reader, she finds her voice as a writer.

Visual Summary

Main Idea
"Language is the tool of my trade. And I use them all—all the Englishes I grew up with."

Supporting Details

Tan's mother comes to one of her talks. Her mother's presence makes Tan realize that she uses different English in her talks from the English she uses with her mother.	Tan has to make phone calls for her mother. People don't take her mother as seriously because her English is limited.	Tan thinks students with parents who speak limited English have trouble with standardized tests. Tan herself always had trouble with achievement tests, SATs, and IQ tests.	When Tan decides to imagine a reader for her writing, she picks her mother. Tan has succeeded when her mother reads her first book and says, "So easy to read."

 © **Pearson Education**, Inc.

LITERARY ANALYSIS

Reflective Essay

What is a **reflective essay?**
- A **reflective essay** is a short work of nonfiction.
- It tells a writer's personal view of a topic.
- The topic of the essay might be a personal experience or an important event.
- The writer sometimes explores an experience or event to find a deeper meaning.

In "Mother Tongue," Tan shares her thoughts about the English language. In this passage from the essay, Tan, the daughter of a Chinese immigrant, explains why she values the written and spoken word:

> I am a writer. And by that definition, I am someone who has always loved language. I am fascinated by language in daily life. I spend a great deal of my time thinking about the power of language. . . . Language is the tool of my trade.

READING STRATEGY

Evaluating a Writer's Message

In a reflective essay, a writer often explores the meaning of his or her personal experiences. When you read a reflective essay, first identify the message, or main point, the writer is trying to make about these experiences. Then **evaluate a writer's message** by judging whether you do or do not agree with it. Use a chart like the one below to make your evaluation.

On the chart, list facts, reasons, or examples Tan uses to support her views about the challenges faced by people who speak "limited" English. When you finish reading, tell whether you agree or disagree with Tan's message.

Tan's Message	Supporting Evidence	Your Response
People who speak "limited" English are often judged unfairly.	They are not taken seriously by people in department stores, banks, and restaurants.	

© Pearson Education, Inc.

Mother Tongue

Amy Tan

◆ **Literary Analysis**

Underline three words, phrases, or sentences in the bracketed paragraphs that let you know this will be a **reflective essay**.

I am not a scholar of English or literature. I cannot give you much more than personal opinions on the English language and its variations in this country or others.

I am a writer. And by that definition, I am someone who has always loved language. I am fascinated by language in daily life. I spend a great deal of my time thinking about the power of language—the way it can <u>evoke</u> an emotion, a visual image, a complex idea, or a simple truth. Language is the tool of my trade. And I use them all—all the Englishes I grew up with.

◆ **Reading Check**

What makes Tan aware of the "different Englishes" she uses?

_____

_____

_____

_____

Recently, I was made <u>keenly</u> aware of the different Englishes I do use. I was giving a talk to a large group of people, the same talk I had already given to half a dozen other groups. The nature of the talk was about my writing, my life, and my book, *The Joy Luck Club.*[1] The talk was going along well enough, until I remembered one major difference that made the whole talk sound wrong. My mother was in the room. And it was perhaps the first time she had heard me give a lengthy speech, using the kind of English I have never used with her.

◆ ◆ ◆

Tan realizes that she is using complicated English—the kind of standard English she learned in school.

◆ ◆ ◆

Vocabulary Development

evoke (ee VOHK) *v.* call forth or draw out
keenly (KEEN lee) *adv.* strongly

---

1. **The Joy Luck Club** Amy Tan's highly praised 1989 novel about four Chinese American women and their mothers.

© Pearson Education, Inc.

Just last week, I was walking down the street with my mother, and I again found myself conscious of the English I was using, the English I do use with her. We were talking about the price of new and used furniture and I heard myself saying this: "Not waste money that way." My husband was with us as well, and he didn't notice any switch in my English. And then I realized why. It's because over the twenty years we've been together I've often used the same kind of English with him, and sometimes he even uses it with me. It has become our language of intimacy, a different sort of English that relates to family talk, the language I grew up with.

◆ ◆ ◆

Tan shares a conversation she had with her mother, demonstrating what her "family talk" sounds like. When Tan's mother speaks, she does not use Standard English. However, Tan's mother understands more than her limited use of English suggests. For example, Tan's mother follows complicated business and finance news. While Tan's friends do not always completely understand her mother, Tan understands her mother's English because it is what she grew up with. Tan explains that the way her mother speaks English influences the way she views the world.

◆ ◆ ◆

Lately, I've been giving more thought to the kind of English my mother speaks. Like others, I have described it to people as "broken," or "fractured" English. But I <u>wince</u> when I say that. It has always bothered me

© Pearson Education, Inc.

How does Tan's language change when she speaks with her mother?

_____

_____

_____

◆ English Language Development

A **sentence** is a group of words that expresses a complete thought. A sentence has two basic parts: a **subject** that answers the question *Who?* or *What?* and a **verb** that tells what the subject does, what is done to the subject, or what the condition of the subject is. A group of words expresses a complete thought if it can stand by itself and still make sense. Which group of words in the bracketed paragraph does not express a complete thought?

_____

_____

_____

◆ Literary Analysis

Underline one sentence in this paragraph that points to the fact that this essay is **reflective**.

Mark the Text

Vocabulary Development

wince (WINS) *v.* draw back slightly as if in pain

that I can think of no way to describe it other than "broken," as if it were damaged and needed to be fixed, as if it lacked a certain wholeness and soundness. I've heard other terms used, "limited English," for example. But they seem just as bad, as if everything is limited, including people's perceptions of the limited English speaker.

I know this for a fact, because when I was growing up, my mother's "limited" English limited my perception of her. I was ashamed of her English. I believed that her English reflected the quality of what she had to say. That is, because she expressed them imperfectly her thoughts were imperfect. And I had plenty of <u>empirical</u> evidence to support me: the fact that people in department stores, at banks, and at restaurants did not take her seriously, did not give her good service, pretended not to understand her, or even acted as if they did not hear her.

◆　◆　◆

Tan explains that her mother herself also realized how her limited use of English created problems. When Tan was fifteen, she was asked to call people to get information for her mother. For example, Tan once called a stockbroker to find out about a missing check. More recently, Tan's mother went to the hospital to learn the results of a brain scan. After the hospital claimed to have lost the scan, Mrs. Tan refused to leave until the doctor called her daughter. Tan arranged to get the information her mother wanted. She also received an apology for the hospital's mistake.

◆　◆　◆

◆ Reading Check

Circle one word or phrase in this paragraph that reveals how Tan used to feel about her mother's use of the English language.

◆ Stop to Reflect

As she was growing up, Tan thought her mother's English reflected the quality of her thoughts. What evidence seemed to support Tan's thoughts?

_____

_____

_____

_____

Vocabulary Development

empirical (em PEER i kul) *adj.* obtained from observation or experiment

© Pearson Education, Inc.

I think my mother's English almost had an effect on limiting my possibilities in life as well. Sociologists[2] and linguists[3] probably will tell you that a person's developing language skills are more influenced by peers. But I do think that the language spoken in the family, especially in immigrant families which are more <u>insular</u>, plays a large role in shaping the language of the child. And I believe that it affected my results on achievement tests, IQ tests, and the SAT.[4] While my English skills were never judged as poor, compared to math, English could not be considered my strong suit.

◆ ◆ ◆

Tan did fairly well in English in school. However, she always had higher scores in math and science achievement tests. Tan believes she did well on math tests because there was only one right answer. On the other hand, she had problems with English tests because she felt that the answers depended on personal experience and opinions. Tan could not sort through all the vivid images that came to mind when she tried to answer fill-in-the-blank sentence completions or word analogies.

◆ ◆ ◆

I have been thinking about all this lately, about my mother's English, about achievement tests. Because lately I've been

---

Vocabulary Development

insular (IN syoo lahr) *adj.* suggestive of the isolated life of an island

---

2. **sociologists** (SOH see AHL uh jists) *n.* people who study human social behavior.
3. **linguists** (LING gwists) *n.* people who study human speech.
4. **SAT** Scholastic Aptitude Test; national college entrance exam.

© Pearson Education, Inc.

◆ **Reading Strategy**

What point about developing language skills is Tan making in the bracketed paragraph? What evidence does Tan give to support her point? To **evaluate the message,** tell whether you agree or disagree with her and why.

_____

_____

_____

_____

_____

◆ **Culture Note**

Tan believes that her performance on standardized tests reflected the fact that she grew up listening to her mother's "broken" English. With a group of classmates, discuss the kinds of standardized tests with which you are familiar. Speak to your teacher or use the Internet to find out more about standardized tests.

• What is the overall purpose of standardized tests?

_____

_____

• List 2 or more types of standardized tests.

_____

_____

◆ **Vocabulary and Pronunciation**

Tan says, "English could not be considered my strong suit." The compound noun *strong suit* means "a quality, an activity, or a skill at which a person excels." Write a sentence about Tan or her mother in which you use the noun *strong suit.*

_____

_____

_____

Tan wonders why so few Asian-Americans appear in literature. With a group of classmates, share what you know about Asian-American writers. Look at a library book, a literature textbook, or the Internet to find out more about Asian-American authors.

• List the names of two Chinese American writers.

_____

_____

• List one title by each author.

_____

_____

• List the names of two Japanese American writers.

_____

_____

• List one title by each author.

_____

_____

◆ Read Fluently

Read the bracketed paragraph here and on the next page aloud. What four kinds of "Englishes" does Tan use in her writing?

1. _____

2. _____

3. _____

4. _____

asked, as a writer, why there are not more Asian Americans represented in American literature. Why are there few Asian Americans enrolled in creative writing programs? Why do so many Chinese students go into engineering? Well, these are broad sociological questions I can't begin to answer. But I have noticed in surveys—in fact, just last week—that Asian students, as a whole, always do significantly better on math achievement tests than in English. And this makes me think that there are other Asian-American students whose English spoken in the home might also be described as "broken" or "limited." And perhaps they also have teachers who are <u>steering</u> them away from writing and into math and science, which is what happened to me.

◆ ◆ ◆

Tan describes how she rebelled against Asian-American stereotypes to become a writer. First, she chose to study English rather than science in college. Then she became a freelance writer after an employer told her that she could not write. In 1985 Tan started writing fiction. At first, she wrote difficult sentences to prove she could use English well.

◆ ◆ ◆

Fortunately, for reasons I won't get into today, I later decided I should <u>envision</u> a reader for the stories I would write. And the reader I decided upon was my mother, because these were stories about mothers. So with this reader in mind—and in fact she did read my early drafts—I began to write stories using all the Englishes I grew up with: the English I spoke

Vocabulary Development

steering (STEER ing) *v.* guiding; directing
envision (en VIZH uhn) *v.* picture in the mind; imagine

© Pearson Education, Inc.

to my mother, which for lack of a better term might be described as "simple"; the English she used with me, which for lack of a better term might be described as "broken"; my translation of her Chinese, which could certainly be described as "watered down"; and what I imagined to be her translation of her Chinese if she could speak in perfect English, her internal language, and for that I sought to preserve the essence, but neither an English nor a Chinese structure. I wanted to capture what language ability tests can never reveal: her intent, her passion, her imagery, the rhythms of her speech and the nature of her thoughts.

Apart from what any critic had to say about my writing, I knew I had succeeded where it counted when my mother finished reading my book and gave me her verdict: "So easy to read."

◆ Stop to Reflect

What are three words you would use to describe Tan's relationship with her mother?

1. _____

2. _____

3. _____

© Pearson Education, Inc.

1. Why is language important to Tan?

   _____

   _____

2. What are two "Englishes" that Tan uses?

   1. _____

   2. _____

3. What are three things that happened to Tan as a result of her mother's use of "limited" English? List them on a chart like this one.

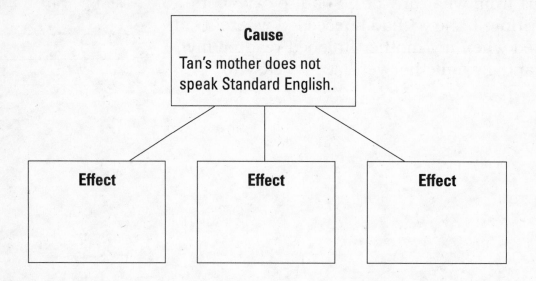

4. What influence do you think Tan's mother has had on her daughter's writing?

   _____

   _____

5. **Literary Analysis:** Name one personal experience Tan explores in this reflective essay.

   _____

   _____

© Pearson Education, Inc.

6. **Reading Strategy:** In your own words, restate Tan's message about how people who do not speak Standard English are often treated. Then **evaluate the message** by deciding whether you do or do not agree with it. Explain why you feel this way.

_____

_____

_____

Listening and Speaking

Speech

What challenges did Tan face in becoming a writer? What experiences helped her learn about different uses of English? Write three points that Tan might include in a **speech** for young people who want to become writers.

- Write one main point for your speech.

_____

- Give one fact, reason, or example to support this main point.

_____

- Write another main point.

_____

- Give one fact, reason, or example to support the second main point.

_____

- Write a third main point.

_____

- Give one fact, reason, or example to support your third point.

_____

- Write out the speech on index cards. List each main point and its supporting evidence on a separate card.
- Then practice the speech before giving it to an audience of your classmates.
- When you give the speech, speak slowly and clearly. Remember to make eye contact with your audience.

© Pearson Education, Inc.

Part 2

Selection Summaries in English and Spanish with Alternative Reading Strategies

Part 2 contains summaries of all selections in *Prentice Hall Literature: Timeless Voices, Timeless Themes*. An alternative reading strategy follows each summary.

- Use the summaries in Part 2 to preview or review the selections.

- Use the alternative reading strategies in Part 2 to guide your reading or to check your understanding of the selection.

© Pearson Education, Inc.

"The Earth on Turtle's Back" (Onondaga),
"When Grizzlies Walked Upright" (Modoc),
from *The Navajo Origin Legend* (Navajo),
from *The Iroquois Constitution* (Iroquois)

Summary These four selections offer insights into the beliefs and attitudes of several Native American groups. "The Earth on Turtle's Back" tells of a time before the Earth existed. It explains how the Earth was brought out of the water and how life on Earth began. "When Grizzlies Walked Upright" tells how the daughter of the Chief of the Sky Spirits came to Earth and married a grizzly bear. Their children became the first Indians. The excerpt from *The Navajo Origin Legend* tells how the wind breathed life into corn to form the First Man and the First Woman. In this excerpt from *The Iroquois Constitution*, Dekanawidah speaks of the Tree of Great Peace that shelters the Iroquois nations. He explains why and how the Five Nations should form a confederacy for the common good.

Resumen Estas cuatro selecciones nos dan una idea de las creencias y actitudes de varios grupos de indígenas americanos. *The Earth on Turtle's Back*, habla de un tiempo cuando la Tierra no existía. Explica cómo la Tierra fue sacada del agua y cómo comenzó la vida. *When Grizzlies Walked Upright*, cuenta como la hija del Jefe de los Espíritus del Cielo bajó a la Tierra y se casó con un oso pardo. Sus hijos fueron los primeros indígenas americanos. El pasaje de *Navajo Origin Legend*, cuenta cómo el viento sopló vida en el maíz para formar al primer hombre y la primera mujer. En la selección tomada de *Iroquois Constitution*, Dekanawidah habla del Árbol de la Gran Paz que cobija a las naciones iroquesas. Explica por qué y cómo las Cinco Naciones deberían formar una confederación por el bien común.

Summarize Main Idea To understand what you read, you should pause from time to time to summarize the main ideas you have met so far. For example, this paragraph from "The Earth on Turtle's Back" can be summarized in one sentence.

Before this Earth existed, there was only water. It stretched as far as one could see, and in that water there were birds and animals swimming around. Far above, in the clouds, there was a Skyland. In that Skyland there was a great and beautiful tree. It had four white roots which stretched to each of the sacred directions, and from its branches all kinds of fruits and flowers grew.

Main Idea: Once there was only water and a Skyland.

Supporting Details: Water stretched as far as one could see; birds and animals were swimming around; Skyland had a great and beautiful tree; all kinds of fruits and flowers grew from its branches.

Apply this strategy to other paragraphs from "The Earth on Turtle's Back," "When Grizzlies Walked Upright," *The Navajo Origin Legend*, and *The Iroquois Constitution*. Summarize the main idea and list some supporting details.

© Pearson Education, Inc.

"A Journey Through Texas" by Alvar Núñez Cabeza de Vaca
"Boulders Taller Than the Great Tower of Seville" by García López de Cárdenas

Summary These accounts of the early explorations of America are written for different purposes: to tell about the experiences of the explorers and to generate enough interest so that further exploration would be financed by interested parties in Spain. In "A Journey Through Texas," the author describes his interactions with the Native Americans. He tells where they lived, what they ate, how they cooked, and how they reacted to the deaths of loved ones. He also tells of their generosity in helping the explorers in their journey "towards sunset." In "Boulders Taller Than the Great Tower of Seville," the author describes his experiences as the first European to explore the Grand Canyon and the difficulties he faced in trying to get down into the gorge to explore the river below.

Resumen Estas historias de las primeras exploraciones de América se escribieron por diferentes razones: para contar las experiencias de los exploradores y generar así suficiente interés y apoyo financiero en España para continuar las exploraciones. En *A Journey Through Texas*, el autor describe su relación con los americanos nativos. Nos dice dónde vivían, qué comían, cómo cocinaban y cómo reaccionaban frente a la muerte de seres queridos. También habla de su generosidad y ayuda hacia los exploradores en su "viaje hacia la puesta del sol". En *Boulders Taller Than the Great Tower of Seville*, el autor describe sus experiencias como el primer europeo en explorar el Gran Cañón, y de las dificultades que enfrentó para tratar de llegar al fondo del cañón y explorar el río que corría abajo.

Sequence of Events Use this sequence organizer to record the main events in "A Journey Through Texas." Some information has already been provided. When you are finished, make your own sequence organizer for "Boulders Taller Than the Great Tower of Seville."

The Indians sent two women to tell other Indians farther west that the explorers were coming.

↓

While waiting for the women to return,

↓

After that, Castillo and Estevanico

↓

When Castillo and Estevanico returned, they said that

↓

The explorers then

↓

After that, they

↓

© Pearson Education, Inc.

Name _____ Date _____

from *The Interesting Narrative of the Life of Olaudah Equiano*
by Olaudah Equiano

Summary This excerpt from a slave narrative tells of the experiences of a young slave during the middle passage, or the trip across the ocean. Olaudah Equiano describes the horrors of the journey, telling of the sickening smells in the hold, where people were crowded so much "that each had scarcely room to turn." He tells of the cruelty of the whites, who starved the captives and kept them in chains. When two captives managed to jump overboard, preferring death to slavery, one was saved and then flogged unmercifully for trying to escape. He also tells of seeing flying fishes along the journey, and about being shown the use of the quadrant. Upon arrival in Bridgetown, the captives were put into small groups so they could be examined more easily by potential buyers.

Resumen Este pasaje del relato de un esclavo cuenta su viaje a través del océano. Olaudah Equiano describe los horrores de la travesía, cuenta del repugnante olor en la bodega del barco, donde la gente estaba tan amontonada que "apenas tenían espacio para darse vuelta". Habla de la crueldad de los blancos, quienes apenas alimentaban a los cautivos y los mantenían en cadenas. Cuando dos de los cautivos lograron arrojarse por la borda, prefiriendo morir a ser esclavos, uno fue rescatado y azotado sin piedad por tratar de escapar. También habla de los peces voladores que vio durante el viaje, y de cuando le enseñaron a usar el cuadrante. Al llegar a Bridgetown, los cautivos fueron separados en pequeños grupos para poder ser examinados más fácilmente por potenciales compradores.

Classify Descriptive Details *The Interesting Narrative of the Life of Olaudah Equiano* is full of descriptive details. Read the following passage. Use the chart to tell what you see and hear. List sights, sounds, smells, and other details. One example has been provided in each category. Complete this passage, and then practice the strategy by doing this exercise with another passage from the story.

> This produced copious perspirations, so that the air soon became unfit for respiration, from a variety of loathsome smells, and brought on a sickness among the slaves, of which many died. . . . This wretched situation was again aggravated by the galling of the chains, now become insupportable, and the filth of the necessary tubs, into which the children often fell, and were almost suffocated. The shrieks of the women, and the groans of the dying, rendered the whole a scene of horror almost inconceivable.

Sights	slaves, _____
	_____
Sounds	shrieks, _____
	_____
Smells	copious perspirations, _____
	_____
Other details	wretched situation, _____
	_____

© Pearson Education, Inc.

Name _____ Date _____

from *Journal of the First Voyage to America* by Christopher Columbus

Summary The excerpt from Columbus's journal details the ninth day after reaching land in 1492. Columbus describes the beauty and fertility of the island he is exploring. He writes about the specimens he is bringing home to his sponsors. He tells how he met and traded with the natives, exchanging bells and beads for fresh water. He writes of his intention to sail to a nearby island, which he believes to be Japan. He ends with the optimistic statement that he will proceed to the continent and meet with the emperor of China.

Resumen El sumario del diario de Colón da detalles del noveno día luego de alcanzar tierra en 1492. Colón describe la belleza y fertilidad de la isla que está explorando. Escribe sobre los especímenes que llevará de vuelta a los reyes. Habla también de cómo se encontró con los indígenas y los trueques que hizo con ellos, cambiando campanillas y cuentas por agua potable. Continúa hablando de su decisión de navegar a una isla cercana, la que él cree que es Japón. Termina en un tono optimista diciendo que continuará hasta el continente y se encontrará con el emperador de China.

Break Down Sentences Many of the sentences in the story are four or five lines long—or even longer. To help you understand these long sentences, break them down into shorter ones. For example:

Sentence: After having dispatched a meal, I went ashore, and found no habitation save a single house, and that without an occupant; we had no doubt that the people had fled in terror at our approach, as the house was completely furnished.

Sentence broken into parts: After eating, I went ashore. I found only one house, completely furnished, but no one was home. We had no doubt that the people had fled in terror at our approach.

Find at least four more sentences that are four or more lines long. Break them into parts. Compare your sentences with those of your classmates.

1. _____

_____

2. _____

_____

3. _____

_____

4. _____

_____

_____

© Pearson Education, Inc.

Name _____ Date _____

from *The General History of Virginia* by John Smith
from *Of Plymouth Plantation* by William Bradford

Summary This excerpt from *The General History of Virginia* tells of the hardships of the Jamestown colony. Fifty colonists die between May and September. When Captain John Smith goes on an expedition, he and his men are attacked by Indians. Smith's life is spared because he gives the Indians his compass and because Pocahontas, Chief Powhatan's daughter, saves him. After six weeks as a captive, Smith is allowed to return to Jamestown. Pocahontas brings the settlers food, saving their lives. The first excerpt from *Of Plymouth Plantation* describes the Puritans' voyage. The second describes their first winter in the New World. The third explains how the English-speaking Indians Samoset and Squanto help the settlers make a peace treaty with the Indian leader Massasoit.

Resumen Este pasaje de *The General History of Virginia*, cuenta las penurias pasadas por los colonos de Jamestown. Cincuenta de ellos murieron entre mayo y septiembre. Cuando el capitán John Smith sale de expedición, él y sus hombres son atacados por los indígenas. Smith salva su vida porque le da a los indígenas su brújula, y porque Pocahontas, la hija del jefe Powhatan, lo rescata. Luego de ser prisionero por seis semanas, Smith puede volver a Jamestown. Pocahontas lleva comida a los colonos, salvándoles la vida. El primer pasaje de *Of Plymouth Plantation*, describe el viaje por mar de los puritanos. El segundo describe su primer invierno en el Nuevo Mundo. El tercero cuenta cómo los indígenas Samoset, y Squanto, que hablaban inglés, ayudan a los colonos a hacer un acuerdo de paz con el jefe indígena Massasoit.

Paraphrase Some of the sentences in these selections are hard to understand because they seem to have so many ideas. One way to make them clear is to paraphrase, or restate, the main idea in the sentence. Choose three sentences from the selections to paraphrase. Use the example as a guide.

Example:

> With this lodging and diet, our extreme toil in bearing and planting palisades so strained and bruised us and our continual labor in the extremity of the heat had so weakened us, as were cause sufficient to have made us as miserable in our native country or any other place in the world.

Paraphrase: We were working so hard in the heat that we were weak and miserable.

Sentence 1 Paraphrase:

_____

_____

_____

Sentence 2 Paraphrase:

_____

_____

_____

Sentence 3 Paraphrase:

_____

_____

_____

"To My Dear and Loving Husband" by Anne Bradstreet
"Huswifery" by Edward Taylor

Summary "To My Dear and Loving Husband" expresses the poet's deep love for her husband. She prays that they may live together forever in the next life when their life on earth is over. "Huswifery" is an extended comparison between the transformation of wool into clothing and the transformation of an imperfect person into a glorious servant of God. The speaker first asks God to make him into a spinning wheel (on which raw wool is spun into yarn); and then into a loom (on which the yarn is woven into cloth). God's sacraments will clean the cloth, which is then dyed, decorated, and made into glorious robes. God, the poet says, is the spinner, weaver, cleaner, and dyer, working His will, transforming the speaker, clothing him in grace to prepare him for salvation.

Resumen *To My Dear and Loving Husband*, expresa el profundo amor de la poeta por su esposo. Ella reza para que puedan pasar juntos la próxima vida, cuando terminen sus vidas terrenas. *Huswifery*, es una detallada comparación entre la conversión de la lana en ropas y la transformación de una persona imperfecta en un glorioso sirviente de Dios. El narrador primero pide a Dios que lo convierta en una rueca (en la que la lana se hila) y luego en un telar (donde la lana pasa a ser paño). Los sacramentos limpiarán la lana, que luego será teñida, decorada y convertida en gloriosos mantos. Dios, dice el poeta, es como el hilandero, el tejedor y los teñidores, haciendo su voluntad, transformando al poeta, arropándolo en gracia, preparándolo para su salvación.

Restate Poetic Language Sometimes poets use poetic language in place of more familiar language. The words themselves might be unfamiliar, or the order of the words might be unusual. Read these poems to identify and list examples of poetic language. Then write more familiar words or word order for the phrases you list. Create a chart like the one below. A few phrases from Anne Bradstreet's poem have been modeled for you. Choose other phrases from her poem, as well as from Edward Taylor's.

Poetic Language	More Familiar Language
If ever two were one, then surely we.	If two were ever one, we are.
If ever man were lov'd by wife, then thee:	If a man were ever loved by his wife, you are.
The riches that the East doth hold	The riches of the East
My love is such that rivers cannot quench	My love is deeper than the rivers

© **Pearson Education**, Inc.

from *Sinners in the Hands of an Angry God* by Jonathan Edwards

Summary This excerpt from Edwards's sermon describes God's rising anger against the sinners in the congregation. These sinners are like spiders that their angry God holds over the "wide and bottomless . . . furnace" of hell. Edwards tells his listeners that they can save their souls from eternal suffering only if they beg God's forgiveness now and experience the saving grace of conversion, which will ensure them a place among the elect.

Resumen Este pasaje del sermón de Edward describe la creciente furia de Dios hacia los pecadores en la congregación. Estos pecadores son como arañas que su furioso Dios sostiene sobre el "ancho y sin fondo . . . horno" del infierno. Edwards le dice a su audiencia que ellos pueden salvar sus almas del sufrimiento eterno sólo si imploran a Dios su perdón y experimentan la gracia salvadora de la conversión, la cual les asegurará un lugar entre los elegidos.

Question Author's Purpose As you read a nonfiction work, you should ask yourself why the writer gives you the information in the way he or she does. Make a record of this excerpt from *Sinners in the Hands of an Angry God* by asking a question for each paragraph and writing an answer to your question. A sample question and answer for the first three paragraphs have been modeled for you.

1. **Q:** How can those who are "out of Christ" (that is, sinners) avoid falling into Hell?

    A: Sinners avoid Hell only through the power and pleasure of God.

2. **Q:** What do sinners think is responsible for keeping them out of Hell?

    A: They think it is their own good health and how they take care of themselves that keeps them out of Hell.

3. **Q:** What would happen if God decided to let you go?

    A: You would immediately plunge into Hell.

_____

_____

_____

_____

_____

_____

_____

_____

_____

_____

_____

© Pearson Education, Inc.

from *The Autobiography* and
from *Poor Richard's Almanack* by Benjamin Franklin

Summary In *The Autobiography*, Franklin describes his plan for "arriving at moral perfection" by listing thirteen virtues. They are temperance, silence, order, resolution, frugality, industry, sincerity, justice, moderation, cleanliness, tranquillity, chastity, and humility. He proposes to work on one virtue at a time, recording his progress in a notebook. In *Poor Richard's Almanack*, Franklin gives advice about how people should behave. These are a few examples: "Fools make feasts, and wise men eat them." "Keep thy shop, and thy shop will keep thee." "Three may keep a secret if two of them are dead." He finds his plan to be helpful and instructive, though not entirely successful.

Resumen Franklin describe su plan para "llegar a la perfección moral" enumerando trece virtudes. Éstas son: sobriedad, silencio, orden, resolución, frugalidad, laboriosidad, sinceridad, justicia, moderación, limpieza, tranquilidad, castidad y humildad. Franklin se propone dedicarse a una virtud por vez, y anotar el progreso alcanzado en su diario. En *Poor Richard's Almanack*, Franklin nos aconseja sobre lo que es importante y sobre como debemos comportarnos. Estos son unos ejemplos: "Los tontos preparan banquetes y los sabios se los comen". "Cuida de to negocio y tu negocio cuidara a ti". "Tres pueden guardar un secreto si dos estan muertos". El autor encuentra que este plan es útil e instructivo, si bien no completamente exitoso.

Identify Paragraph Topics One good way to understand nonfiction is to identify the topic of each paragraph as you go along. That way, you can see how the topic of the first paragraph leads into the topic of the second, how the second leads into the third, and so on. Identify the topic of each paragraph in *The Autobiography*. Then, for each topic, list the supporting details. The first paragraph has been modeled for you.

Topic for first paragraph: Franklin decides to try to achieve "moral perfection."
Supporting details:
1. Since he knows what is right and what is wrong, he thinks he can just do the one and avoid the other.
2. He finds out that it is not so easy.
3. Bad habits get the better of him when he isn't paying attention.
4. He decides that he must break bad habits and establish good ones.

_____

_____

_____

_____

_____

_____

_____

_____

_____

_____

 © **Pearson Education**, Inc.

The Declaration of Independence by Thomas Jefferson
from *The Crisis, Number 1,* by Thomas Paine

Summary The Declaration opens by saying it is important to give reasons why America should separate from Britain. It states that all men are created equal, and they have certain "unalienable rights." Governments exist to protect those rights. When government destroys those rights, the people may start a new government. It lists the English king's abuses of those rights. It declares the colonists independent of Britain. The colonists pledge support for the Declaration with their lives, fortunes, and honor.

In his essay, Paine urges the colonists to fight against the British. He assures his readers of God's support for the American cause. Paine states that a good father will fight so his child may live in peace. Paine appeals to all Americans in all states to unite.

Resumen La Declaración comienza enumerando las razones por las cuales América debe separarse de Inglaterra. Declara que todos los hombres han sido creados iguales y que tienen ciertos "derechos inalienables". Que los gobiernos existen para proteger esos derechos y que, cuando los destruyen, el pueblo debe crear un nuevo gobierno. Enumera los abusos cometidos por el rey inglés en contra de esos derechos y declara la independencia de los colones del gobierno inglés. Los colonos se comprometen a apoyar la Declaración con sus vidas, fortunas y honor.

En su ensayo, Paine urge a los colonos a luchar contra los ingleses y dice que Dios apoya a la causa americana. Añade que un buen padre luchará para que sus hijos vivan en paz y exhorta a todos los americanos en todos los estados a unirse.

Simplify Long Sentences Some of the sentences in these selections are long, which might make them difficult to understand. To understand them more easily, you can simplify them. Listen to the audiocassette recording of these selections as you read along. Then work with a partner to simplify any sentences that seem long to you. Use the example as a model.

Example:

When in the course of human events, it becomes necessary for one people to dissolve the political bands which have connected them with another, and to assume among the powers of the earth, the separate and equal station to which the laws of nature and of nature's God entitle them, a decent respect to the opinions of mankind requires that they should declare the causes which impel them to the separation.

Simplified Sentence:

When one group of people wants to break away from another group, they should state their reasons for wanting to do so.

_____

_____

_____

_____

_____

_____

© **Pearson Education, Inc.**

"An Hymn to the Evening" and "To His Excellency, General Washington"
by Phillis Wheatley

Summary In "An Hymn to the Evening," Wheatley talks about the beauty of the sunset. She hopes that people may glow with virtue, just as the sky glows with the beautiful colors of the setting sun. She sees night as a time that soothes "each weary mind." After sleep, we can wake "more pure." "To His Excellency, General Washington" uses the goddess Columbia as a symbol of America. Wheatley describes the bravery and goodness of America. Washington is praised as "first in peace and honors." America is seen as defended by heaven, while all other nations hope that she will win the war against Britain. Washington is asked to proceed guided by the goddess. The poet suggests that he will be rewarded with a crown, a mansion, and a golden throne.

Resumen En *An Hymn to the Evening*, Wheatley habla de la belleza de la puesta de sol. Ella ve a la noche como un tiempo que "calma la mente cansada". Luego del sueño, podemos despertar "más puros". *En To His Excellency, General Washington*, Wheatley usa a la diosa Columbia como símbolo de América y describe el valor y bondad de América. Elogia a Washington como "el primero en paz y honores". Ve a América defendida por los cielos, mientras todas las otras naciones esperan que gane su lucha contra Inglaterra. Le pide a Washington que proceda guiado por la diosa. La poeta sugiere que Washington será recompensado con una corona, una mansión y un trono dorado.

Restate Poetic Language Sometimes poets use poetic language instead of more familiar language. As you read Wheatley's poems, look for examples of poetic language. Create a chart like the one below. A few phrases have been modeled for you. Apply this strategy to the rest of "To His Excellency, General Washington" and to "An Hymn to the Evening."

Poetic Language	More Familiar Language
Columbia's scenes of glorious toils	I write about glorious work in America
See mother earth her offspring's fate	See mother earth cry about her children's
bemoan thick as leaves in Autumn's golden reign	thick as leaves in the fall
high unfurl'd the ensign waves in air	the flag waves

© Pearson Education, Inc.

"Speech in the Virginia Convention" by Patrick Henry
"Speech in the Convention" by Benjamin Franklin

Summary Patrick Henry begins by saying that, without disrespect, he must disagree with the previous speeches. Judging by their conduct, he says, the British are preparing for war. We have tried discussing the problem. We are being ignored; there is no retreat but into slavery. The time for going along peacefully is over. The war has already begun. "Give me liberty or give me death" is his strong closing. Benjamin Franklin opens by saying he does not "entirely approve" of the Constitution as it is written. Even so, he encourages every member of the Convention to sign it. He gives several reasons for this. He doubts that a better Constitution can be written. A united front will win respect and confidence. If the government is well administered, the Constitution will work.

Resumen Patrick Henry dice que, con todo respeto, él está en desacuerdo con los anteriores discursos. A juzgar por su conducta, los ingleses se están preparando para la guerra. Dice que han tratado de discutir el problema, pero que los han ignorado, que retirarse sería igual a la esclavitud. El momento de proceder pacíficamente ya ha pasado y que la guerra ya ha comenzado. En un poderoso final, dice: "Denme la libertad o denme la muerte". Franklin dice que no "aprueba completamente" el lenguaje de la Constitución. A pesar de eso, alienta a los miembros de la Convención a firmarla por varias razones. Duda que se pueda escribir una Constitución mejor y dice que un frente unido ganará respeto y confianza en sí mismo. Si el gobierno es administrado correctamente, la Constitución funcionará.

List Key Ideas To understand persuasive speeches, you must find the key ideas and take note of the details that the speaker uses to support them. Working with a partner, list the key ideas in these speeches. Then find and list the supporting details for each key idea. The opening of Patrick Henry's speech has been modeled for you.

Key Idea of Paragraph 1:

Even though I respect others' opinions, I must voice my own on this matter of great importance.

Supporting Details:

The men who spoke before me are patriotic and able.
I mean no disrespect, but I must disagree with them.
This matter is so important that I cannot worry about offending others.
Because it is so important, freedom of debate must be allowed.
If I hold back my opinion, I would consider myself guilty of treason.

_____

_____

_____

_____

_____

_____

_____

_____

© Pearson Education, Inc.

"Letter to Her Daughter From the New White House" by Abigail Adams
from *Letters From an American Farmer* by Michel-Guillaume Jean de Crèvecoeur

Summary Abigail Adams describes her journey to Washington as First Lady. Washington is barely settled, with just a few public buildings. The White House is huge, but there are no bells to ring for servants. There is very little firewood. She tells her daughter to tell others that she finds the house and city beautiful. She closes by saying that Mrs. Washington has just invited her to visit Mount Vernon. Crèvecoeur tells of the opportunities for American immigrants. In Europe, these people were starving and unemployed. The protective laws of this new land let people "take root and flourish." Europeans from all nations come together in America. Everyone can work for his own self-interest. Here, free from involuntary dependence and hunger, they can start a new life.

Resumen Abigail Adams describe su viaje a Washington como Primera Dama. Washington está apenas habitado, con muy pocos edificios públicos. La Casa Blanca es enorme, pero no hay campanillas para llamar a los sirvientes y hay poca leña para el hogar. Abigail pide a su hija que diga a otros que ella encuentra a la casa y a la ciudad muy hermosas. Cierra diciendo que la señora Washington la acaba de invitar a Mount Vernon. Crèvecoeur habla de las oportunidades para los inmigrantes. En Europa, estaban sin trabajo y muriéndose de hambre. Las leyes de esta nueva tierra los protegen y les permiten "echar raíces y prosperar". Europeos de todas las naciones se unen en América. Todos pueden trabajar para su propio provecho. Aquí, libres de toda dependencia y del hambre, pueden comenzar una nueva vida.

Summarize Main Idea To follow the ideas in nonfiction, you should pause often to summarize the main ideas you have read so far. In a very long paragraph, you might pause several times. For example, part of the first paragraph in Crèvecoeur's letter can be summarized in one sentence.

In this great American asylum, the poor of Europe have by some means met together, and in consequence of various causes; to what purpose should they ask one another what countrymen they are? Alas, two thirds of them had no country. Can a wretch who wanders about, who works and starves, whose life is a continual scene of sore affliction or pinching penury, can that man call England or any other kingdom his country? A country that had no bread for him, whose fields procured him no harvest, who met with nothing but the frowns of the rich, the severity of the laws, with jails and punishments; who owned not a single foot of the extensive surface of this planet? No! Urged by a variety of motives, here they came.

Main Idea: The poor of Europe have come together in a new country that, unlike their old country, they can call their own.

Supporting Details: In Europe, these people were starving. The country had no bread for them. The fields gave them no harvest. They were frowned on by the rich. They were punished by severe laws. They owned no land.

Apply this strategy to other paragraphs from these two letters. Summarize the main ideas and list some supporting details. Use an additional sheet of paper for your summaries and supporting details.

_____

_____

© Pearson Education, Inc.

"The Devil and Tom Walker" by Washington Irving

Summary Tom Walker meets the Devil ("Old Scratch") in a thickly wooded swamp. He is offered Captain Kidd's treasure "on certain conditions." Tom's wife encourages him to accept, but Tom refuses to do it. She leaves with the house's valuables to find the Devil and make her own bargain. After her second attempt, she does not return. Later, Tom finds her apron with a heart and liver in it. He assumes that the Devil has slain her. Almost grateful, Tom seeks out the Devil again. This time, he makes a deal: Tom will get the pirate's treasure if he becomes a moneylender. Later, Tom regrets his deal and starts going to church often. But the Devil returns and sends Tom off on horseback into a storm. Tom never returns, though his "troubled spirit" appears on stormy nights.

Resumen Tom Walker se encuentra con el diablo ("Old Scratch") en un pantano. El diablo le ofrece el tesoro del Capitán Kidd "bajo ciertas condiciones". La esposa de Tom le dice que acepte la oferta, pero Tom no lo hace. La esposa sale de la casa para hacer ella un trato con el diablo. Luego de su segundo intento, la mujer no regresa. Más tarde, Tom halla su delantal con un corazón e hígado. Tom supone que el diablo la ha matado. Casi agradecido, Tom busca al diablo y hace un trato con él: Tom recibirá el tesoro del pirata si se convierte en un prestamista. Luego, Tom se arrepiente del trato y comienza a ir frecuentemente a la iglesia. Pero el diablo regresa y hace que Tom salga a caballo, en una tormenta. Tom nunca regresa, pero su "angustiado espíritu" aparece en noches tormentosas.

Summarize Paragraphs To make it easier to follow the plot in a story, you should pause from time to time to summarize what has happened so far. For example, the first paragraph of the story can be summarized in one sentence.

A few miles from Boston in Massachusetts, there is a deep inlet, winding several miles into the interior of the country from Charles Bay, and terminating in a thickly wooded swamp or morass. On one side of this inlet is a beautiful dark grove; on the opposite side the land rises abruptly from the water's edge into a high ridge, on which grow a few scattered oaks of great age and immense size. Under one of these gigantic trees, according to old stories, there was a great amount of treasure buried by Kidd the pirate. The inlet allowed a facility to bring the money in a boat secretly and at night to the very foot of the hill; the elevation of the place permitted a good look-out to be kept that no one was at hand; while the remarkable trees formed good landmarks by which the place might easily be found again. The old stories add, moreover, that the Devil presided at the hiding of the money, and took it under his guardianship; but this it is well known he always does with buried treasure, particularly when it has been ill-gotten.

Main Idea: Some say that Captain Kidd buried his stolen treasure in a grove near Boston, and the Devil now looks after the money.

Supporting Details: A deep inlet leads to the grove, the inlet allowed the money to be brought in by boat, the elevation allows for a good look-out, the huge trees provide a visual landmark, the Devil is known to guard stolen buried treasure.

Apply this strategy to other paragraphs from "The Devil and Tom Walker. Summarize the main idea and list some supporting details. Use an additional sheet of paper for your summaries and supporting details.

_____

_____

_____

© Pearson Education, Inc.

Name _____ Date _____

"A Psalm of Life" and "The Tide Rises, The Tide Falls"
by Henry Wadsworth Longfellow

Summary In "A Psalm of Life," the speaker refuses to accept the idea that life is only a dream with the grave as its only goal. The soul is eternal. Heroic action in life is important because life is short. The lives of heroes who have gone before us remind us that we, too, can be examples of courage and achievement for others. In "The Tide Rises, The Tide Falls," a traveler walks quickly on the beach, hurrying toward town. Darkness falls, and the sea erases the traveler's footprints in the sand. At dawn, the horses and their handler can be heard, but the traveler will never be heard. Only the cycles of nature, as symbolized by the tide, are eternal.

Resumen En *A Psalm of Life*, el poeta se rehusa a aceptar la idea de que la vida es solo un sueño y la tumba su única meta. El alma es inmortal y las acciones heroicas son importantes porque la vida es corta. Las vidas de los héroes que nos han precedido, nos recuerdan que nosotros también podemos ser ejemplos de coraje y logro para otros. En *The Tide Rises, The Tide Falls*, un viajero camina rápidamente en una playa, hacia un pueblo. Cae la noche y el mar borra las huellas que dejó el viajero en la arena. Al amanecer, se pueden escuchar caballos y voces, pero no se vuelve a escuchar al viajero. Sólo los ciclos de la naturaleza, simbolizados por la marea, son eternos.

Recognize Metaphors Poets often use metaphors, or comparisons of two unlike things. They also use similes, which also compare unlike objects but use the word *like* or *as* in each comparison. Think about the metaphors and similes in these two poems. Explain what the two things compared in each case have in common. Follow the example in the chart.

Items Compared	What They Have in Common
our hearts and muffled drums	both beat their way to the grave
a bivouac and everyday life	
people and cattle	
a person's life and footprints in the sand	
the rising tide and life	
the falling tide and death	
waves on the beach and death	

© **Pearson Education, Inc.**

Name _____ Date _____

"Thanatopsis" by William Cullen Bryant
"Old Ironsides" by Oliver Wendell Holmes
"The First Snowfall" by James Russell Lowell
from *Snowbound* by John Greenleaf Whittier

Summary In "Thanatopsis," nature brings joy and comfort to those who love her. When people think of death, nature teaches that everyone and everything must die and become part of the earth again. In "Old Ironsides," Holmes remembers the battles fought under the ship's flag. He suggests that a good ending for the ship would be to let it sink during a storm. In "The First Snowfall," the speaker describes a snowfall that has covered the land. He thinks of a grave now covered with snow. He kisses his surviving child as he thinks of her dead sister. In this excerpt from *Snowbound*, everyday objects assume strange shapes under the snow. The boys shovel a path to the barn and feed the animals. On the second evening, the family sits around the fire to enjoy cider, baked apples, and nuts.

Resumen En *Thanatopsis*, la naturaleza brinda alegría y consuelo a quienes la aman. Al pensar en la muerte, la naturaleza nos enseña que todos y todo debemos morir y volver a la tierra. En *Old Ironsides*, Holmes recuerda las batallas luchadas en su barco y sugiere que un buen final para el barco sería dejar que se hundiera durante una tormenta. En *The First Snowfall*, el que habla describe una nevada y piensa en una tumba cubierta por la nieve. Él besa a la hija que ha sobrevivido y piensa en la hermana muerta. En este pasaje de *Snowbound*, objetos de la vida diaria toman formas extrañas bajo la nieve. Los chicos limpian un camino hasta el granero para alimentar a los animales. En la segunda tarde, la familia se reúne alrededor del fuego, y disfruta de sidra, manzanas asadas y nueces.

Explain Poetic Phrases Some of the phrases in these poems might be confusing. One way to understand unfamiliar language is to explain the references in everyday language. Work with two or three of your classmates, and discuss what the following lines from the poem mean. An example from each poem has been given. Choose four more examples, and explain the meaning of each.

Confusing Phrases Explanation

1. When thoughts of the last bitter hour come like a blight/Over thy spirit (from "Thanatopsis")
   The "last bitter hour" is death. A blight is disease of plants that causes them to die. The word "thy" means "your." Thinking about death causes your spirit to sink as if you were ill.

2. And many an eye has danced to see (from "Old Ironsides)
   The word "danced" suggests that it made the viewer happy to see the flag.

3. Every pine and fir and hemlock/Wore ermine too dear for an earl (from "The First Snowfall")
   Pine, fir, and hemlock are types of trees. Ermine is a white fur, to which the snow is being compared. "Dear" means costly. The trees looked more expensively dressed than the aristocracy.

4. A sadder light than waning moon (from *Snowbound*)
   After a full moon, the moon gradually appears to become smaller, until only a crescent is visible. We call this a waning moon. The sun is giving less light than a crescent moon.

5. _____

6. _____

7. _____

8. _____

© Pearson Education, Inc.

"Crossing the Great Divide" by Meriwether Lewis
"The Most Sublime Spectacle on Earth" by John Wesley Powell

Summary Reports on the early explorations of the West, these selections say much about their writers. In "Crossing the Great Divide," Meriwether Lewis speaks about his dealings with the Indians who helped him find his way. He tells about explaining to the Indians that the only reason he wanted to explore the land was to find a "more direct way to bring merchandise to them." In "The Most Sublime Spectacle on Earth," John Wesley Powell speaks of the awesome beauty of the Grand Canyon. He describes its depth and complexity, explaining that the gorges were formed by erosion. He also describes the cloud formations and explains their role in forming the mountains. Rather than speaking about himself, Powell focuses entirely on the majesty of the Grand Canyon.

Resumen Estos relatos sobre las primeras expediciones al Oeste, revelan mucho de sus autores. En *Crossing the Great Divide*, Meriwether Lewis habla sobre sus tratos con los indígenas que lo guiaron. Dice cómo les explicó que la única razón de su viaje era para hallar "una manera más directa de llevarles mercaderías". En *The Most Sublime Spectacle on Earth*, John Wesley Powell habla de la impresionante belleza del Gran Cañón. Describe su profundidad y complejidad, explica que sus gargantas fueron formadas por la erosión. También describe las formaciones de nubes y explica su función en la formación de las montañas. En vez de hablar de sí mismo, Powell se concentra en la majestuosidad del Gran Cañón.

Outline Main Idea and Supporting Details To understand nonfiction, you must find the main ideas and study the details that support them. Working with a partner, list the main ideas and supporting details in each of these selections. Identify the main idea for each paragraph. Then list the details that support it. The first paragraph of "The Most Sublime Spectacle on Earth" has been modeled for you.

Main Idea: The Grand Canyon is the most sublime spectacle on Earth.
Details About the Main Idea:

1. It is composed of many canyons.
2. There are tens of thousands of gorges.
3. Each wall of the canyon is composed of many walls with no repetition in design.
4. Mt. Washington is not as tall as the Grand Canyon is deep.
5. The Blue Ridge Mountains would not fill the Grand Canyon.

_____

_____

_____

_____

_____

_____

_____

_____

 © **Pearson Education**, Inc.

"The Fall of the House of Usher" and "The Raven" by Edgar Allan Poe

Summary The narrator in "The Fall of the House of Usher" is visiting his friend, Roderick Usher, who is ill. Within days, Roderick says his sister Madeline has died. They put her body in a vault to await burial. About a week later, the narrator awakens in terror during a storm. Roderick enters. Soon they hear strange noises. Roderick says that Madeline is alive, has broken out of her coffin, and is at the door. The door opens, Madeline falls upon her brother, and they both die. The narrator flees into the storm, looks back, and sees the house split and fall into the lake.

In "The Raven," the speaker is reading at night. A mysterious raven arrives. To all the speaker's questions, the raven says "Nevermore!" The speaker demands that the raven leave, but it stays, forever haunting him.

Resumen En *The Fall of the House of Usher*, el narrador visita a su amigo, Roderick Usher, que está enfermo. En unos días, Roderick dice que su hermana Madeline ha muerto. Los amigos ponen el cuerpo en una bóveda. Una semana más tarde, el narrador se despierta aterrorizado durante una tormenta. Roderick entra y pronto escuchan ruidos extraños. Roderick dice que Madeline está viva, que ha salido de su ataúd y está en la puerta. La puerta se abre, Madeline cae sobre su hermano y ambos mueren. El narrador huye, se vuelve para mirar y ve a la casa partirse y hundirse en el lago.

En *The Raven*, el narrador está leyendo de noche, cuando llega un cuervo misterioso. A todas las preguntas del narrador, el cuervo responde "¡Nunca mas!" El narrador le ordena irse, pero el cuervo se queda, atormentándolo.

Sequence of Events Use this sequence organizer to record the main events in "The Fall of the House of Usher." Some information has already been provided. When you are finished, make your own sequence organizer for "The Raven."

The narrator enters the gloomy old house, and a servant takes him to see Roderick Usher.

↓

Roderick tells the narrator about the lady Madeline's illness.

↓

Roderick and the narrator carry her body to a vault deep in the building.

↓

One stormy night,_____

↓

Finally, _____

"The Minister's Black Veil" by Nathaniel Hawthorne

Summary One Sunday, Reverend Mr. Hooper appears with a black veil over his face. Everyone in his congregation is filled with dread. They wonder if he has lost his reason or is hiding a secret sin. Only his fiancée, Elizabeth, dares to ask him about it. Even she becomes terrified when he refuses to remove the veil. Hooper's congregation continues to fear and avoid him, although he becomes a more effective clergyman. Years later, on his deathbed, he is attended by Elizabeth. The Reverend Mr. Clark asks Parson Hooper if he wishes to remove the veil, but he refuses. Mr. Clark then asks him if he wants to confess his sins. The parson tells the spectators that he sees a black veil on every face. Everyone, he says, hides secret sins. He dies and is buried with the veil still covering his face.

Resumen Un domingo, el Reverendo Mr. Hooper aparece con un velo negro sobre su cara. Todos los feligreses se aterrorizan y se preguntan si Mr. Hooper ha perdido la razón o si oculta un pecado. Sólo su novia, Elizabeth, se atreve a preguntarle qué sucede. Ella también se aterroriza cuando Mr. Hooper se rehusa a quitarse el velo. La congregación continúa aterrorizada y lo evita, a pesar de que Mr. Hooper se ha convertido en un mejor pastor. Años más tarde, Mr. Hooper está muriendo, atendido por Elizabeth. El Reverendo Mr. Clark le pregunta si quiere confesar sus pecados. Mr. Hooper dice que ve un velo negro en todas las caras. Todos, dice, ocultan pecados. Muere y es enterrado con su velo.

Analyze Characters' Behavior Read "The Minister's Black Veil" with a partner, one or two paragraphs at a time. As you read, make a character analysis chart like the one below. In the first column of the chart, write the name of the character. In the second column, write what he or she does. In the third column, write the reason for the character's behavior. The first entry has been done for you.

Character	What the Character Does	Why the Character Does It
The sexton	He pulls at the bell rope.	He is calling the people to church.

   © Pearson Education, Inc.

from *Moby-Dick* by Herman Melville

Summary Captain Ahab paces the deck for hours. Near sunset, he orders Starbuck, the first mate, to send everyone on deck. Ahab nails a sixteen-dollar gold piece to the mainmast, saying that the first man to see Moby-Dick will win it. He says he wants revenge on the white whale who took off his leg. On the third day of the chase, Moby-Dick is sighted, and Ahab gets into a whale boat to chase him. Starbuck begs Ahab to stop, but Ahab follows Moby-Dick and gets his harpoon into the whale. The line breaks, and Moby-Dick suddenly turns and attacks the ship. Ahab strikes the whale again, but the harpoon line catches him around the neck and pulls him down into the water, the *Pequod* sinks, taking a sky hawk with her. Ahab's whale boat sinks in the whirlpool. The whale disappears into the sea.

Resumen El capitán Ahab se pasea por la cubierta por horas. Al atardecer, ordena a Starbuck, su primer oficial, que llame a todos a cubierta. Ahab clava una moneda de oro al mástil principal, y dice que es para el primer hombre que vea a Moby-Dick. Añade que quiere vengarse de la ballena blanca que le había costado una pierna. En el tercer día, ven a Moby-Dick, y Ahab la persigue en un bote. Starbuck le ruega a Ahab que se detenga, pero Ahab sigue a Moby-Dick y la arponea. La línea se rompe y súbitamente Moby-Dick se da vuelta y ataca al barco. Ahab la arponea nuevamente pero la línea del arpón se enreda en su cuello y lo arrastra al agua, el *Pequod* se hunde, junto con un halcón. El bote de Ahab gira en el remolino y la ballena desaparece en el mar.

Identify Chain of Events As you read a story, you probably anticipate, or think about what will happen next. Part of the excitement of a good story is finding out what will happen next and learning the outcome. While reading this excerpt from *Moby-Dick*, use a Chain-of-Events organizer like the one below to keep track of what happens.

Begin with the scene on the quarter-deck, when Ahab is pacing for hours. Then draw boxes joined by arrows to mark each event in the story. The first two boxes have been modeled for you.

Event 1: Ahab spends the whole day pacing the deck or staying in his cabin.

↓

Event 2: Ahab tells Starbuck to send the entire crew to the deck.

↓

Event 3: _____

↓

Event 4: _____

↓

Event 5: _____

© Pearson Education, Inc.

Name _____ Date _____

from *Nature*, from *Self-Reliance*, "The Snowstorm," and "Concord Hymn"
by Ralph Waldo Emerson

Summary In *Nature*, Emerson says he feels great joy outdoors. He feels linked with the Universe, God, and every living thing. Yet nature, he finds, mirrors human emotions. In *Self-Reliance*, Emerson says that every person is unique. To be great, people must rely on themselves, not conform, and not be afraid to be misunderstood. "The Snowstorm" is about a snowstorm that covers everything and brings all activity to a halt. The speaker praises the beautiful snow forms created by the wind. "Concord Hymn" is about a monument to the farmers who once fought at a bridge. They fired the symbolic first shot of the Revolutionary War. The winners and the losers are all dead, and the bridge itself has been swept away. The poet hopes that time and nature may spare the monument.

Resumen En *Nature*, Emerson dice experimentar gran alegría cuando está en la naturaleza porque se siente vinculado con el Universo, Dios y todo lo vivo. Sin embargo, Emerson encuentra que la naturaleza, imita las emociones humanas. En *Self Reliance*, dice que cada uno es único. Para ser una gran persona, debemos depender sólo en nosotros mismos, no aceptar convenciones y no temer que no nos entiendan. En *The Snowstorm*, una nevada lo cubre todo y detiene toda actividad. El poeta admira las figuras que crea el viento con la nieve. *Concord Hymn*, es sobre un monumento a unos granjeros que una vez habían luchado sobre un puente. Ellos habían hecho el primer disparo de la Guerra Revolucionaria. Ya todos han muerto y el puente ya no existe. El poeta desea que el tiempo y la naturaleza no hagan lo mismo con el monumento.

Reword Author's Ideas Some of the ideas in these essays and poems might be hard to understand because the words are unfamiliar. One way to make the ideas easier to understand is to reword them, using language that is simpler. Choose one sentence from each essay or poem, and put it in your own words. Use the example as a guide.

Example: Nature is a setting that fits equally well a comic or a mourning piece.

Reworded: Whether you're in a happy mood or a sad one, you will find your feelings reflected in the natural world.

From *Nature*: _____

Reworded: _____

_____

From *Self-Reliance*: _____

Reworded: _____

_____

"The Snowstorm": _____

Reworded: _____

_____

"Concord Hymn": _____

Reworded: _____

_____

© Pearson Education, Inc.

Name _____ Date _____

from *Walden* and from *Civil Disobedience* by Henry David Thoreau

Summary Thoreau almost bought one farm because it was far from its neighbors, but he decided it was too much of a commitment. Instead he builds a cabin in the woods because he wants to deal only with the essentials of life. His cabin is open and airy, allowing him to live in touch with nature. He urges his readers to simplify their lives, not fritter them away in details. So-called improvements only make our lives more complicated. In "The Conclusion," Thoreau decides to leave the woods because he is forming habits. He wants to avoid tradition and conformity. Live confidently, he says, and follow your own dream. Step to whatever music you hear. Simplicity and poverty force us to deal with the most basic and important everyday experiences.

Resumen Thoreau casi compra una granja para alejarse de sus vecinos pero decidió que era un gran compromiso. En vez, construyó una cabaña en el bosque porque quería vivir una vida simple. La cabaña era abierta y aireada, permitiéndolo vivir en contacto con la naturaleza. Thoreau urge a sus lectores que simplifiquen sus vidas. Dice que los aparentes adelantos sólo hacen más complicadas a nuestras vidas. Thoreau decide dejar el bosque porque se da cuenta que está creando hábitos y quiere evitar la tradición y la conformidad. Hay que vivir con confianza en nosotros mismos, dice, y trabajar por nuestros sueños. Añade que cada uno debe seguir la música que escucha internamente y que la simplicidad y la pobreza nos fuerzan a encarar las experiencias más básicas e importantes diariamente.

Identify Key Ideas Thoreau talks about what he thinks is important in life. In a small group, take turns reading the selections aloud, one paragraph at a time. As you read Thoreau's essays, make a list of the key ideas in each essay. When you are finished, compare your lists with those of your classmates. The first entry has been started for you.

from *Walden*

1. Wherever I sat, there I might live.

2. What is a house but a seat? It's better if it's a country seat.

3. A man is rich in proportion to the number of things which he can afford to let alone.

4. A poet can enjoy the most valuable part of a farm.

5. _____

6. _____

7. _____

8. _____

9. _____

10. _____

© Pearson Education, Inc.

Name _____ Date _____

Emily Dickinson's Poetry

Summary In "I heard a Fly buzz—when I died—," the poet imagines herself dying. In "Because I could not stop for Death," she is taken by Death in a carriage to her grave. In "My life closed twice before its close—," two terrible events have occurred and she waits now for a third. In "The Soul selects her own Society—," she says the soul chooses one person and ignores all others. In "There's a certain Slant of light," she talks about a depressing winter light. In "There is a solitude of space—," she says the solitude of one soul is more private than the solitude of space, sea, and death. In "The Brain—is wider than the Sky—," she says that the brain can contain the sky with ease. In "Water, is taught by thirst," the poet says that various things are taught by what seem to be opposites.

Resumen En *I heard a Fly buzz—when I died*, la poeta se imagina muriendo. En *Because I could not stop for Death*, la Muerte la lleva en un carruaje a la tumba. En *My life closed twice before its close*, han ocurrido dos terribles sucesos y ella espera por el tercero. En *The Soul selects her own Society*, Dickinson dice que el alma elige una persona e ignora a todas las otras. En *There is a certain Slant of light*, habla sobre una depresiva luz invernal. En *There is a solitude of space*, la poeta dice que el alma es más privada que la soledad del espacio, el mar y la muerte. En *The Brain is wider than the Sky*, dice que el cerebro puede contener fácilmente al cielo. En *Water, is taught by thirst*, menciona que varias cosas se enseñan por lo que pareciera ser opuestos.

Form a Mental Picture A good way to understand literature is to form a picture in your mind's eye of what the author describes. Listen to the audiocassette recording of these poems as you read along. Picture each scene as you listen. Use this page to jot down notes to describe what you see in your mind. Then work with a partner to draw sketches of what Dickinson describes in each of the following scenes.

1. the poet dying, with mourners standing around, when a fly buzzes in the room

2. death coming in a carriage for the poet, who wears a thin, light gown and fine netting around her shoulders

3. the soul selecting her own society and turning her back on an Emperor kneeling upon her mat

4. the poet reliving the event that causes her to say, "Parting is all we know of heaven. / And all we need of hell."

5. the poet learning about water because of thirst

_____

_____

_____

_____

_____

_____

_____

© **PEARSON** Education, Inc.

Walt Whitman's Poetry

Summary In the *Preface to the 1855 Edition of Leaves of Grass*, Whitman says the United States is a great poem. In "Song of Myself," he describes himself, and then considers the grass, a symbol of immortality. He then identifies himself with a farm laborer, animals, and people who work with animals. In "I Hear America Singing," he lists the various songs he hears: of mechanics, carpenters, masons, and other workers in America. In "A Noiseless Patient Spider," the poet compares a spider's work with that of a soul trying to become attached to something. In "By the Bivouac's Fitful Flame," he looks out at the sleeping army and thinks of life and death. In "When I Heard the Learn'd Astronomer," he is bored with a lecture on the stars. He goes out and looks up "in perfect silence."

Resumen En el *prefacio a la edición de 1855 de Leaves of Grass*, Whitman dice que los Estados Unidos son un gran poema. En *Song to Myself*, se describe y considera a la yerba un símbolo de inmortalidad. Más tarde, Whitman se identifica con un trabajador de campo, los animales y la gente que trabaja con los animales. En *I Hear America Singing*, enumera las muchas canciones que escucha: la de los mecánicos, carpinteros, albañiles y otros trabajadores. En *A Noiseless Patient Spider*, el poeta compara el trabajo de una araña con el de un alma tratando de unirse a algo. En *By the Bivouac's Fitful Flame*, el poeta mira al ejército durmiendo y piensa sobre la vida y la muerte. En *When I Heard the Learn'd Astronomer*, se aburre en una conferencia sobre las estrellas. Sale y mira hacia arriba "en perfecto silencio".

Identify Theme To understand literature, you must find the theme and study the details that support that theme. Working with a partner, identify the theme and list the details that relate to the theme in each selection. The first selection has been modeled for you. Follow this example for the other selections.

Theme of the excerpt from *Preface to the 1855 Edition of Leaves of Grass*:

Accepting the lessons of the past, America knows that the old ways are passing and new ways are approaching.

Details Relating to the theme:

1. America does not repel the past.

2. America accepts the lessons of the past with calmness.

3. Americans have the fullest poetical nature.

4. The United States are essentially the greatest poem.

5. Other nations of the past appear tame and orderly compared to movement in America.

_____

_____

_____

_____

_____

© Pearson Education, Inc.

"An Episode of War" by Stephen Crane
"Willie Has Gone to the War" words by George Cooper, music by Stephen Foster

Summary In "An Episode of War," a young lieutenant is dividing his company's supply of coffee when he gets shot in the arm. It is in the middle of the Civil War, and treatment of the wounded is very poor. The lieutenant makes his way to the field hospital. Before he gets there, an officer ties his handkerchief over the wound. When the lieutenant sees a doctor, the doctor assures him that he will not amputate the arm. When the lieutenant gets home, his mother, sisters, and wife sob "for a long time at the sight of the flat sleeve." In "Willie Has Gone to the War," the song lyrics tell the feelings of the person left behind. She is waiting by the brook where they had spent their last moments together. She is now waiting, hoping for his safe return, and pining "like a bird for its mate."

Resumen En *An Episode of War,* un joven teniente está dividiendo la provisión de café de su compañía cuando lo balean en el brazo. Esto ocurre durante la Guerra Civil, cuando no había elementos para tratar bien a los heridos. El teniente llega a un hospital de campaña y se ata la herida con un pañuelo. Al ver a un doctor, éste le asegura que no le amputará el brazo. Cuando el teniente regresa a casa, su madre, hermanas y esposa lloran "por mucho tiempo al ver la manga vacía". En *Willie Has Gone to War,* la letra de la canción habla de los sentimientos de la persona que se queda atrás. Ella está esperando cerca del arroyo, donde pasaron sus últimos momentos juntos. Ahora ella está esperando, deseando que vuelva sano y salvo, y languideciendo, "como un ave por su pareja".

Form a Mental Picture When you read, it is helpful to picture in your mind a scene that an author is describing. Listen to the audiocassette recordings of the story and of the song lyrics as you read. Picture each scene as you listen. Use this page to jot down notes to describe what you picture in your mind. Then work with a partner to draw sketches of each of the following scenes:

1. the lieutenant dividing the coffee supply

2. the lieutenant's first reaction when he is shot

3. the lieutenant trying to put his sword back in its scabbard

4. the lieutenant protesting when the doctor says he'll "tend" to him

5. the scene in which the lieutenant returns home

6. Willie's loved one, visiting the brook and thinking of Willie

_____

_____

_____

_____

_____

_____

_____

© Pearson Education, Inc.

"Swing Low, Sweet Chariot" and "Go Down, Moses" Spirituals

Summary In "Swing Low, Sweet Chariot," the chorus describes a chariot coming to take the singer home to heaven. Verses 2 and 3 tell of angels coming across the Jordan River. If a listener gets to heaven first, he or she should tell everyone that the singer is coming, too. In "Go Down, Moses," the chorus sings God's command: Tell pharaoh to let my people go. Verses 2 and 4 tell the story: The Israelites were held in bondage by the Egyptians. Moses told pharaoh of God's command. Moses said that if the Israelites were not freed, God would kill the Egyptians' firstborn children.

Resumen En el espiritual *Swing Low, Sweet Chariot,* el coro describe a un carro de caballos que llega para llevar al cantante a los cielos. Los versos 2 y 3 hablan de ángeles cruzando el río Jordan. Si alguien que escucha llega a los cielos primero, debe decirle a todos que el cantante también va a ir. En *Go Down, Moses,* el coro canta un mandato de Dios: Di al faraón que deje ir a mi pueblo. Los versos 2 y 4 cuentan una historia: Los israelitas eran cautivos de los egipcios. Moisés le dijo al faraón el mandato de Dios. Moisés le dijo que si no dejaba libres a los israelitas, Dios mataría a los primogénitos egipcios.

Explain Poetic Phrases Some of the phrases in these poems are symbols, that is, they do not mean exactly what they say. For example, there is no "sweet chariot" coming to carry the singer away. The chariot symbolizes a means of escape from slavery. It might represent an escape by traveling over the Ohio River to freedom, or it might symbolize an escape through death.

Look for other poetic phrases that can be seen as symbols. Explain them in the chart below.

Poetic Phrase	What It Means or Symbolizes

© Pearson Education, Inc.

from *My Bondage and My Freedom* by Frederick Douglass

Summary Frederick Douglass learned to read and write in spite of great disadvantages. Mrs. Auld, his owner's wife and a kind woman, began teaching him, but her husband stopped her. He convinced her that it was not a good idea to educate slaves, and Mrs. Auld became a different person. She kept young Frederick from reading whenever she could. He continued to learn from young white boys, paying them with bread. At the age of thirteen, he bought a copy of a schoolbook, *The Columbian Orator*. He learned to hate slavery and realized that he, as well as Mrs. Auld, had changed. They were both victims of slavery, he said. It was because of slavery that they were enemies rather than friends.

Resumen Frederick Douglass aprendió a leer y escribir a pesar de grandes inconvenientes. La Sra. Auld, la esposa del dueño, una buena mujer, comenzó a enseñar a Douglass, pero su marido la detuvo. El marido la convenció que no era una buena idea el educar a los esclavos, y la Sra. Auld se convirtió en una persona diferente. Siempre que pudo, evitó que el joven Douglass leyera. Pero Frederick continuó aprendiendo de jóvenes blancos, pagándoles con pan. A los trece años, Douglass compró un ejemplar de un libro de texto, *The Columbian Orator*. El joven Frederick aprendió a odiar la esclavitud y se dio cuenta de que, tanto él como la Sra. Auld, habían cambiado. Ambos habían sido víctimas de la esclavitud, dijo el autor. La esclavitud fue la razón por la que eran enemigos en vez de amigos.

Reword Author's Ideas As you read, it is a good idea to pause now and then and put the author's ideas into your own words. Choose ten sentences that seem especially difficult. Reword them in a way that is easier to understand. Follow the example in the model. When you finish, compare your sentences with those of your classmates.

Model: On entering upon the career of a slaveholding mistress, Mrs. Auld was singularly deficient; nature, which fits nobody for such an office, had done less for her than any lady I had known.

Reworded: Mrs. Auld was too kind-hearted to be a good slaveowner.

_____
_____
_____
_____
_____
_____
_____
_____
_____
_____
_____
_____

 © Pearson Education, Inc.

"An Occurrence at Owl Creek Bridge" by Ambrose Bierce

Summary A civilian southern plantation owner is about to be hanged by Union soldiers, having apparently tried to burn a railroad bridge. The prisoner imagines that he escapes and returns home. Just as he is about to embrace his wife, his dream ends with his death by hanging.

Resumen Soldados del ejército de la Unión están a punto de ahorcar a un civil, dueño de una plantación en el Sur. La razón era que, aparentemente, este hombre había tratado de quemar un puente para trenes. El prisionero imagina que escapa y regresa a su casa. Justo cuando está a punto de abrazar a su esposa, la muerte interrumpe el sueño, al morir ahorcado.

Plot a Story Map One way to understand a story better is to make a story map. Complete the one below by filling in the second column.

"An Occurrence at Owl Creek Bridge"	
Setting	
Characters	
What the characters want	
What blocks their wants	
Main events	
Climax (high point)	
Conclusion	

© Pearson Education, Inc.

"The Gettysburg Address" and "Second Inaugural Address"
by Abraham Lincoln
"Letter to His Son" by Robert E. Lee

Summary In "The Gettysburg Address," Lincoln reminds us that our nation was founded on the principle of equality. The war tests whether the nation can last. The battlefield is already consecrated by the men who fought. Lincoln says his words will soon be forgotten but the soldiers' struggle will be remembered. In the "Second Inaugural Address," Lincoln talks of the war. He says that slavery was a cause of the war and he hopes that the war may soon end. In "Letter to His Son," Lee writes that he hopes civil war can be avoided. He is proud of his country and will sacrifice everything but honor to keep it whole. In his view, states have no right to secede, but he does not want to be part of a Union that can be maintained only with guns. If the Union is broken, he will fight only to defend his state.

Resumen En *The Gettysburg Address,* Lincoln nos recuerda que nuestra nación está basada en el principio de igualdad. La guerra es una prueba de su perdurabilidad. El campo de batalla ya ha sido consagrado por los hombres que lucharon en él. Lincoln dice que sus palabras pronto serán olvidadas, pero que la lucha de los soldados no. En *Second Inaugural Address,* Lincoln habla de la guerra y dice que una de sus razones fue la esclavitud. En *Letter to His Son,* Lee dice tener la esperanza de evitar la guerra civil. Él está orgulloso de su país y sacrificará todo, menos su honor, para mantenerlo unido. Según Lee, los estados no tienen derecho a la secesión, pero él no quiere ser parte de una Unión que sólo se puede mantener por medio de las armas. Si la Unión se rompe, él sólo luchará para defender a su estado.

Summarize Main Idea To follow the ideas in nonfiction, you should pause occasionally and summarize the main ideas you have read so far. For example, the first paragraph of "The Gettysburg Address" can be summarized in fewer words.

Original: Four score and seven years ago our fathers brought forth on this continent, a new nation, conceived in Liberty, and dedicated to the proposition that all men are created equal.

Summary: Eighty-seven years our nation was founded on the principles of freedom and equality.

Follow the example and apply this strategy to other sentences, passages, or paragraphs from "The Gettysburg Address," "Second Inaugural Address," and "Letter to His Son."

_____

_____

_____

_____

_____

_____

_____

_____

_____

_____

_____

_____

 © Pearson Education, Inc.

Name _____ Date _____

from Civil War Diaries, Journals, and Letters

Summary Mary Chesnut writes about the attack on Fort Sumter in April, 1861. She is at home while her husband is out in the middle of the fight. She can see and hear the shells bursting in the night. Confusion is all around. At one point, she sits down on a chimney and her dress catches on fire. She finally hears that Fort Sumter has surrendered. Warren Goss writes about the excitement and nervousness he feels when he enlists in the Union army. His uniform doesn't fit. He gives advice to the drill sergeant. He quickly finds out that his job is to obey. Randolph McKim, a Confederate soldier, writes about his side's terrible and costly defeat at Gettysburg. Stonewall Jackson writes to his wife about his important role in the Battle of Bull Run.

Resumen Mary Chestnut relata el ataque al Fort Sumter en abril de 1861. Ella estaba en casa, mientras su marido estaba peleando. Mary podía ver y oír los proyectiles estallando en la noche. Todo es confusión. En un momento, Mary se sienta en una chimenea y su vestido se prende fuego. Finalmente, se entera que Fort Sumter se ha rendido. Warren Goss habla del entusiasmo y nerviosismo que sintió cuando se enlistó en el ejército de la Unión. El uniforme no era de su medida y él trata de darle consejos al sargento instructor. Warren se da cuenta rápidamente de que su trabajo es obedecer. Randolph McKim, un soldado confederado, relata la terrible y costosa derrota de su bando en la batalla de Gettysburg. Stonewall Jackson le escribe a su esposa sobre su importante actuación en la batalla de Bull Run.

Identify Chain of Events Use this chain-of-events organizer to record the main events in this excerpt from *Mary Chesnut's Civil War*. Some information has already been provided. When you are finished, make your own chain-of-events organizers for the other selections.

April 7, 1861. Mary Chesnut's husband tells her that Fort Sumter may be attacked tonight.

↓

April 12, 1861. Mr. Chesnut returns after an interesting meeting with Colonel Anderson, the commander of the Union troops at Fort Sumter. He doesn't say what happened.

↓

That night,

↓

April 13, 1861.

↓

Finally,

© Pearson Education, Inc.

"The Boys' Ambition" from *Life on the Mississippi* and "The Notorious Jumping Frog of Calaveras County" by Mark Twain

Summary In "The Boys' Ambition," Twain tells why he and his friends always wanted to work on steamboats. When the steamboats came to the wharf, the whole town came alive. In "The Notorious Jumping Frog of Calaveras County," the narrator asks a talkative old man, Simon Wheeler, about a Leonidas W. Smiley. Wheeler tells a tall tale about a Jim Smiley. Jim loves to gamble and will bet on anything. He bets a stranger that his frog can outjump any frog in Calaveras County. The stranger accepts the bet, but he needs a frog. Jim goes to find one, and the stranger fills Jim's frog with birdshot. This makes him too heavy to jump, so the stranger wins the bet. Jim Smiley discovers the trick, but he can't catch up with the stranger. Wheeler is about to keep on talking, but the narrator leaves.

Resumen En *The Boys' Ambition*, Mark Twain dice que él y sus amigos querían trabajar en los barcos de vapor porque cuando éstos llegaban, toda la ciudad se animaba. En *The Notorious Jumping Frog of Calaveras County*, el narrador le pregunta a un parlanchín viejo, Simon Wheeler, sobre Leonidas W. Smiley. Wheeler le cuenta una historia exagerada. A Jim le gustaba apostar y un día le apostó a un desconocido que su rana podía saltar más que cualquier otra en Calaveras County. El desconocido acepta, pero no tiene una rana. Jim va a buscar una y el desconocido llena la rana de Jim con munición. Esto hace que la rana pese mucho y no salte lejos, y el desconocido gana la apuesta. Jim Smiley descubre la trampa, pero no puede alcanzar al desconocido. Wheeler quiere hablar más, pero el narrador se va.

Recognize Humor Mark Twain is known as a humorist. As you read, look for lines that make you laugh. Think about why they are funny. Then complete the chart. When you are finished, make another chart for "The Notorious Jumping Frog of Calaveras County."

Funny Line from "The Boys' Ambition"	Why It's Funny
"now and then we had a hope that if we lived and were good, God would permit us to be pirates."	Pirates are not approved of by society. They make their living by stealing.

© Pearson Education, Inc.

"The Outcasts of Poker Flat" by Bret Harte

Summary The town of Poker Flat rids itself of four "undesirable characters": a gambler, two prostitutes, and a thief. The group travels half a day into the foothills of the Sierras. Then they stop to rest and drink whiskey. Two innocent young lovers, Tom Simson and Piney Woods, find the outcasts and they set up camp together. The next day, snow begins to fall. Mr. Oakhurst, the gambler, discovers that "Uncle Billy," the thief, has stolen the mules. Snowed in, the others tell stories and become good friends. One of the prostitutes starves herself to death so Piney can have more to eat. Tom leaves to get help. Two days later, the "law" from Poker Flat finds the women dead in each other's arms. Under a tree they find the body of Mr. Oakhurst, who shot himself.

Resumen El pueblo de Poker Flats se libra de cuatro "indeseables:" un jugador, dos prostitutas y un ladrón. El grupo viaja medio día en las Sierras, luego se detienen para descansar y beber whiskey. Tom Simson y Piney Woods, dos inocentes enamorados, hallan a los indeseables y acampan con ellos. Al día siguiente, comienza a nevar. Mr. Oakhurst, el jugador, descubre que "Uncle Billy", el ladrón, se ha robado las mulas. Atrapados por la nieve, se cuentan historias y se hacen amigos. Una de las prostitutas se deja morir de hambre para que Piney tenga más para comer. Tom se va a buscar ayuda. Dos días después, la "ley" de Poker Flat halla a las mujeres muertas y abrazadas. Bajo un árbol encuentran el cuerpo de Mr. Oakhurst, que se había pegado un tiro.

Make a Character Chart Read "The Outcasts of Poker Flat" with a partner, one paragraph at a time. As you read, make a character chart like the one below. In the first column of the chart, identify a character. In the second column, write the character's action. In the third column, write the reason for the character's action.

Character	Character's Action	Reason for Character's Action
John Oakhurst	He steps into the main street of Poker Flat.	It is morning, and he is ready to start the day.

"Heading West" by Miriam Davis Colt
"I Will Fight No More Forever" by Chief Joseph

Summary In "Heading West," Miriam Davis Colt writes about her decision to move from Antwerp, New York, to Kansas with her husband. They will be part of a group that calls itself the Vegetarian Company. They will work together and cooperate to make a better life for themselves and their children by living as vegetarians. She describes the difficult parting from her mother and friends. She tells about the hardships of the month-long journey. When they arrive, they find that the settlement is not as well developed as they had hoped. In "I Will Fight No More Forever," Chief Joseph says that his heart is heavy. He is concerned for his starving, freezing people. He is tired of fighting, and he "will fight no more forever."

Resumen En *Heading West*, Miriam Davis Colt habla de su decisión de mudarse con su marido de Antwerp, New York, a Kansas. Iban con un grupo llamado Vegetarian Company, a trabajar juntos y cooperar para tener una mejor vida, ellos y sus hijos, viviendo como vegetarianos. Describe el difícil momento cuando se separa de su madre y amigos y de las penurias pasadas durante el viaje, que duró un mes. Cuando llegan, hallan que el asentamiento no estaba tan bien desarrollado, como ellos habían esperado. En *I Will Fight No More Forever*, Chief Joseph dice que su corazón está agobiado. Chief Joseph está preocupado por su gente, hambrienta y con frío. Él está cansado de luchar y "no va a luchar nunca más".

Use a Chain-of-Events Organizer As you read, ask yourself what happened before and what will happen next. Sometimes you have to infer, or make assumptions, about events that happened before. In "I Will Fight No More Forever," for example, you can infer that Chief Joseph and his people have been fighting with the Federal troops. You can also infer that he has lost many of his loved ones.

One way to keep track of events is write them in a chain-of-events organizer. Complete this one for "Heading West." Then make another one for "I Will Fight No More Forever."

Event 1: Miriam Davis Colt and her husband decide to go to Kansas.

↓

Event 2:

↓

Event 3:

↓

Event 4:

© Pearson Education, Inc.

Name _____ Date _____

"To Build a Fire" by Jack London

Summary A man and a dog set off on a Yukon trail at dawn. The man is a newcomer to Alaska. He is traveling alone on a very cold day; the temperature is about seventy-five degrees below zero. The dog knows that the weather is too cold for travel, but the man does not. After stopping for lunch, the man is making good time when he suddenly falls through the snow into a spring. He gets wet up to his knees. He builds a fire to dry out, but snow slides off the tree and puts it out. The man tries to start another fire but fails. He thinks of killing the dog to warm his hands in the dog's blood, but his frozen hands are useless. The man keeps trying to walk, but he finally falls and freezes to death. When the dog realizes that the man has died, he leaves to find another man who can provide food and a fire.

Resumen Un hombre y su perro inician un viaje una madrugada en el Yukon. El hombre está recién llegado a Alaska y viaja solo en un día muy frío. Hacen aproximadamente 75° grados bajo cero. El perro sabe que hace demasiado frío para viajar, pero el hombre no lo sabe. Luego de parar para comer, reanudan el viaje cuando el hombre cae en un arroyo. Se moja hasta las rodillas y enciende una fogata para secarse. El calor hace que se derrita la nieve en un árbol. La nieve cae y apaga la fogata. El hombre trata de encender otra pero no puede. Piensa en matar al perro para calentarse las manos, pero no puede usar sus manos porque están congeladas. El hombre trata de caminar, pero finalmente cae y muere. Cuando el perro se da cuenta de que el hombre ha muerto, va en busca de otro hombre que le pueda dar comida y una fogata.

Identify Sensory Images Jack London uses a great deal of sensory language to describe the man's experience in the snow. This language helps the reader to see, hear, feel, taste, and smell what the author is describing. As you read, look for sensory words and phrases. Think about the sense to which they appeal. Record them in the proper columns on the chart. Remember that some words can appeal to more than one sense. When you are finished, compare your chart with those of your classmates. A few examples from the first paragraph have been given.

Sight	Sound	Touch	Taste	Smell
gray		cold		
dim				
gloom				
spruce				
peep				

© **Pearson Education, Inc.**

"The Story of an Hour" by Kate Chopin

Summary When Mrs. Mallard hears that her husband has been killed in a train accident, she weeps and goes to her room. Alone there, she realizes that she is free from the control of her husband. As she leaves her room, she is very happy. Just then, her husband, who had not been on the train after all, comes in the door. Mrs. Mallard dies of a heart attack.

Resumen Cuando La Sra. Mallard se entera de que su marido ha muerto en un accidente de tren, llora y se a va a su cuarto. Allí, sola, se da cuenta de que ahora está libre del control de su marido. Cuando sale de su cuarto, está muy contenta. En ese momento, su marido, quien no estaba en el tren después de todo, entra. La Sra. Mallard muere de un ataque al corazón.

Analyze Characters' Behavior To understand the characters in the stories you read, keep track of their actions in a character chart. Read "The Story of an Hour" with a partner, one or two paragraphs at a time. As you read, complete a chart like the one below. In the first column, identify a character. In the second column, list a character's action. In the third column, explain the reason for the character's action. An example has been given. When you are finished, compare your character chart with those of your classmates.

Character	Character's Action	Reason for Character's Action
Josephine	She hints that her sister's husband is dead, rather than telling her directly.	Mrs. Mallard has heart trouble, and Josephine doesn't want to shock her.

© **Pearson Education, Inc.**

"April Showers" by Edith Wharton

Summary Theodora writes a novel called *April Showers* and sends it to *Home Circle* magazine for publication. Some time later, she receives word that the novel has been accepted. She is overjoyed. Finally the magazine comes out, and Theodora finds that another author is given credit for it, and then she sees that it is not even her story. She travels to Boston and goes to the editorial offices of *Home Circle* for an explanation. She is told that a famous author had sent a novel with the same title. The editor had meant to reject Theodora's, but accidentally sent an acceptance letter to both authors. Heartbroken, Theodora takes back her manuscript. Her father tells her a similar thing happened to him when he was young.

Resumen Theodora escribe una novela titulada *April Showers*, y la envía a la revista *Home Circle*, para que la publiquen. Un tiempo después, recibe la noticia de que la novela ha sido aceptada, lo que la alegra mucho. Finalmente la revista sale con la novela y Theodora descubre que dicen que otra persona es el autor, y luego ve que la novela no es la suya. Theodora viaja a Boston y va a las oficinas de *Home Circle*, para pedir una explicación. Le dicen que un autor famoso había mandado una novela con el mismo título. El publicador había tenido la intención de rechazar la novela de Theodora, pero, accidentalmente había mandado una carta de aceptación a ambos. Desconsolada, Theodora recibe su manuscrito. Su padre le dice que algo parecido le había pasado a él cuando era joven.

Identify a Chain of Events One way to keep track of events in a story is to write them in a chain-of-events organizer. Complete this one for "April Showers."

Event 1: Theodora finishes her novel and ties the pages with a blue satin ribbon.

↓

Event 2:

↓

Event 3:

↓

Event 4:

↓

↓

↓

"Douglass" and "We Wear the Mask" by Paul Laurence Dunbar

Summary "Douglass," a sonnet, is addressed to Frederick Douglass. It describes the present racial conflict as worse than that of the past. The speaker wishes that Douglass were still alive to guide his people. In "We Wear the Mask," the poet says that we hide our feelings of grief and pain behind smiles and jokes. We reveal our true selves only to Christ.

Resumen *Douglass*, es un soneto dirigido a Frederick Douglass, y le dice que en ese momento el conflicto racial es peor que en el pasado. El poeta desearía que Douglass estuviera todavía vivo para guiar a su gente. En *We Wear the Mask*, el poeta dice que ocultamos nuestros sentimientos de pena y dolor detrás de sonrisas y bromas. Añade que sólo revelamos nuestras verdaderas identidades a Cristo.

Rephrase Poetry as Prose Sometimes poetic language is difficult to understand. One way to make it clearer is to rephrase it as prose, in everyday language. Read these poems with a partner. When you come to end punctuation (a period, a question mark, or an exclamation point) or a semicolon, stop and rephrase that part in your own words. For example, the first sentence of "Douglass" is the first two lines. Your rephrasing of that sentence might be something like this:

Douglass, now is a much more evil time than the time in which you lived.

Take turns reading the poems and writing the sentences in your own words. When you finish, compare your sentences with those of your classmates.

_____

_____

_____

_____

_____

_____

_____

_____

_____

_____

_____

_____

_____

_____

_____

_____

_____

_____

© Pearson Education, Inc.

Name _____ Date _____

"Luke Havergal" and "Richard Cory" by Edwin Arlington Robinson
"Lucinda Matlock" and "Richard Bone" by Edgar Lee Masters

Summary In "Luke Havergal," the speaker urges Luke Havergal to go to the western gate. There, he should listen for the voice of the woman he has loved. The woman has apparently died. The speaker encourages Luke also to die. In "Richard Cory," the townspeople admire and envy Richard Cory. Yet one night Cory shoots himself. In "Lucinda Matlock," the speaker says she had a full life. She was married for seventy years and had twelve children. She died at ninety-six and rests easily. She ends by scolding the next generation for complaining. She says, "It takes life to love Life." The speaker in "Richard Bone" made the headstones for the townspeople. He carved whatever he was told, without knowing if it was true. Now dead himself, he knows the epitaphs were true.

Resumen En *Luke Havergal*, el poeta exhorta a Luke a ir al portal del oeste. Allí, deberá escuchar la voz de la mujer que ha amado. Aparentemente, esta mujer ha muerto. El poeta también alienta a Luke a morir. En *Richard Cory*, la gente del pueblo admira y envidia a Richard Cory. Sin embargo, una noche éste se suicida. *Lucinda Matlock*, dice que ha vivido una vida plena. Estuvo casada por setenta y cinco años y tuvo doce hijos. Ella murió a los noventa y seis años y descansa en paz. Termina reprochando a la siguiente generación por sus quejas. La mujer dice: "Hace falta vida para amar a la vida". En *Richard Bone*, el personaje talla las lápidas para la gente del pueblo. Talla cualquier cosa que le pidan, sin saber si es verdad o no. Ahora que él mismo está muerto, sabe que los epitafios eran ciertos.

Gather Evidence About Characters Each character in these poems has special qualities. As you read, look for evidence of those qualities. Keep track of the evidence in lists. Identify the line in the poem in which you found the proof of each quality. A list is started below for "Lucinda Matlock." Complete this list, and then make other lists for the other characters.

"Lucinda Matlock"	
Quality	**Proof**
liked to dance	"I went to the dances at Chandlerville"
liked to play	"and played snap-out at Winchester"
was a loyal, loving wife	"We were married and lived together for seventy years"

© Pearson Education, Inc.

"A Wagner Matinée" by Willa Cather

Summary The narrator's aunt has inherited a small legacy. She comes to Boston to settle the estate and to visit her nephew. Many years before, she had been a music teacher at the Boston Conservatory. She had given up her profession when she married and moved to the Nebraska prairies. The narrator remembers all his aunt taught him when he spent time with her. The day after his aunt's arrival, the narrator takes her to a matinée performance of music by Wagner. She cries with joy at the music and with grief at the beauty she has missed.

Resumen En *Wagner Matinée*, la tía del narrador ha heredado una pequeña fortuna. La mujer llega a Boston a recibir el dinero y visitar a su sobrino. Muchos años antes, ella había enseñado música en el Conservatorio de Boston, pero había dejado su profesión al casarse y mudarse a las praderas de Nebraska. El narrador recuerda todo lo que su tía le había enseñado en su tiempo juntos. El día después de la llegada de su tía, el narrador la lleva a un concierto de música de Wagner. La tía llora de alegría al escuchar la música y de pena por toda la belleza que había perdido.

Outline Main Idea and Supporting Details To understand what you read, you must find the main ideas and notice the details that support them. Working with a partner, list the main ideas and supporting details of each paragraph in "A Wagner Matinée." The first paragraph has been modeled for you.

Main Idea: The narrator receives a letter saying that his aunt is arriving in Boston the next day and he is to pick her up at the station.

Details About the Main Idea:

1. The letter is written in pale ink, on glassy blue-lined notepaper.
2. The letter comes from a little Nebraska village, where the narrator's aunt and uncle live.
3. The letter is from the narrator's Uncle Howard.
4. The narrator's aunt is coming to settle the estate of a bachelor relative of hers.
5. The narrator is to meet her at the station on the following day.
6. The narrator's uncle has waited until the last minute to write the letter. If the narrator had been away from home for a day, he would have missed his aunt.

_____

_____

_____

_____

_____

_____

_____

_____

_____

_____

© Pearson Education, Inc.

"The Love Song of J. Alfred Prufrock" by T. S. Eliot

Summary The opening quotation, from Dante's *Inferno*, suggests that what follows will be like a guided visit to Hell, finding no meaning to life. Prufrock invites a companion to enter a modern city in the evening. The atmosphere he describes is smoky and degenerate. It is a place in which talking of spiritual and artistic values no longer seems to make any sense. Then Prufrock asks a series of questions about himself, his past and present life: Could he and should he have done more with his life? Can he even express love for a woman when they are alone together? Is he capable of any grand human action? Does the answer matter? Prufrock answers in the negative. He sees himself and others as drowning in a sea of troubles.

Resumen Esta selección comienza con una cita del *Inferno*, de Dante, que sugiere que lo que sigue será como una visita guiada al Infierno. Prufrock, que no encuentra sentido a la vida, invita a un acompañante a ir a una ciudad moderna. La atmósfera que describe es una llena de humo y degeneración. Es un lugar donde hablar de valores espirituales y artísticos ya no parece tener ningún sentido. Luego, Prufrock, se hace una serie de preguntas sobre sí mismo, su pasado y su vida actual: ¿Podría y debería haber hecho más con su vida? ¿Puede expresar amor por una mujer cuando están solos? ¿Es capaz de una acción humana importante? ¿Importa realmente la respuesta? Prufrock contesta no a todo esto. Él se ve a sí mismo y a otros ahogándose en un mar de problemas.

Paraphrase Sometimes the best way to understand the ideas in a poem is to break it up by sentences or main ideas. Then you can paraphrase, or restate, that part in your own words. In a small group, take turns reading aloud "The Love Song of J. Alfred Prufrock." When you get to the end of a sentence or main idea—that is, to a period, a question mark, a semicolon, or ellipses— stop and paraphrase that section. For example, the first main idea of this poem is the first three lines, to the semicolon. Your paraphrase of that section might be something like this:

> Let's go out this still evening.

Follow this example by writing sentences of your own for each of the main ideas in the poem. When you finish, compare your sentences with those of your classmates.

_____

_____

_____

_____

_____

_____

_____

_____

_____

_____

_____

© **Pearson Education, Inc.**

Imagist Poets

Summary In "A Few Don'ts by an Imagiste," Pound discusses rules for writing poetry. In "The River-Merchant's Wife: A Letter," a young Chinese woman writes to her absent husband, longing for his return. In "In a Station of the Metro," the speaker compares faces in a crowded subway station to flower petals on a black bough. In "The Red Wheelbarrow," Williams creates an image of a rain-slicked wheelbarrow and a chicken. In "The Great Figure," the speaker describes a moving fire truck. "This Is Just to Say" is in the style of a personal, informal note. The speaker apologizes for eating plums from the refrigerator. In "Pear Tree," H. D. talks about seeing the tree in blossom. In "Heat," she addresses the wind, asking it to attack and break up the heat, so the fruit can drop.

Resumen En *A Few Dont's by an Imagiste*, Pound habla sobre reglas para escribir poesía. En *The River-Merchant's Wife: a Letter*, una joven mujer china le escribe a su marido ausente, ansiosa por que regrese. En *In a Station of the Metro*, el que habla compara las caras en una estación de metro llena a pétalos de flores en una rama de árbol negra. En *The Red Wheelbarrow*, Williams crea una imagen de una carretilla lustrosa por la lluvia y un pollo. En *The Great Figure*, el narrador describe un camión de bomberos en movimiento. *This Is Just to Say*, está escrito en un estilo personal e informal. El narrador se disculpa por comer ciruelas de la nevera. En *Pear Tree*, H. D. habla de cuando vio un peral en flor. En *Heat*, la poeta le pide al viento que sople y quiebre una ola de calor, para que la fruta pueda caer.

Identify Sensory Images Poets often use sensory language to create images in the reader's mind. This language helps readers to see, hear, feel, taste, and smell what the poet describes.

Some of the sensory words in "The Great Figure" have been identified and classified below. Look for other sensory words in this poem, and write them in the proper column or columns. (Remember that some words can appeal to more than one sense.) Then choose another poem and practice this strategy.

Among the *rain*

and lights

I saw the *figure 5*

in *gold*

on a red

fire truck

moving

tense

unheeded

to gong clangs

siren howls

and wheels rumbling

through the dark city.

Sight	Sound	Touch	Taste	Smell
rain lights figure 5 gold	rain	rain		rain

© **Pearson Education**, Inc.

Name _____ Date _____

"Winter Dreams" by F. Scott Fitzgerald

Summary Dexter Green, son of a grocer in a small Minnesota town, is in love with Judy Jones, daughter of a very wealthy local family. Dexter and Judy meet at a country club when he is fourteen and she is eleven. He is attracted to her and quits his caddying job to avoid the humiliation of carrying her clubs. After college they meet again. She invites him home and begins a serious romance for one summer. Judy, however, starts seeing other men, and Dexter decides to marry the more sensible Irene Scheerer. On the eve of the engagement, Judy returns. She renews the relationship, causes Dexter to lose Irene, and leaves again. Years later, Dexter's idealized image of Judy is shattered when he learns that Judy is now trapped in an unhappy marriage and has lost her beauty.

Resumen Dexter Green, el hijo del tendero en un pueblo de Minnesota, está enamorado de Judy Jones, la hija de una familia muy rica. Dexter y Judy se encuentran cuando él tiene catorce años y ella once. Dexter se enamora de Judy y deja su trabajo de caddy para evitar la humillación de llevarle los palos de golf. Luego de la universidad, los dos se encuentran nuevamente. Ella lo invita a la casa e inician un romance. Judy, sin embargo, comienza a salir con otros hombres, y Dexter decide casarse con la más razonable Irene Scheerer. El día antes del compromiso, Judy regresa y reanuda su relación con Dexter. Esto hace que Dexter pierda a Irene, y ella se va de nuevo. Años más tarde, la imagen idealizada que tiene Dexter de Judy se rompe cuando se entera que está atrapada en un matrimonio infeliz y ya no es bella.

Respond to Characters' Actions In "Winter Dreams," the characters behave in ways that may not be for their own good. As you read, you might say to yourself, "I would never do that," or "I understand why the character did that," or "I would have advised the character to act differently." To record your responses to the actions of the characters, complete the chart below. Share your chart with your classmates. An example has been modeled for you.

Character	What Character Does	My Response
Dexter	quits job as a caddy	not a good idea, since he didn't have another job

© Pearson Education, Inc.

"The Turtle" from *The Grapes of Wrath* by John Steinbeck

Summary Near a concrete highway is a mass of tangled, dry grass full of seeds of every kind. The seeds are waiting for a means to travel—it might be a woman's skirt or a passing animal. Over the grass a land turtle crawls toward the highway. A head of wild oats attaches itself to the front legs of the turtle. With great effort, the turtle gets onto the pavement. A sedan driven by a forty-year-old woman swerves to avoid the turtle. A light truck driven by a man swerves to hit it. The front wheel hits the turtle's shell. The turtle spins and rolls off the highway. After a long time, the turtle pulls itself over. The head of wild oats falls off and the seeds spill out. As the turtle pulls itself along, its shell drags dirt over the seeds.

Resumen Cerca de una carretera hay un montón de pastos secos, entrelazados y llenos de semillas de todas clases. Las semillas están esperando por un medio de transporte—una falda de mujer o un animal que pasa. Una tortuga se dirige a paso lento hacia la carretera. Unas semillas de avena silvestre se pegan a las patas delanteras de la tortuga. Con gran esfuerzo, la tortuga llega al pavimento. Un sedán, conducido por una mujer de cuarenta años, se desvía para evitar a la tortuga. Un camión, conducido por un hombre, se desvía para golpearla, su rueda delantera golpea el caparazón de la tortuga. Ésta rueda fuera de la carretera. Luego de un largo rato, la tortuga se endereza y las semillas de avena caen a la tierra. Cuando la tortuga comienza a caminar, su caparazón cubre las semillas con tierra.

Outline Main Idea and Supporting Details To understand what you read, you must find the main ideas and then take note of the supporting details. Working with a partner, find the main idea for each paragraph of "The Turtle." Then list the details that support it. The first paragraph has been modeled for you.

Main Idea: Seeds of all kinds in the dry grass by the highway were waiting for some way to be spread and dispersed.

Details About the Main Idea:

1. Oat beards were waiting to catch on a dog's coat.
2. Foxtails were waiting to tangle in a horse's hair.
3. Clover burrs were waiting to fasten in sheep's wool.
4. Some seeds were waiting to be carried by the wind.
5. Other seeds were waiting to be caught on the hem of a woman's skirt.

_____
_____
_____
_____
_____
_____
_____
_____
_____

    © Pearson Education, Inc.

Name _____ Date _____

"anyone lived in a pretty how town" and "old age sticks"
by E. E. Cummings
"The Unknown Citizen" by W. H. Auden

Summary In "anyone lived in a pretty how town," Cummings focuses on the eternal rhythms of life and the seasons of nature. The anonymity of "anyone" and "a pretty how town" shows these experiences to be universal. In "old age sticks," the poet says that the warnings of the elderly about the dangers of age are ignored by the carefree young. He suggests that although the young tear down warning "signs," one day they will be posting such "signs" themselves. "The Unknown Citizen" honors JS/07/M/378, a model citizen of his society. The speaker calls this man a saint, for he served the Greater Community by meeting ordinary expectations. The speaker shows how the man always conformed. When asked whether the man lived freely or happily, the speaker responds with disinterest.

Resumen En *anyone lived in a pretty how town*, Cummings trata de los eternos ritmos de la vida y de las estaciones. El anonimato de "anyone" y " a pretty how town", muestra que estas experiencias son universales. En *old age sticks*, el poeta dice que las advertencias de los ancianos sobre la vejez son ignoradas por los jóvenes. Añade que, si bien los jóvenes rompen las señales de advertencia, un día los jóvenes estarán haciendo las mismas advertencias. *The Unknown Citizen*, honra a JS/07/M/378, un ciudadano modelo. El narrador llama santo a este hombre, por haber servido a la Gran Comunidad al haber satisfecho expectaciones comunes. El narrador muestra cómo este hombre siempre se ajustó a las reglas. Cuando le preguntan si el hombre fue libre o feliz, el narrador responde sin interés.

Interpret Poetic Images Poets present images that represent ideas and feelings. In order to understand what these images represent, you must first form a mental picture of the images, and then decide how that image makes you feel. Here are some images, or word pictures, from the poems. Describe the picture that forms in your mind as you read each image, and then tell how it makes you feel. The first one has been modeled for you.

"anyone lived in a pretty how town"

1. he sang his didn't he danced his did

   He sang and danced no matter what. The feeling in this image is one of happiness, of being carefree and young.

2. sun moon stars rain _____

3. she laughed his joy she cried his grief _____

"old age sticks"

1. old age sticks/up Keep/Off signs _____

2. youth yanks them/down _____

3. youth laughs _____

"The Unknown Citizen"

1. He worked in a factory and never got fired _____

2. The press are convinced that he bought a paper every day _____

3. A phonograph, a radio, a car and a frigidaire _____

© Pearson Education, Inc.

Name _____ Date _____

"The Far and the Near" by Thomas Wolfe

Summary Daily for twenty years, the engineer of a train blows the whistle when he approaches a certain pleasant little cottage near the tracks. A woman and her daughter, both otherwise strangers to him, come out and wave to him as he passes. He has increasingly more tender feelings about them and the little house, which become symbols of happiness for him. At last, when he retires, he goes to visit the spot, to be near what he has seen only from afar for so long. But the town is strange to him when seen at close range, the house is unattractive, and the women are hostile. He leaves, feeling disillusioned, sad, and old.

Resumen A diario, por veinte años, un conductor de tren hace pitar a su locomotora cada vez que se acerca a una pequeña y hermosa casa cerca de las vías. Una mujer y su hija, a quienes el conductor no conoce, salen de la casa y lo saludan cuando pasa. El conductor tiene sentimientos cada vez más tiernos hacia ellas y la pequeña casa, las que se convierten para él en símbolos de felicidad. Al fin, cuando el conductor se jubila, va a visitar ese lugar, para estar cerca de lo que sólo había visto a la distancia por tanto tiempo. Pero el pueblo le es extraño cuando lo ve de cerca, la casa es fea y las mujeres hostiles. El conductor se retira, desilusionado, triste y viejo.

Identify Key Ideas To understand better what you read, it is a good idea to identify the key ideas as you go along. In a small group, take turns reading the paragraphs of this story aloud. After reading each paragraph, stop and think about the key idea in it. Make a list of those key ideas. When you are finished, compare your list with those of other groups. An entry for the first paragraph of "The Far and the Near" has been done for you. Follow this example for the rest of the story.

Paragraph 1: A tidy little cottage sat on a small hill within sight of the railroad tracks.

_____

_____

_____

_____

_____

_____

_____

_____

_____

_____

_____

_____

_____

_____

© Pearson Education, Inc.

Name _____ Date _____

"Of Modern Poetry" and "Anecdote of the Jar" by Wallace Stevens
"Ars Poetica" by Archibald MacLeish
"Poetry" by Marianne Moore

Summary In "Of Modern Poetry," Stevens says that a poem "has to be living" and use the language of its own time. In "Anecdote of the Jar," the wilderness is given order by the presence of the jar on a hill in Tennessee. Nevertheless, the jar is "gray and bare" in its lush surroundings. In "Ars Poetica," MacLeish compares a poem to globed fruit, old medallions, a worn stone, and the flight of birds. He says a poem should be "motionless in time," like the moon. He says that the image, not its meaning, makes the poem. In "Poetry," Moore sympathizes with those who do not like poetry. She says that the best poets can or should express "the genuine," such as hands, eyes, and hair that are real enough to express emotion.

Resumen: En *Of Modern Poetry*, Stevens dice que un poema "tiene que estar vivo" y usar el lenguaje de su época. En *Anecdote of the Jar*, el tumulto de la naturaleza es ordenado por un frasco en una colina de Tennessee. Sin embargo, el frasco es "gris y sin adornos," en medio de un exhuberante ambiente. En *Ars Poetica*, MacLeish compara a un poema con una fruta redonda, con viejos medallones, con piedra gastada y el vuelo de los pájaros. Él dice que un poema debe estar "inmóvil en el espacio," como la luna. Añade que la imagen, no su significado, es lo que constituye el poema. En *Poetry*, Moore entiende a los que no gustan de la poesía. Dice que los mejores poetas pueden, o deberían expresar "lo genuino," como manos, ojos y pelo, que son lo suficientemente reales para expresar emociones.

Explain and Respond to Poetry Some of the ideas in these poems may be hard to understand. One way to make them clearer is to explain or restate the ideas in everyday language. Get together with two or three of your classmates, and discuss how the following lines from the poems might be restated in everyday language. Then choose two more lines to explain at the end of the list. An example has been given.

Confusing Phrases	Translation
It has to be living, to learn the speech of the place.	Poetry should use modern language.
It has to face the men of the time	
I placed a jar in Tennessee, And round it was, upon a hill	
The wilderness rose up to it	
A poem should be palpable and mute As a globed fruit	
A poem should not mean But be.	
I, too, dislike it: there are things that are important beyond/all this fiddle.	
One discovers in/it after all, a place for the genuine	

© Pearson Education, Inc.

"In Another Country" by Ernest Hemingway
"The Corn Planting" by Sherwood Anderson
"A Worn Path" by Eudora Welty

Summary In "In Another Country," an American officer recovering from a war injury meets three young Italian officers and an older major, all wounded. The major helps the American with his Italian grammar, advises him not to marry, and mourns the death of his own wife. In "The Corn Planting," an old farmer and his wife have two things they love: their farm and their son. One night, a telegram arrives telling of their son's death in a car accident. They spend the rest of that night planting corn, their way of dealing with grief. In "A Worn Path," an old woman makes her way along a country path. Once in town, she goes to a doctor's office to get medicine for her grandson. She alone has been taking care of him since he swallowed lye some years before.

Resumen En *In Another Country,* un oficial americano, recuperándose de una herida de guerra, se encuentra con tres jóvenes oficiales italianos y un viejo mayor, todos heridos. El mayor lo ayuda a estudiar la gramática italiana, le aconseja que no se case y lamenta la muerte de su esposa. En *Corn Planting,* un viejo granjero y su esposa tienen dos cosas que aman, su granja y su hijo. Una noche llega un telegrama anunciando la muerte del hijo en un accidente de carro. Los dos pasan el resto de la noche plantando maíz, que es su manera de bregar con su pena. En *A Worn Path,* una vieja mujer camina por un sendero en el campo. Una vez que llega a la ciudad, la mujer va al consultorio de un médico para obtener medicinas para su nieto. Ella sola ha estado cuidándolo, desde que el muchacho había tomado lejía años antes.

Make a Character Chart Read "In Another Country" with a partner, one paragraph at a time. As you read, complete the character chart below. Then make similar charts for "The Corn Planting" and "A Worn Path." An example has been given.

Character	Character's Action	Reason for Character's Action
narrator	goes to hospital every day	to be treated for a leg injury

© Pearson Education, Inc.

Name _____ Date _____

"Chicago" and "Grass" by Carl Sandburg

Summary In "Chicago," the poet praises the city by personifying it as a strong, energetic worker. He says that there is some justification in calling Chicago wicked, crooked, and brutal. Yet he also sees the city's good side. The young worker who is the city is singing, cursing, working, and—above all—laughing. In "Grass," the grass itself addresses those who bury the dead in various wars. It tells them that because the grass will cover the graves, future passers—by will not recognize these places of carnage. Sandburg here repeats a common theme in his war poetry—namely, that the dead should rest but that the earth mocks their struggles.

Resumen En *Chicago*, Sandburg elogia a la ciudad personificándola como un obrero fuerte y enérgico. El poeta dice que hay cierta razón en decir que Chicago es mala, deshonesta y brutal. Pero él ve también el lado bueno de la ciudad. El joven obrero es la ciudad que canta, maldice, trabaja, y sobre todo, ríe. En *Grass*, es la hierba la que se dirige a los que enterraron a los muertos de varias guerras. Les dice que, porque ella cubrirá las tumbas, los que pasen no reconocerán esos lugares de matanza. Aquí, Sandburg repite un tema común en su poesía sobre la guerra—que los muertos deberían descansar, pero que la tierra se burla de sus luchas.

Reword Poet's Ideas Sometimes the ideas in a poem are difficult to understand, even if the language itself is not really difficult. One way to make the ideas clearer is to reword the lines in your own words. As you read these two poems by Carl Sandburg, choose four or five sections and put them into your own words. An example has been provided.

Poem	Lines	Rewording of lines
"Chicago"	1—5	Chicago provides pork, tools, and wheat to the world. It also handles the nation's railroad freight. It is a strong city.

© Pearson Education, Inc.

Name _____ Date _____

"The Jilting of Granny Weatherall" by Katherine Anne Porter

Summary Ellen Weatherall, almost eighty, has taken to her bed and is dying. She thinks back on her life. She recalls George, who jilted her, and John, who became her husband but died when their children were still young. She recalls with pleasure her raising of the children, and she thanks God for a full life. The only thing that still bothers her is having been jilted sixty years before. In the evening, the doctor returns. The priest says the last rites, and some of the children arrive. In her final moments, Granny thinks about what she is leaving done and undone. As she watches the "light" of her life dwindle away, she asks God for a sign. Receiving no answer, she blows out the "light" herself.

Resumen Ellen Weatherall, de casi ochenta años, está en cama, muriendo. Ella piensa sobre su vida. Recuerda a George, que la abandonó, y a John, que fue su marido, pero murió cuando sus hijos eran niños. Recuerda con placer cómo crió a sus niños, y agradece a Dios una vida plena. La única cosa que la molesta es haber sido abandonada sesenta años atrás. El médico vuelve por la tarde; el sacerdote le da los últimos sacramentos; y llegan algunos de sus hijos. En sus últimos momentos, Granny piensa que está por partir con cosas acabadas y cosas inacabadas. Mientras observa disminuir la "luz" de su vida, le pide a Dios una señal. Al no recibir una respuesta, ella misma apaga la "luz".

Make a Timeline In some stories, the narrative jumps back and forth from the present to the past and back again. This might make it difficult to follow the story. One way to keep the timing of the events clear in your mind is to make a timeline. As events are described, enter them in the proper place on the timeline. For this story, make a timeline labeled 20, 40, 60, and 80, to represent the various ages of Granny Weatherall. You might have to estimate Granny Weatherall's age when various events happened. As you read, enter each event in the proper place on the timeline. An example has been done.

20 _____

_____

_____

_____

_____

40 _____

_____

_____

_____

_____

60 _____

_____

_____

_____

_____

80   Doctor Harry checks her.

"Race at Morning" and "Nobel Prize Acceptance Speech"
by William Faulkner

Summary In "Race at Morning," a boy is the first to spot the buck swimming up the river. This deer usually leaves the day before hunting season opens and returns the day after, but this year he is off by one day. The boy and Mister Ernest, his guardian, chase the deer the next morning. When it comes time to shoot, Mister Ernest has no bullets. He explains to the boy later that it's better for the deer to stay alive, so they can hunt him again next year. In accepting his Nobel Prize, Faulkner tells young writers to set aside fear of world destruction and address the basic problems of love, honor, and compassion. It is the writer's duty to remind man of the glory of his past, to help him endure and prevail.

Resumen En *Race at Morning*, un chico es el primero que ve al ciervo nadando en el río. El animal generalmente se va un día antes de que empiece la temporada de caza y vuelve un día después que termine, pero este año está atrasado un día. A la mañana siguiente, el chico y Mr. Ernest, su tutor, persiguen al ciervo. Cuando llega el momento de disparar, Mr. Ernest no tiene balas, y le explica al chico que es mejor así, que el ciervo continúe vivo, para que ellos puedan cazarlo el próximo año. Al aceptar el premio Nobel, Faulkner se dirige a los escritores jóvenes. Dice que deben poner de lado su miedo de la destrucción del mundo y tratar los temas básicos de amor, honor y compasión. Añade que es la obligación del escritor recordar a la humanidad de su glorioso pasado, para ayudarla a sobrellevar y prevalecer.

Understand Dialect/Summarize the Main Idea In "Race at Morning," Faulkner uses dialect, a way of speaking that is unique to certain people and places. Sometimes, the best way to understand dialect is to read it out loud, listening for words that might be misspelled, or incorrect verb forms. For example, if you read the phrase "him and Uncle Ike would sholy manage," you can hear that *sholy* must mean *surely*. For the passage below, rewrite the dialect the way you would speak, as shown in the example. Then practice the strategy by rewriting another passage from the story.

When you finish, summarize the main idea in each paragraph of Faulkner's "Nobel Prize Acceptance Speech."

(1) I was in the boat when I seen him. (2) It was jest dust-dark; (3) I had jest fed the horses and clumb back down the bank to the boat and shoved off to cross back to camp when I seen him. . . . (4) But I could see that rocking chair he toted on it (5) and I knowed it was him, going right back to that canebrake in the fork of the bayou . . . (6) like the game wardens had give him a calendar, when he would clear out and disappear, nobody knowed where. . . .

1. I was in the boat when I saw him. _____

2. _____

3. _____

4. _____

5. _____

6. _____

Robert Frost's Poetry

Summary In "Birches," Frost sees himself as one who swings on imaginary birch trees that carry him to heaven and return him to earth, where he is content to stay. In "Mending Wall," Frost describes the up-keep of stone walls that separate neighbors. "Out, Out—" tells of the death of a boy in a farm accident. The speaker of "Stopping by Woods on a Snowy Evening" stops to watch the falling snow, but he must move on, for he has "promises to keep" and "miles to go" before he can sleep. In "Acquainted with the Night," Frost suggests that the moon reminds us that we cannot expect to understand everything now. "The Gift Outright" refers to the land on which our country is built.

Resumen En *Birches*, Frost se ve columpiándose en abedules imaginarios que lo llevan al cielo y lo devuelven a la tierra, donde él está contento en quedarse. En *Mending Wall*, el poeta describe el mantenimiento de las paredes de piedras que separan a los vecinos. *Out, Out*, cuenta la muerte de un niño en un accidente en una granja. El narrador de *Stopping by Woods on a Snowy Evening*, se detiene para mirar caer la nieve, pero debe continuar porque tiene "promesas que cumplir" y "millas para caminar", antes de poder irse a dormir. En *Acquainted with the Night*, Frost sugiere que la luna nos recuerda que no podemos esperar entender todo ahora. *The Gift Outright*, se refiere a la tierra sobre la que se construyó nuestro país.

Restate Poetry as Prose Sometimes poetic language is difficult to understand. One way to make it clearer is to restate it as prose, in everyday language. Read these poems with a partner. When you come to the end of a complete thought (for instance, the end of a sentence), stop and rephrase that part in your own words. For example, the first sentence of "Mending Wall" is the first three lines. Your restating of that sentence might be something like this:

> Sometimes acts of nature can destroy walls.

Take turns reading the poems and writing the sentences or complete thoughts in your own words. When you finish, compare your sentences with those of your classmates.

_____

_____

_____

_____

_____

_____

_____

_____

_____

_____

_____

_____

 © Pearson Education, Inc.

"The Night the Ghost Got In" by James Thurber
from *Here Is New York* by E. B. White

Summary In "The Night the Ghost Got In," the narrator hears footsteps and wakes his brother. The footsteps come upstairs, but the boys can see no one. The mother appears, throws a shoe through a neighbor's window, and asks the startled man to call the police, who arrive with reporters. They break down the door and ransack the house. In the attic, the grandfather shoots a policeman in the shoulder. In the morning the family can only wonder at what has happened. This excerpt from *Here Is New York* tells why New York is such a special city. Outsiders are often uncomfortable in the city because it seems so big. People who live there know that the city has thousands of tiny neighborhoods, where everybody knows everybody else.

Resumen En *The Night the Ghost Got In*, el narrador escucha pisadas y despierta a su hermano. Las pisadas llegan arriba, pero los chicos no ven a nadie. Aparece la madre, arroja un zapato por la ventana de un vecino, y le pide al sorprendido hombre que llame a la policía, la que llega con periodistas. Rompen la puerta y destrozan la casa. En el ático, el abuelo le dispara a un policía y lo hiere en un hombro. Por la mañana, la familia se pregunta qué pudo haber pasado. Este pasaje de *Here is New York*, dice por qué New York es una ciudad tan especial. Los que no son de New York, con frecuencia se sienten incómodos en ella porque parece tan grande. Pero la gente que vive en ella sabe que la ciudad tiene miles de pequeños barrios, donde todo el mundo se conoce.

Identify Paragraph Topics Whether you are reading fiction or nonfiction, it is a good idea to stop from time to time and ask yourself what you've read so far. With a partner, read "The Night the Ghost Got In," stopping after each paragraph. Identify the topic, or the main idea, of that paragraph before going on to the next. When you are finished, follow the same procedure for the excerpt from *Here Is New York*.

The topic of the first paragraph of "The Night the Ghost Got In" might be expressed in the following way:

A ghost got into our house on November 17, 1915, and caused a great deal of confusion.

_____

_____

_____

_____

_____

_____

_____

_____

_____

_____

_____

© **Pearson Education, Inc.**

from *Dust Tracks on a Road* by Zora Neale Hurston

Summary In this excerpt from *Dust Tracks on a Road*, Zora Neale Hurston describes life in a small Florida town and herself as a child. Self-assured and filled with curiosity, she often stopped white travelers and asked to accompany them for a short distance. Hurston talks about her first real interaction with white people and the role they played in developing her literary tastes. During a school visit of two white women from the North, Zora reads very well, and the visitors later invite her to visit them at their hotel. There they reward her with exotic sweets and a hundred new pennies. Later she receives an Episcopal hymn book, clothing, and a number of books that please her more than anything else.

Resumen En este pasaje de *Dust Tracks on a Road*, Zora Neale Hurston describe la vida en un pequeño pueblo de Florida y a ella misma cuando niña. Con confianza en sí misma y llena de curiosidad, con frecuencia detenía a viajeros blancos y les pedía acompañarlos un trecho. Hurston habla de sus primeros tratos con personas blancas y del papel que éstas tuvieron en el desarrollo de sus preferencias literarias. Durante una visita de dos mujeres blancas del Norte a su escuela, Zora lee muy bien y las mujeres la invitan a visitarlas más tarde en su hotel. Allí la agasajan con dulces exóticos y un centenar de monedas nuevas de un centavo. Más tarde Nora recibe un libro de himnos episcopales, ropas y un número de libros, que la complacen más que ninguna otra cosa.

Analyze Characters Read this excerpt from *Dust Tracks on a Road* with a partner, one or two paragraphs at a time. As you read, complete the character chart below. A few examples are given. When you are finished, compare your chart with those of your classmates.

Character	Character's Action	Reason for Character's Action
Zora	sits on gatepost	to watch the world go by
Zora	asks to go along with white travelers	to take a ride in a car or carriage
Grandmother	tells Zora not to do it	to protect Zora from harm

© **Pearson Education**, Inc.

"The Negro Speaks of Rivers," "Ardella," "Dream Variations"
and "Refugee in America," by Langston Hughes
"The Tropics in New York" by Claude McKay

Summary In "The Negro Speaks of Rivers," the speaker recalls ancient rivers and the peoples who lived along their shores. He compares the depth of his soul to that of the rivers. "Ardella" describes a woman who defies comparison because of her eyes and her songs. "Dream Variations" expresses the poet's wish to dance all day and then rest in the night that comes tenderly, "Black like me." In "Refugee in America," Hughes tells how the words *Freedom* and *Liberty* cause his heart to sing and almost make him cry. He says that the reader would understand if "you had known what I knew." In "The Tropics in New York," the sight of tropical fruits in a window brings back memories of the poet's home in the tropics, causing him to bow his head and weep.

Resumen En *The Negro Speaks of Rivers*, el narrador recuerda antiguos ríos y a los pueblos que vivieron a sus orillas. También compara la profundidad de su alma con la de los ríos. *Ardella,* describe a una mujer que desafía toda comparación debido a sus ojos y canciones. *Dream Variations,* expresa el deseo del poeta de bailar todo el día y luego descansar cuando la noche llegue suavemente, "Negra como yo". En *Refugee in America*, Hughes dice cómo las palabras *Freedom* y *Liberty,* hacen que su corazón cante y a él casi lo hacen llorar. Dice que el lector entendería si "supiera lo que él sabe". En *The Tropics in New York*, unas frutas tropicales en una ventana le recuerdan al poeta su hogar en los trópicos, haciéndolo bajar la cabeza y llorar.

React to Poetry Poetry often causes an emotional response in the reader. As you read these poems, think about how they make you feel. Does a certain line make you feel sad, happy, joyful, or peaceful? Does it make you wish you could go back to a certain time or place? Does it make you feel like crying or laughing? Does it make you curious about the characters speaking or described in the poem? Complete the chart below. Write about how certain lines in each poem makes you feel. An example has been given.

Poem	Lines	How the Lines Make Me Feel
"Refugee in America"	"If you had known what I knew You would know why"	I feel sad for the narrator. I wonder what makes him want to cry.

© Pearson Education, Inc.

Name _____ Date _____

"From the Dark Tower" by Countee Cullen
"A Black Man Talks of Reaping" by Arna Bontemps
"Storm Ending" by Jean Toomer

Summary In "From the Dark Tower," the poet seems to say that better times are coming for those who plant "while others reap." He says the night is no less lovely because it is dark, and that some flowers cannot bloom in the light. He closes by referring to waiting in the dark, tending "our agonizing seeds." In "A Black Man Talks of Reaping," the poet describes his careful planting of a large crop from which he reaped only a small harvest. While his brother's sons gather the bounty of his fields, his own children eat bitter fruit gathered from fields they have not sown. In "Storm Ending," thunder and the storm are compared with huge, hollow flowers blossoming overhead. As the flowers bleed rain and drip like honey, the sweet earth flies from the storm.

Resumen *From the Dark Tower,* parece decir que vienen mejores tiempos para aquéllos que plantan "mientras otros cosechan". Dice que la noche no es menos encantadora por ser negra, y que muchas flores no pueden abrirse en la luz. Termina refiriéndose a una espera en la oscuridad, cuidando a "nuestras agonizantes semillas". En *A Black Man Talks of Reaping,* el poeta describe cómo plantó cuidadosamente lo que él esperaba fuera una gran cosecha, pero resultó una cosecha pequeña. Mientras los hijos de su hermano recogen el tesoro de sus campos, sus propios hijos comen fruta amarga, recogida de campos que no habían cultivado. En *Storm Ending,* los truenos y tormentas son flores enormes y huecas. A medida que las flores se desangran en lluvia y gotean como la miel, la dulce tierra huye de la tormenta.

Explain Poetic Images Many poets use strong images to suggest ideas, emotions, or thoughts. One way to understand poetry is to form a mental picture of the image and then ask yourself how that mental picture makes you feel. That is probably what the poet is trying to get you to feel.

Here are some images from the poems. Describe the picture that forms in your mind when you read each one, and tell how it makes you feel. An example has been given.

"From the Dark Tower"

1. The night whose sable breast relieves the stark, / White stars

   The word *sable,* which can mean a costly fur, suggests softness and warmth. It also means the color black, so I see a contrast to the white stars. It gives me a feeling of luxury.

2. tend our agonizing seeds

_____

"A Black Man Talks of Reaping"

1. my children glean in fields/they have not sown

_____

2. and feed on bitter fruit

_____

"Storm Ending"

1. Thunder blossoms gorgeously above our heads
   Dripping rain like golden honey

_____

 © Pearson Education, Inc.

Name _____ Date _____

"The Life You Save May Be Your Own" by Flannery O'Connor

Summary An old woman and her daughter, both named Lucynell Crater, are sitting on their porch when a one-armed man named Mr. Shiftlet appears. He says he is a carpenter. He agrees to fix up the old woman's property in exchange for food and a place to sleep. Within a week, he has not only made the needed repairs but has taught the girl, who is deaf and mute, to say "bird." After fixing the car, he agrees to marry the daughter. The old woman gives him money to take an overnight trip with his new bride. He leaves the girl at a roadside eatery and heads toward Mobile in the old woman's car. On the way, he picks up a hitchhiker and begins to talk to him about mothers. The boy insults both their mothers and jumps out of the car. Mr. Shiftlet continues on his way as the rain begins to fall.

Resumen Una anciana y su hija, ambas llamadas Lucynell Crater, están sentadas en su porche, cuando aparece un hombre con un solo brazo, que dice ser carpintero. Acuerda con la anciana hacer algunos trabajos a cambio de comida y un lugar para dormir. En una semana, el hombre no solo hizo las reparaciones necesarias, también le enseñó a la hija, que es sordomuda, a decir "pájaro". Luego de arreglar el carro, el hombre acepta casarse con la hija, y la anciana le da dinero para que hagan un viaje de un día. El hombre deja a la joven en un restaurante y se va con el carro a Mobile. De camino, recoge a un muchacho y comienzan a hablar sobre madres. El muchacho insulta a su madre y a la del hombre y salta del carro. Mr. Shiflet, que así se llamaba el hombre, continúa su viaje, cuando empieza a llover.

Analyze Characters' Behavior Read "The Life You Save May Be Your Own" with a partner, one or two paragraphs at a time. As you read, make a character analysis chart like the one below. The first entry has been done as an example.

Character	Character's Action	Reason for Character's Action
old woman	She shades her eyes with her hand.	She wants to block the sun so she can better see the stranger.

Name _____ Date _____

"The First Seven Years" by Bernard Malamud

Summary Feld, a shoemaker, wants his nineteen-year-old daughter, Miriam, to go out with a local college boy named Max. One day Max brings in some shoes for repair. Feld persuades him to ask Miriam out. When Max leaves, Sobel, Feld's helper, breaks the last with his heavy pounding and flees from the store. Feld hires a new but less trustworthy helper. After their second date, Miriam reports that Max is a soulless bore. When Feld learns that his new helper has been stealing from him, he has a heart attack. When he recovers, he goes to see Sobel. He learns that Sobel has worked for him for five years only because he is in love with Miriam. Feld tells Sobel to wait two more years before asking Miriam to marry him. The next morning, Sobel is at work, "pounding leather for his love."

Resumen Feld, un zapatero, quiere que Miriam, su hija de 19 años, salga con Max, un estudiante universitario. Un día Max trae unos zapatos para arreglar y Feld lo convence de que invite a salir a Miriam. Cuando Max se va, Sobel, el ayudante de Feld, rompe una horma de zapatos con su martilleo y huye de la zapatería. Feld contrata a un nuevo ayudante, no tan fiable como Sobel. Luego de su segunda cita, Miriam dice que Max es terriblemente aburrido. Cuando Feld se entera que su nuevo ayudante le roba, va a ver a Sobel. Ahí se entera que Sobel ha trabajado para él por cinco años, solamente porque está enamorado de Miriam. Feld le dice que espere dos años más antes de pedir la mano de Miriam. A la mañana siguiente, Sobel está en el trabajo, "golpeando cuero por su amor".

Make a Timeline One way to follow the plot of a story is to make a timeline. Work with a partner to divide the story into sections. Use a chart like the one below to record the events that take place during each section. When you have finished your chart, summarize the events you have recorded. Share your summaries with your classmates.

Section 1 Events	Section 2 Events	Section 3 Events

Summary:

_____

_____

_____

_____

_____

_____

© Pearson Education, Inc.

"The Brown Chest" by John Updike

Summary A big wooden chest had always been in a family's house. Until the narrator was thirteen, the chest was on the second floor. When the family moved to a smaller house, the chest was put into the attic, where it stayed for over forty years. Inside the chest were souvenirs of the family's life. When the narrator's grandmother died, the chest was moved again. He and his brother carried it to the moving van. The chest, along with some of the old furniture, came to rest in the narrator's barn. Years later, his youngest son came to the house to claim some of the furniture. He brought with him the girl he was planning to marry. When she opened the chest, "the smell of family, family without end," filled the air, astonishing him.

Resumen Un arcón grande de madera había estado siempre en la casa de la familia. Hasta que el niño tuvo trece años, el arcón había estado en el segundo piso. Cuando la familia se mudó a una casa más pequeña, pusieron al arcón en el ático, donde permaneció por cuarenta años. Dentro del arcón había recuerdos familiares. Cuando la abuela murió, movieron de nuevo al arcón. El muchacho y su hermano lo llevaron al camión de mudanzas. El arcón, junto con los viejos muebles, terminó en un granero. Años más tarde, el hijo más joven llegó a la casa a reclamar algunos de los muebles. Traía con él a una joven, con la que pensaba casarse. Cuando la joven abrió el arcón, "el olor de familia, de familia sin fin", llenó el aire, sorprendiéndolo.

Form a Mental Picture If you picture in your mind's eye what an author describes, you will not only get more enjoyment out of what you read, you will also understand it better. Listen to the audiocassette recording of the story as you read along. Picture each scene as you listen. Use this page to jot down notes to describe what you picture in your mind. Then work with a partner to draw sketches of what Updike describes in each of the following scenes.

1. the brown chest in the first house the narrator lived in

2. the narrator looking into the brown chest the week before the family's move when he was thirteen

3. the brown chest as it appeared in the attic of the second house

4. the narrator and his brother taking the chest to the moving van, after their mother died

5. the narrator's youngest son and his fiancée opening the chest in the narrator's barn

_____

_____

_____

_____

_____

_____

_____

_____

© Pearson Education, Inc.

"Hawthorne" by Robert Lowell
"Gold Glade" by Robert Penn Warren
"Traveling Through the Dark" by William Stafford
"The Light Comes Brighter" and **"The Adamant"** by Theodore Roethke

Summary In "Hawthorne," the speaker walks along the streets of Salem, trying—and failing—to picture Hawthorne in that setting. The speaker compares the blond Hawthorne, who wore a mustache, with the dark-bearded faces of other New England authors. In "Gold Glade," the speaker recalls an autumn walk through the woods. In a glade, he sees a beautiful hickory tree giving forth gold light. No matter where the poet goes, he knows the tree still stands in the glade. "Traveling Through the Dark" reminds readers of the dangers created by expanding civilization. In "The Light Comes Brighter," the poet describes the arrival of spring, when the "light comes brighter from the east." "The Adamant" tells of the strength of the truth. It can bear the "the hammer's weight," for its "core lies sealed."

Resumen En *Hawthorne*, el narrador camina por las calles de Salem, tratando, sin poder, de imaginarse a Hawthorne en ese ambiente. El narrador compara al rubio Hawthorne, quien sólo tenía bigotes, con las caras oscuras y barbadas de otros escritores de New England. En *Gold Glade*, el que habla recuerda una caminata por los bosques en otoño. En un claro, ve a un hermoso nogal. que despide una luz dorada. El poeta sabe que, no importa donde vaya, él sabe que el árbol está ahí. "Traveling Through the Dark" le recuerda a los lectores los peligros creados por la expansión de la civilización. En *The Light Comes Brighter*, el poeta describe la llegada de la primavera, cuando "la luz llega más luminosa del este". *The Adamant*, habla de la fuerza de la verdad, que puede soportar "el peso del martillo," porque "su centro está sellado".

Restate Poetry as Prose In order to understand a poem better, it often helps to rewrite it as if it were prose. For each line, reword the poem in ordinary language, the kind of language you would use for speaking. For example, the first few lines of "Gold Glade" might be reworded like this:

> One autumn, I wandered through the same woods I had known in boyhood. Thick, black cedar trees covered the ridge.

Rephrase each line of the poem as prose. Then sum up the idea of the poem in your own words. When you are finished with "Gold Glade," do the same for the other poems.

_____

_____

_____

_____

_____

_____

_____

_____

_____

_____

_____

© **PEARSON** Education, Inc.

"Average Waves in Unprotected Waters" by Anne Tyler

Summary Bet wakes Arnold, her nine-year-old son, dresses him, and tries to give him breakfast. She picks up his suitcase and takes him to the train station. On the train, she thinks about her unsuccessful marriage, which ended when Avery left her alone to raise their severely retarded son. Bet and Arnold take a taxicab from the Parkinsville railroad station to the state hospital. There, a nurse takes him to a hallway lined with cots. Bet is quickly ushered out and advised not to return for six months. She takes the cab back to the station and is horrified to learn that her train will be twenty minutes late. She listens to the mayor as he gives a speech, observing as if it were a private play performed for her benefit.

Resumen Bet despierta a Arnold, su hijo de nueve años, lo viste y trata de servirle el desayuno. Bet recoge la maleta y lleva a su hijo a la estación de tren. En el tren, piensa sobre su desdichado matrimonio, que terminó cuando Avery la abandonó, y ella tuvo que criar sola a su hijo, quien estaba severamente incapacitado mentalmente. Bet y Arnold toman un taxi de la estación de Parkinsville hasta el hospital estatal. Allí, una enfermera acompaña a Arnold por un pasillo lleno de camas. A Bet la hacen salir rápidamente del hospital y le dicen que no vuelva por seis meses. Ella toma el taxi de vuelta a la estación y se horroriza al enterarse que su tren está atrasado veinte minutos. Escucha al alcalde dar un discurso, observando todo como si fuera una obra que están representando sólo para ella.

Identify Chain of Events Use this sequence organizer to record the main events in "Average Waves in Unprotected Waters." Some information has already been provided. You may want to continue the organizer on another piece of paper.

```
┌─────────────────────────────────────────────────────────────────────┐
│                                                                       │
└─────────────────────────────────────────────────────────────────────┘
                                   ↓
┌─────────────────────────────────────────────────────────────────────┐
│ Bet and Arnold come down the stairs, and Mrs. Puckett gives Arnold    │
│ some cookies.                                                         │
└─────────────────────────────────────────────────────────────────────┘
                                   ↓
┌─────────────────────────────────────────────────────────────────────┐
│                                                                       │
└─────────────────────────────────────────────────────────────────────┘
                                   ↓
┌─────────────────────────────────────────────────────────────────────┐
│ Arnold is nervous on the train at first, but he soon calms down.      │
└─────────────────────────────────────────────────────────────────────┘
                                   ↓
┌─────────────────────────────────────────────────────────────────────┐
│ Bet thinks back on her marriage to Avery.                             │
└─────────────────────────────────────────────────────────────────────┘
                                   ↓
┌─────────────────────────────────────────────────────────────────────┐
│                                                                       │
└─────────────────────────────────────────────────────────────────────┘
                                   ↓
┌─────────────────────────────────────────────────────────────────────┐
│                                                                       │
└─────────────────────────────────────────────────────────────────────┘
```

from *The Names* by N. Scott Momaday
"Mint Snowball" by Naomi Shihab Nye
"Suspended" by Joy Harjo

Summary In this excerpt from *The Names*, the narrator tells about a horse his parents gave him when he was thirteen. He names it Pecos. He and Pecos have many interesting adventures together. Years later, he still thinks of Pecos, whom he finally sold to an old man. In "Mint Snowball," the author recalls the drugstore that her great-grandfather used to own. She especially remembers an ice cream treat that he invented. Before he died, he sold the recipe to someone in town. Nobody in the family could ever make the syrup the same way. In "Suspended," the author remembers a moment in her life before she could talk. She was in a car with her parents, and they were listening to jazz on the radio. At that moment she recognized music as a way to communicate.

Resumen En *The Names*, el narrador habla de un caballo que sus padres le regalaron cuando él tenía trece años y al que había nombrado Pecos. El narrador y Pecos tuvieron muchas e interesantes aventuras. Años más tarde, el autor todavía piensa en Pecos, a quien finalmente había vendido a un anciano. En *Mint Snowball*, la autora recuerda la farmacia que tenía su bisabuelo, especialmente un helado que él había inventado. Antes de morir, el bisabuelo vendió la receta del helado a alguien del pueblo. Nadie en la familia pudo hacer el jarabe de la misma manera. En *Suspended*, la autora recuerda un momento en su vida, antes de que aprendiera a hablar. Ella estaba en un carro con sus padres, y estaban escuchando jazz en el radio. En ese momento ella se dio cuenta de que la música era una forma de comunicación.

Summarize Paragraphs One way to follow the ideas in an essay is to summarize paragraphs as you read. With a partner, read these essays. At the end of each paragraph, stop and discuss the main idea in that paragraph. Then write a sentence that summarizes the main idea. Follow the example that is given for "Mint Snowball."

Paragraph beginning . . .	Summary
My great-grandfather on . . .	My great-grandfather had an old-fashioned drugstore.

© **PEARSON** Education, Inc.

Name _____ Date _____

"Everyday Use" by Alice Walker

Summary A mother and her daughter Maggie await a visit from the older daughter, Dee. The mother is a hard-working, undereducated woman who lives in a modest rural home. Maggie is shy and badly scarred from a fire that burned down their previous house. As they wait, the mother recalls how Dee had resented their poverty. Dee arrives with a long-haired male companion. She says she has changed her name to Wangero. She asks for some of the family belongings, including two handmade quilts. She wants to use them as pieces of art even though her mother has planned to give them to Maggie when she marries. The mother snatches the quilts and gives them to Maggie. Dee and her companion leave in a huff. The story ends with Maggie and her mother sitting contentedly on the porch.

Resumen Una madre y su hija, Maggie, esperan la visita de la hija mayor, Dee. La madre es una mujer trabajadora, de poca educación, que vive en una casa modesta. Maggie es tímida y con cicatrices, consecuencias del incendio que había destruido su previa casa. Mientras esperan, la madre recuerda como Dee había resentido ser pobre. Dee llega acompañada por un hombre de pelo largo. Dice que se ha cambiado el nombre a Wangero y pide algunas posesiones familiares, incluidas dos mantas hechas a mano. Las quiere usar como objetos de arte, a pesar de que la madre pensaba dárselas a Maggie, cuando ésta se casara. La madre arrebata las mantas y se las da a Maggie. Dee y su acompañante se van enojados. La historia termina con Maggie y su madre contentas, sentadas en su porche.

Analyze Characters Read "Everyday Use" with a partner, one or two paragraphs at a time. As you read, complete the character analysis chart below. You may want to continue this chart on another piece of paper.

Character	Character's Action	Reason for Character's Action
Maggie	helped her mother sweep the yard	to prepare for her sister's visit

© Pearson Education, Inc.

Name _____   Date _____

from *The Woman Warrior* by Maxine Hong Kingston

Summary Brave Orchid is waiting at San Francisco International Airport for her sister to arrive from Hong Kong. She has not seen Moon Orchid for thirty years. Brave Orchid has been awake since the plane took off, for she must concentrate and "add her will power to the forces that keep an airplane up." She has brought her niece, Moon Orchid's only daughter, with her. She has also brought two of her own children, and enough blankets and food for everyone. They wait at the airport for more than nine hours. Finally the plane lands, but they must wait another four hours for the passengers to get past the "Immigration Ghosts." When she finally sees her sister, Brave Orchid cannot believe how old she looks. Her sister feels the same way about her.

Resumen Brave Orchid está en el aeropuerto de San Francisco, esperando a su hermana, Moon Orchid, que viene de Hong Kong, y a quien no ha visto en treinta años. Brave Orchid no ha podido dormir porque cree que debe concentrarse para "sumar su fuerza de voluntad a las fuerzas que mantienen al avión en el aire". Brave Orchid espera con su sobrina, la única hija de Moon Orchid, con sus dos hijos, y suficiente comida y mantas para todos. Habían estado esperando el avión por más de nueve horas. Finalmente el avión llega, pero tienen que esperar otras cuatro horas hasta que los pasajeros pasen por los "Fantasmas de Inmigración". Cuando Brave Orchid finalmente ve a su hermana, no puede creer lo vieja que se ve. La hermana piensa lo mismo de Brave Orchid.

Identify Paragraph Topics A good way to understand what you read is to identify the topic of each paragraph as you go along. Working with a partner, list the topics of each paragraph in this excerpt from *The Woman Warrior*. The first paragraph has been modeled for you.

Paragraph 1: Brave Orchid waited for over nine hours at the airport for her sister to arrive from Hong Kong, using her will power to help keep the plane in the air.

_____
_____
_____
_____
_____
_____
_____
_____
_____
_____
_____
_____
_____
_____

   © Pearson Education, Inc.

"Antojos" by Julia Alvarez

Summary Yolanda is looking for guavas, which she has been craving. Her aunts, who live in the capital, are afraid for her safety. They tell her a woman should not travel alone, for "This is not the States." Yolanda stops at a roadside stand and arranges to pick some guavas, with the help of some boys who want a ride in her car. They pick guavas for an hour, and all but one of the boys disappear. By now it is almost dark. Yolanda and the remaining boy, Jose, find that she has a flat tire. He goes for help, leaving her at the car. Suddenly two men appear, carrying machetes. Yolanda is frightened, although the men seem friendly. They change her tire and refuse any payment, saying it was their pleasure. She stuffs money into one of the men's pockets, picks up Jose, drives him home, and leaves.

Resumen Yolanda busca guayabas, de las que tiene antojo. Sus tías, que viven en la capital, temen por ella. Le dicen que una mujer no viaja sola, porque "esto no son los Estados". Yolanda se detiene en una frutería de la ruta y hace arreglos con unos muchachos, que quieren un viaje en carro, para recoger guayabas. Recogen guayabas por una hora, y todos, menos uno de los muchachos, desaparecen. Ya es de noche, y Yolanda y José, el muchacho, encuentran que el carro tiene una llanta pinchada. José va a buscar ayuda, dejando a Yolanda en el carro. De repente, aparecen dos hombres con machetes, pero aparentemente amistosos. Los hombres cambian la llanta y rehusan dinero, diciendo que había sido un placer. Yolanda da dinero a uno de los hombres, recoge a José, lo lleva a su casa, y se va.

Sequence Events One way to keep track of events in a story is to write them in a chain-of-events organizer. Complete this organizer for "Antojos." You may have to continue it on another piece of paper.

Event 1: Yolanda pulls her car to the side of the road.

↓

Event 2:

↓

Event 3:

↓

Event 4:

↓

Event 5:

↓

Event 6:

↓

Event 7:

↓

© Pearson Education, Inc.

"**Freeway 280**" by Lorna Dee Cervantes
"**Who Burns for the Perfection of Paper**" by Martín Espada
"**Most Satisfied by Snow**" by Diana Chang
"**Hunger in New York City**" by Simon Ortiz
"**What For**" by Garrett Hongo

0Summary In "Freeway 280," the speaker returns to her old neighborhood, which has been torn down and replaced by a highway. There, she finds new signs of life. In "Who Burns for the Perfection of Paper," the speaker describes a job he had at sixteen, making yellow legal pads. In "Most Satisfied by Snow," fog can press against the window, but snow has a stronger physical presence. The speaker, learning this lesson, flowers in self-knowledge. In "Hunger in New York City," hunger is a presence that comes to you. It asks you to remember the world you once knew. In the city, one cannot feed oneself. So the speaker is feeding himself with the soul of the earth. In "What For," the speaker recalls what was important to him as a child in Hawaii.

Resumen: En *Freeway 280*, la narradora regresa al sitio de su viejo vecindario, el que había sido reeemplazado por una carretera. Allí, halla nuevas señales de vida. En *Who Burns for the Perfection of Paper*, el narrador describe un trabajo que tenía a los dieciséis años, haciendo bloques de papel amarillo. En *Most Satisfied by Snow*, la niebla se puede apretar contra la ventana, pero la nieve tiene una presencia física más fuerte. El narrador, al aprender esta lección, florece en autoconocimiento. En *Hunger in New York City*, el hambre es una presencia que te visita. Te pide que recuerdes al mundo que conociste una vez. En la ciudad, uno no se puede alimentar, por lo que el narrador se alimenta con el alma de la tierra. En *What For*, el narrador recuerda lo que fue importante para él, cuando era un niño en Hawaii.

Reword Poet's Ideas Sometimes the ideas in a poem are difficult to understand, even if the language itself is not really difficult. One way to make the ideas clearer is to reword the lines in your own words. As you read these poems, choose four or five sections and put them into your own words. An example has been provided.

Poem	Lines	Rewording of lines
"Freeway 280"	1–5	The little houses and flowers near the cannery are gone now. A freeway has replaced them.

© **Pearson Education**, Inc.

from *The Mortgaged Heart* by Carson McCullers
"Onomatopoeia" by William Safire
"Coyote v. Acme" by Ian Frazier

Summary This excerpt from *The Mortgaged Heart* talks about the isolation many people in cities feel. From infancy to death, we all want to claim our identity and belong. After our identity is established, we wish to lose our sense of moral isolation. Love is the bridge from *I* to *we*. In "Onomatopeia," Safire gives a history of this name for the use of words that imitate sounds. He then talks about the word *zap*, which takes the concept one step further. It imitates an imaginary noise—the sound of a paralyzing ray gun. "Coyote v. Acme" is the opening statement of a lawyer defending Wile E. Coyote, the cartoon character, against the Acme Company. The case concerns faulty equipment sold by Acme, which caused Mr. Coyote to be injured in his job of chasing the Roadrunner.

Resumen *The Mortgaged Heart*, habla de la aislación de mucha gente en las ciudades. Desde la infancia hasta la muerte, queremos establecer nuestra identidad y pertenecer. Luego, todos queremos librarnos de la sensación de aislación moral. El amor es el puente del *yo al nosotros*. *En Onomatopeia*, Safire cuenta la historia de las palabras que imitan sonidos. Luego, habla de la palabra *zap*, la que va aún más allá. *Zap* imita a un sonido imaginario—el de un arma de rayos paralizantes. *Coyote v. Acme*, es la declaración inicial en el juicio de Wile E. Coyote, el personaje de la tira cómica, en contra de la Acme Company. El caso trata de la venta a Coyote de equipo defectuoso por parte de la compañía Acme. Este equipo causó lesiones a Coyote en su trabajo de perseguir al Roadrunner.

Paraphrase Sometimes the ideas in an essay might seem hard to understand. This is especially true when the sentences are long. A good way to make an essay's ideas clearer is to paraphrase, or restate them in simpler language and shorter sentences. In a small group, take turns reading aloud these essays. When you get to the end of a paragraph, paraphrase it, or put it into your own words. For example, your paraphrase of the first paragraph of "Onomatopoeia" might be something like this:

The word *onomatopoeia* refers to words that sound like the action they describe.

Take turns reading the essays and rewriting the ideas in each paragraph in your own words. When you finish, compare your sentences with those of your classmates.

_____

_____

_____

_____

_____

_____

_____

_____

_____

_____

"Straw Into Gold: The Metamorphosis of the Everyday" by Sandra Cisneros
"For the Love of Books" by Rita Dove
"Mother Tongue" by Amy Tan

Summary Cisneros opens with a humorous story about her first try at making tortillas. She compares this to spinning a roomful of straw into gold. She lists other things she has done that she didn't think she could. She says there is a wealth of straw in the world just waiting for someone with imagination to spin it into gold. In "For the Love of Books," Dove says her love of books began in childhood. She read everything from Shakespeare to science fiction. When her eleventh-grade English teacher took her to a book-signing, she realized writers were real people. In "Mother Tongue," Amy Tan talks about "all the Englishes" she uses as a Chinese American. When she began to think of her mother as her reader, she found her voice as a writer.

Resumen Cisneros abre con una historia cómica sobre su primer intento de hacer tortillas. Compara esta tarea a hilar un cuarto lleno de paja en oro. Enumera otras cosas que ha hecho que no creía que podía hacer. Dice que en la paja del mundo hay riquezas en espera de alguien con la imaginación para hilarla en oro. En *For the Love of Books*, Dove dice que su amor por los libros comenzó en su niñez. Ella había leído todo, desde Shakespeare hasta ciencia ficción. Cuando su maestra de inglés del grado once la llevó a un firma de libros, Dove se dio cuenta de que los escritores eran personas reales. En *Mother Tongue*, Amy Tan habla de "todo los ingleses" que ella usa como americana de ascendencia china. Cuando ella comenzó a considerar a su madre como a su lectora, Amy encontró su voz de escritora.

Summarize Main Idea To follow the ideas of a nonfiction article, you should pause occasionally and summarize the main ideas you have read so far. For example, the paragraph below from "Straw Into Gold" can be summarized in one sentence:

> When I was living in an artists' colony in the south of France, some fellow Latin-Americans who taught at the university in Aix-en-Provence invited me to share a home-cooked meal with them. I had been living abroad almost a year then on an NEA grant, subsisting mainly on French bread and lentils while in France so that my money could last longer. So when the invitation to dinner arrived, I accepted without hesitation. Especially since they had promised Mexican food.

Main Idea: After I had been living in France for almost a year, I was invited to a home-cooked Mexican meal.

Supporting Details: in an artists' colony, invited by fellow Latin-Americans who were college teachers, had been eating mostly bread and lentils

Apply this strategy to other paragraphs from "Straw Into Gold," "For the Love of Books," and "Mother Tongue." Summarize each main idea and list some supporting details.

_____

_____

_____

_____

_____

_____

© **Pearson Education**, Inc.

Name _____ Date _____

"The Rockpile" by James Baldwin

Summary One Saturday in Harlem in the 1930's, two brothers, Roy and John, are sitting on the fire escape of their family's apartment. Their father, a preacher, is away for the morning. Their mother is sipping tea in the kitchen with a friend. John, the older boy, is responsible for watching Roy. Roy's friends ask him to join them on the rockpile, where fights regularly take place and where the brothers are forbidden to go. John cannot stop Roy from going. Roy says, "I be back in *five* minutes." As John looks on, Roy is injured in the gang fight on the rockpile. A stranger carries Roy home; he is bleeding from a wound near his eye. When their father comes home, he turns on his wife and stepson, John, for allowing this to happen. The parents argue as John looks on, silently.

Resumen: Un sábado, en el Harlem de los años 30, dos hermanos, Roy y John, están sentados en la escalera de incendio de su departamento. Su padre, un predicador, ha salido a la calle y su madre está tomando té en la cocina, con una amiga. John, el mayor, tiene que cuidar a Roy. Los amigos de Roy le piden que se les una en la pila de rocas, donde siempre hay peleas y adonde les prohibieron ir a los hermanos. John no puede impedir que Roy vaya allí. Roy dice "Vuelvo en *cinco* minutos". Bajo los propios ojos de John, hieren a Roy en una pelea. Un extraño lleva a Roy a casa, sangrando de una herida cerca de un ojo. Cuando el padre vuelve a casa, les reprocha a su esposa y a John que haya ocurrido esto. Los padres discuten mientras John los mira, en silencio.

Rephrase Characters' Speech Part of this story consists of dialogue between characters. Some of this dialogue might be hard to understand because it is written in dialect, a way of speaking that is unique to certain people and places. Choose a passage that uses dialect and rewrite it the way you would state it, using your own words and sentences. An example from the story has been started for you. Complete this example, and then find other examples to rewrite.

(1) You better stay where you is, boy. (2) You know Mama don't want you going downstairs.

(3) I be right *back*. (4) She won't even know I'm gone, less you run and tell her.

1. <u>You better stay where you are.</u> _____

2. _____

_____

_____

3. _____

_____

_____

4. _____

_____

_____

© Pearson Education, Inc.

from *Hiroshima* by John Hersey
"Losses" and "The Death of the Ball Turret Gunner"
by Randall Jarrell

Summary This excerpt from *Hiroshima* tells of six people on the morning the atomic bomb was dropped in Hiroshima, Japan, on August 6, 1945. A hundred thousand people died, but these six survived. Hersey tells the story through their eyes, detailing their activities that morning. In "Losses," the speaker is a fighter pilot. When pilots died in training accidents, their deaths seemed an expected part of a familiar world. In combat, death was not an accident but a mistake. The crews bombed foreign cities they had only read about. They won medals if they survived and became statistics if they died. In "The Death of the Ball Turret Gunner," the speaker compares his position within the ball turret to a baby in the womb. He sees fighter planes shooting at him, and he dies in flames.

Resumen Este pasaje de *Hiroshima*, cuenta la historia de seis personas en la mañana del 6 de agosto de 1945, cuando lanzaron la bomba atómica en Hiroshima, Japón. Cien mil personas murieron, pero éstas seis sobrevivieron. Hersey cuenta este acontecimiento histórico a través de estas seis personas, detallando sus actividades esa mañana. En *Losses*, el narrador es un piloto de caza. Cuando los pilotos morían en accidentes durante su entrenamiento, sus muertes parecían ser algo que se esperaba en el mundo en que vivían. Cuando morían en combate, la muerte no era un accidente, era un error. Las tripulaciones bombardeaban ciudades extranjeras que sólo conocían por lecturas. Si sobrevivían, recibían medallas, y si morían se convertían en estadísticas. En *The Death of the Ball Turret Gunner*, el narrador compara su posición dentro de la torreta giratoria a un bebé en el vientre de su madre. Ve a aviones cazas que le disparan, y muere en llamas.

Question Author's Purpose As you read a nonfiction work, you should ask yourself why the writer gives you the information the way he or she does. Make a record of this excerpt from *Hiroshima* by asking a question for each paragraph and writing an answer to your question. A sample question and answer for the first three paragraphs have been modeled below.

1. **Question:** Why does Hersey tell about what each person was doing at the exact moment the bomb fell?

   Answer: He wants the reader to know that the people in Hiroshima were real people with real lives, not just faceless enemies.

2. **Question:** Why is the Reverend Mr. Tanimoto so full of anxiety?

   Answer: He has heard that the Americans are saving something special for his city.

3. **Question:** Why is Mr. Tanimoto moving his things to the rayon manufacturer's house?

   Answer: He wants to protect them by getting them out of the probable target area.

   Continue writing questions and answers for the rest of the excerpt. Then write questions and answers for the two poems by Randall Jarrell.

_____

_____

     © **Pearson Education, Inc.**

Name _____ Date _____

"Mirror" by Sylvia Plath
"In a Classroom" by Adrienne Rich
"The Explorer" by Gwendolyn Brooks
"Frederick Douglass" and "Runagate Runagate" by Robert Hayden

Summary In "Mirror," the speaker is a woman's mirror. It states that it is "not cruel, only truthful." Like a lake, the mirror has drowned the young face of the aging woman, and now rising toward the woman is the face of her old age. In "In a Classroom," the speaker looks at a student, "a presence like a stone." "The Explorer" is about a character who is looking for "a still spot in the noise." He is afraid of all the choices he has. He can find no quiet rooms. "Frederick Douglass" remembers an important African American leader and hopes that Douglass's dream will someday be realized. In "Runagate Runagate," the point of view changes from that of one runaway slave, to that of an owner looking for a runaway slave, to that of Harriet Tubman, who guided slaves to freedom.

Resumen En *Mirror*, un espejo dice que él "no es cruel, sólo veraz". Como un lago, el espejo ha ahogado la cara juvenil de la mujer que envejece, y ahora, la cara de su vejez está subiendo a la superficie, hacia la mujer. *In a Classroom*, el narrador mira a un estudiante, "una presencia como de piedra". *The Explorer*, trata de un personaje que busca "un lugar tranquilo en el ruido", pero teme todas las opciones que tiene. No puede hallar cuartos tranquilos. *Frederick Douglass*, recuerda a un importante líder afroamericano y espera que, algún día, el sueño de Douglass se haga realidad. En *Runagate Runagate*, cambian los puntos de vista, del de un esclavo escapado al de un dueño que persigue a un esclavo que huye, al de Harriet Tubman, quien guiaba a los esclavos hacia la libertad.

Interpret and Explain Poetry Poets often use images or word pictures to express ideas and feelings. To understand these images, you must first form a mental picture and then decide how each picture makes you feel. Some images from the poems have been listed below. Describe the picture that forms in your mind when you read each one, and then tell how it makes you feel. The first one has been modeled for you.

"Mirror"

1. Now I am a lake

   a shiny surface that reflects images—Makes me think of what might be under the water

"In a Classroom"

2. the slant of dust-motes over the table

   _____

"The Explorer"

3. A satin peace somewhere

   _____

"Frederick Douglass"

4. gaudy mumbo jumbo of politicians

   _____

"Runagate Runagate"

5. darkness thicketed with shapes of terror

   _____

Name _____ Date _____

"For My Children" by Colleen McElroy
"Bidwell Ghost" by Louise Erdrich

Summary In the first stanza of "For My Children," the speaker refers to the experiences of her ancestors in both the United States and Africa. Throughout the poem, she tells of her memories of the stories of her ancestors. She looks for connections between these stories and the realities of present-day life. As the poem closes, the speakers talks of the importance of "being and belonging"—the importance of preserving the African American cultural heritage. In "Bidwell Ghost," the speaker describes a ghost that "waits by the road." Twenty years earlier, the person had been killed when her house burned down. The speaker then goes on to describe how the ghost reaches out to the living and expresses its sense of loneliness and longing.

Resumen: Al comienzo de *For My Children*, la narradora habla de sus antepasados en Estados Unidos y en África. Cuenta de cómo recuerda las historias de sus antepasados y busca conexiones entre estas historias y las realidades de la vida actual. Al cerrar, habla de la importancia de "ser y pertenecer"—la importancia de conservar el patrimonio cultural afroamericano. En *Bidwell Ghost*, la narradora describe al fantasma de una persona que "espera en el camino". Veinte años antes, la persona había muerto cuando se incendió su casa. La narradora continúa describiendo cómo el fantasma se acerca a los vivos y expresa su soledad y nostalgia del mundo de los vivos.

Identify Sensory Words Often, a poet uses sensory language to express ideas and feelings. This language helps readers imagine that they see, hear, feel, taste, and smell what the poet expresses.

Some of the sensory words in "For My Children" have been identified and classified in the chart. Look for additional sensory words in this poem, and record them in the proper columns. Remember that some words can appeal to more than one sense. When you are finished with "For My Children," repeat the procedure for "Bidwell Ghost."

Sight	Sound	Touch	Smell	Taste
shackles	shackles	shackles	honey	honey
honey				
ebony				

© Pearson Education, Inc.

Name _____ Date _____

"The Writer in the Family" by E. L. Doctorow

Summary When the narrator's father dies, his ninety-year-old mother is still alive in a nursing home. The family does not want to tell their grandmother, thinking the shock would kill her. They make up a story that her son has moved to Arizona with his wife and children. When the grandmother wonders why she hasn't heard from her son in Arizona, the narrator is asked to write letters as if they are from his father. One of the aunts will read the letters to her aged mother. The narrator writes a few letters, but he does not feel right about it. In the months following his father's death, he learns to understand his father better. His final letter to the grandmother does not please Aunt Frances. She returns it angrily, without having read it to the grandmother.

Resumen Cuando el padre del narrador muere, su madre, de noventa años, está todavía viva en una residencia para ancianos. La familia no le quiere decir de la muerte de su hijo, por temor que la noticia pudiera matarla. Le dicen que su hijo se ha mudado a Arizona con su esposa e hijos. Cuando la anciana se pregunta por qué no tiene noticias de su hijo, le piden al narrador que le envíe cartas como si las hubiera escrito su padre. Una de sus tías se las leerá a la anciana. El narrador escribe unas pocas cartas, pero no se siente bien haciéndolo. En los meses después de la muerte de su padre, el narrador comienza a entenderlo mejor. Su última carta a su abuela no le agrada a su tía Frances, quien se la devuelve enojada, sin habérsela leído a la abuela.

Respond to Characters' Actions Read "The Writer in the Family" with a partner, a paragraph at a time. As you read, make a character analysis chart like the one below. The first entry has been done as an example.

Character	Character's Action	Reasons for Character's Action
aunts	tell grandmother that narrator's father had moved to Arizona	to avoid shocking her by saying he has died

© Pearson Education, Inc.

"Camouflaging the Chimera" by Yusef Komunyakaa
"Ambush" from *The Things They Carried* by Tim O'Brien

Summary In "Camouflaging the Chimera," the poet describes his experiences in Vietnam during the war. He tells how soldiers used branches, mud, and grass to camouflage themselves. He relates his memories of being in combat. In "Ambush," the narrator tells the story of how he killed a "short, slender young man of about twenty" during the Vietnam War. It was dawn, and the light was just beginning to break through the fog. Suddenly, a young man came out of the fog, moving without any hurry. Even though there was "no real peril," the narrator threw a grenade at him. To this day, he hasn't finished sorting it out in his mind. He could have let the man go on. "Almost certainly," he would have passed by. Sometimes the narrator forgives himself. Other times, he doesn't.

Resumen En *Camouflaging the Chimera*, el poeta describe sus experiencias en Vietnam. Cuenta cómo los soldados usaban ramas, barro y pasto como camuflaje en combate. En *Ambush*, el narrador nos cuenta de cuando mató a "un hombre joven delgado y bajo, de unos veinte años" durante la guerra. Ocurrió al alba, cuando la luz empezaba a filtrarse entre la niebla. De repente, un hombre joven salió de entre la niebla, caminando sin prisa. Aunque el joven no representaba "un peligro real", el narrador le arrojó una granada. Hasta el día de hoy, sigue pensando sobre todo esto. Podría haber dejado pasar al hombre. "Casi seguramente" el joven hubiera seguido sin darse cuenta de la presencia del narrador. Éste a veces se perdona por lo que hizo, a veces no.

Form a Mental Picture One way to understand what an author describes is to form a picture in your mind's eye. Listen to the audiocassette recording of "Ambush" as you read along. Picture each scene as you listen. Use this page to jot down notes to describe what you picture in your mind. Then work with a partner to draw sketches of what O'Brien describes in each of the following scenes. When you are finished, follow the same procedure for "Camouflaging the Chimera." Choose a few scenes of your own to sketch.

1. the author answering his nine-year-old daughter's questions about the war

2. the author staying awake for the final watch while his partner sleeps

3. the young man coming out of the fog

4. the author's reaction to seeing the young man

5. what the author imagines would have happened if he had not thrown the grenade

_____

_____

_____

_____

_____

_____

_____

  © Pearson Education, Inc.

The Crucible, Act I, by Arthur Miller

Summary It is 1692 in Salem, Massachusetts. The Reverend Parris is praying for his daughter Betty, who is ill. He says he saw his niece Abigail and Betty dancing in the woods. He asks Abby why no one will hire her as a mother's helper since Mrs. Proctor fired her. John Proctor enters. He sends Mary back to his farm, where she works. Parris and all the girls but Abby leave. Abby wants to resume a love affair with Proctor, but he refuses. Betty begins to wail. Others rush in, including kindly Rebecca Nurse, who calms Betty. Reverend Hale, an expert in witchcraft, enters. He questions Abby, and she shifts the blame to Tituba. Frightened, Tituba says that she saw Sarah Good and Goody Osburn with the Devil. Abby cries out other names, and soon all the girls are crying out names.

Resumen Es el año 1692, en Salem, Massachussetts, el reverendo Parris reza por su hija Betty, que está enferma. Él dice que vio a su sobrina Abigail bailando con Betty en el bosque y le pregunta a Abby por qué nadie la quiere emplear desde que la Sra. Proctor la despidió. John Proctor entra. Parris y todas las muchachas, menos Abby, se van. Abby quiere reiniciar una relación amorosa con Proctor, pero él se niega. Betty comienza a gemir y otras personas entran, entre ellas la bondadosa Rebecca Nurse, quien calma a Betty. El reverendo Hale, un experto en brujería, entra e interroga a Abby, quien acusa a Tituba. Asustada, Tituba dice que vio a Sarah Good y a Goody Osburn con el Diablo. Abby grita otros nombres, y pronto todas las muchachas comienzan a hacer lo mismo.

Make a Character Chart You understand characters by what they say, what they do, and what others say about them. Listen to the audiocassette recording of Act I as you follow along in your text. Listen for what the characters do and say. Listen for what others say about them. With a partner, complete a character chart like the following.

Character	Does	Says	What others say
Tituba			
Reverend Parris			
Abigail Williams			
Mrs. Ann Putnam			
Mercy Lewis			
Mary Warren			
John Proctor			
Rebecca Nurse			
Giles Corey			
Reverend John Hale			
Betty Parris			

The Crucible, Act II, by Arthur Miller

Summary Act II opens in the Proctor home, eight days later. Elizabeth says fourteen people have been arrested, based on what Abigail and the other girls said. She urges John to testify that the girls are frauds. They quarrel over his previous affair with Abigail. Mary, back from court, gives Elizabeth a small doll. Mary says those who confess will not be hanged. She says that Elizabeth's name has been mentioned. Elizabeth says she is sure that Abigail wants her dead. Hale appears at the door. To test John, Hale asks him to list the Ten Commandments. Ironically, John forgets the one about adultery. Then two men burst in. They say their wives have been arrested. The marshall arrives and arrests Elizabeth. Over John's protests, she is taken away in chains

Resumen En casa de los Proctor, ocho días después, Elizabeth dice que hay catorce arrestados por lo que dijeron Abigail y otras muchachas. Ella urge a John a testificar que las jóvenes no dicen la verdad. Los dos pelean sobre la pasada relación amorosa entre John y Abigail. Mary, de regreso del tribunal, le dice a Elizabeth que los que confiesen no serán colgados y que se mencionó el nombre de Elizabeth. Ésta dice que está segura que Abigail la quiere ver muerta. Hale aparece en la puerta y, para probar a John, le pide que diga los Diez Mandamientos. Irónicamente, John se olvida el que habla de adulterio. Luego, dos hombres irrumpen en la casa y dicen que sus esposas fueron arrestadas. Llega el *marshall* y arresta a Elizabeth. A pesar de las protestas de John, se la llevan encadenada.

Paraphrase Dialogue One way to understand the dialogue in a play is to paraphrase, or re-word it. Choose some dialogue from the play that you find especially difficult to understand. Restate it in your own words. Use the example as a guide.

Example:

Elizabeth: I do not judge you. The magistrate sits in your heart that judges you. I never thought you but a good man, John—only somewhat bewildered.

Paraphrase: I do not judge you. You judge yourself. I always thought you were a good man, John—just a bit confused.

Sentence 1: _____

_____

Paraphrase: _____

_____

Sentence 2: _____

_____

Paraphrase: _____

_____

Sentence 3: _____

_____

Paraphrase: _____

_____

© Pearson Education, Inc.

Name _____ Date _____

The Crucible, Act III, by Arthur Miller

Summary Act III opens with Giles Corey pleading for his wife's life. Francis Nurse says the girls are frauds. Danforth tries to scare the men by saying he has jailed almost 400 people and sentenced seventy-two to hang. Proctor leads in a terrified Mary, who admits she never saw any spirits. Danforth tells John that Elizabeth is pregnant and will not be executed until after the baby is born. Abigail swears that Mary is lying. To stop Abigail, John admits his infidelity. Elizabeth is brought in to back up John's claim. Yet she lies about John's affair with Abigail, so John is not believed. Echoed by the girls, Abigail begins pretending that Mary's spirit is bewitching her. Mary hysterically takes back her confession. John is arrested. Hale quits the court.

Resumen El tercer acto comienza con Giles Corey rogando por la vida de su mujer. Francis Nurse dice que las muchachas mienten. Danforth dice que él ha arrestado a casi 400 personas y sentenciado a morir a setenta y dos. Proctor llega con Mary, que está aterrorizada y que admite no haber visto espíritus. Danforth le dice a John que Elizabeth está embarazada y no será ejecutada hasta después del nacimiento del niño. Abigail jura que Mary miente. Para detener a Abigail, John admite su adulterio, pero cuando traen a Elizabeth, ella miente sobre la relación de John con Abigail, por lo que no creen lo que John ha dicho. Respaldada por las jóvenes, Abigail comienza a fingir que el espíritu de Mary la está embrujando. Mary, histéricamente, niega su confesión, John es arrestado y Hale deja el tribunal.

Use a Story Map Organizer Think about the events of the play that have happened before Act III opens. Use a Story Map to record the events that have built the plot so far. For example, you might include the following events: Reverend Parris praying over his daughter Betty, Abigail's conversation with John Proctor, the girls crying out names, John's conversation with Elizabeth about Abigail, Mary giving a doll to Elizabeth and talking about what went on in court, Elizabeth's arrest. Then add other events as you read Act III. Continue this Story Map as you read Act IV. Decide which event should be considered the climax, or high point, of the plot. Compare your Story map with those of your classmates and discuss the differences between them.

Setting:
> Place: Salem, Massachusetts
> Time: 1692

Problem:

Event 1: The Reverend John Parris prays over his daughter Betty, who is ill.

Event 2: _____

Event 3: _____

Event 4: _____

Event 5: _____

Climax
(Turning Point)

The Crucible, Act IV, by Arthur Miller

Summary Act IV opens in the Salem jail. Danforth and Hathorne enter. Parris enters and tells the judges that Abigail and Mercy Lewis have stolen his money and run away. Parris, hoping that John or Rebecca will confess, asks for a postponement of their hangings. Danforth refuses. Hale enters to ask Danforth to pardon the condemned. Elizabeth is brought in. Hale asks her to urge John to confess. John is brought in and the couple is left alone. They express their love, but Elizabeth refuses to advise John about whether he should confess. John decides to confess but refuses to name others. He signs the confession but will not give it to Danforth. In a fury, he rips the paper, crying that he will not destroy his good name. He is taken away to be hanged.

Resumen: El cuarto acto comienza en la cárcel de Salem. Danforth y Hathorne entran. Parris entra y dice a los jueces que Abigail y Mercy Lewis le han robado su dinero y se han escapado. Parris, con la esperanza de que John o Rebecca confiesen, pide que se pospongan sus ejecuciones. Danforth se rehusa a hacerlo. Entra Hale y pide a Danforth que perdone a los condenados. Traen a Elizabeth. Hale urge a John a que confiese. Traen a John y dejan a la pareja solos. Ellos se expresan su amor, pero Elizabeth se rehusa a decir a John que él debe confesar. John decide confesar pero se rehusa a dar otros nombres. Firma su confesión, pero no se la quiere dar a Danforth. Enfurecido, rompe el papel, diciendo que no destruirá su buen nombre. Se llevan a John para colgarlo.

Prepare a Reader's Theater Plays are written to be performed. Reading a play aloud is more rewarding than reading it silently. Plan a Readers' Theater presentation of this play. Assign roles to different members of your group. Practice reading your parts as a group. When you have practiced, present your Readers' Theater to the class or record it to play for the class. Then ask your classmates to evaluate your performance.

Use the lines below to assign roles and to jot down ideas about your performance.

_____

_____

_____

_____

_____

_____

_____

_____

_____

_____

_____

_____

_____

 © Pearson Education, Inc.

Answers: Part 1

Unit 1

The Iroquois Constitution
Translated by Arthur C. Parker

p. 6 English Language Development
A *confederacy* is an alliance or joining together with others.

p. 6 Literary Analysis Students should circle "peace" and "strength." The purpose of the alliance is peace.

p. 6 Culture Note Other repeated words or phrases include "council fire," "roots," and "confederacy."

p. 7 Reading Strategy The eagle is a sentry or a guard who warns the people of evil or danger.

p. 7 Reading Strategy Students should circle "so that other nations who may be allies may see the council fire of the Great Peace."

p. 7 Stop to Reflect All the lords must be honest in all things.

p. 8 Read Fluently Students should read the passage clearly, varying their tone and volume appropriately. Students may circle any three of the following words: "patience, duty, firmness, tenderness, calm, deliberation."

p. 8 Vocabulary and Pronunciation The sentence means that the lords of the council should not discard or ignore any warnings from the young members of their nation. They should always correct their errors and return to the way of the Great Law.

p. 8 Reading Strategy They are concerned about the welfare of future generations.

p. 9 Review and Assess

1. Action 1: planting the Tree of the Great Peace
Action 2: naming the tree the Tree of the Great Long Leaves
Action 3: spreading the soft white feathery down as seats for the cousin lords

2. With its piercing sight, the eagle can warn the people of any approaching evil or danger.

3. The people should have a high opinion of their lords, out of respect for the lords' honorable positions.

4. It helps to explain the origin of the Iroquois Confederacy.

5. *Sample answer:* Qualities of honesty, patience, firmness, calm deliberation, and concern for the welfare of the whole people and of future generations point to a well-balanced society with respect for good leadership.

from The Interesting Narrative of the Life of Olaudah Equiano
by Olaudah Equiano

p. 13 English Language Development The verb is "had got."

p. 13 Vocabulary and Pronunciation Here the word *hold* means the storage area for a ship's cargo.

p. 13 Literary Analysis Three details that show the horrible conditions are "the closeness of the place," "the heat of the climate," and "the number in the ship."

p. 13 Stop to Reflect It would have been in their interest because fewer slaves would have died of sickness.

p. 14 Reading Strategy *Sample summary:* After the white traders caught and ate a number of fish, they threw the leftovers into the sea rather than feed the hungry slaves.

p. 14 English Language Development The correct plural forms are *deer, tigers, wolves,* and *sheep.*

p. 14 Reading Check Students should underline "tried to get fish in secret" and "jumped into the sea."

p. 14 Read Fluently Students should read the passage clearly, varying their tone and volume appropriately. Students should circle "flying fishes" and "quadrant."

p. 15 Stop to Reflect The effect is to shock the reader. The slaves are treated like sheep and crowded together. They are sold and referred to as "parcels."

p. 16 Review and Assess

1. The slave traders are greedy for profits and pack the ship full to bursting. However, the crowded conditions and brutal treatment of the slaves lead to many deaths, so Equiano calls the traders shortsighted.

2. The traders eat until they are satisfied and then throw the leftovers into the sea, ignoring the pleas of the hungry slaves.

3. They whip him unmercifully.

4. *Sample summary:* Two wonders Equiano observed during the journey were flying fish, which jumped across the ship, and the quadrant. When one of the officers let him look through the quadrant, he was amazed.

5. These details show that Equiano is curious. Despite the horrible conditions on board ship, he has retained a childlike sense of wonder.

6. Details include the penning up of all the slaves together like sheep and the rapid selling off of the slaves to buyers who rush into the yard as soon as a signal is given.

© Pearson Education, Inc.

from The General History of Virginia
by John Smith

p. 20 Read Fluently Students should read the passage clearly, varying their tone and volume appropriately. Before the ships left, the colonists were able to obtain food. After the ships departed, the supplies ran out, and the settlers went hungry.

p. 20 English Language Development Students should rewrite the sentence as follows: "If Pocahontas had not pleaded with her father, Smith would have been executed."

p. 21 Reading Check The corn had been in the ship's hold for twenty-six weeks and was full of worms.

p. 21 English Language Development Encourage students to explain the context in which the proverbs or
traditional sayings would be used.

p. 21 Reading Strategy The following words contain the main idea: "
everything of worth is found full of difficulties."

p. 21 Literary Analysis Examples of subjective reporting are "by his own example," "good words," "fair promises," and "neglecting any for himself."

p. 22 Reading Strategy Factual details include the following: the young women sitting on either side of Powhatan; the two rows of men and two rows of women on each side of the house; heads and shoulders painted red; heads decorated with white down of birds; great chains of white beads around the people's necks.

p. 22 Vocabulary and Pronunciation The meaning is "at which."

p. 22 Stop to Reflect He probably spared him because of the intervention of Pocahontas, his "dearest daughter."

p. 23 Vocabulary and Pronunciation The meaning is "account" or "story."

p. 23 Reading Check They were no longer afraid because of Smith's "relation of the plenty he had seen" and because of the "state and bounty of Powhatan."

p.23 Read Fluently Students should read the passage clearly, varying their tone and volume appropriately. Smith claims that God is responsible.

p. 24 Review and Assess

1. They had little to eat.

2. Powhatan's daughter Pocahontas saved Smith.

3. In exchange for guns and a grindstone, Powhatan promised to give Smith land.

4. Smith praises himself when he remarks that he set a good example for the colonists and neglected building any house for himself.

5. *Sample answers:*

Sentence 1	Sentence 2
While the ships stayed, out allowance was somewhat bettered by a daily proportion of biscuit which the sailors would pilfer to sell, give, or exchange with us for money, sassafras, or furs.	Now every once in four or five days, Pocahontas with her attendants brought him so much provision that saved many of their lives, that else for all this had starved with hunger.
Who (Subject)	**Who (Subject)**
allowance	Pocahontas
Did What (Main Verb)	**Did What (Main Verb)**
was bettered	brought
Main Idea	**Main Idea**
We had better conditions while the ships were still present.	Pocahontas brought food that saved the colonists from starvation.

from Sinners in the Hands
of an Angry God
by Jonathan Edwards

p. 28 Literary Analysis Students should underline the words "sinners" and "angry."

p. 28 Reading Strategy The meaning is "open wide."

p. 28 English Language Development The superlative forms are *longest* and *strongest.*

p. 29 Vocabulary and Pronunciation The meaning is "not able to be parted."

p. 29 Stop to Reflect Edwards compares the wrath of God to extremely powerful waters that have been dammed up for the moment but are ready to burst out.

p. 29 Read Fluently Students should read the passage clearly, varying their tone and volume appropriately. (1) bow (2) arrow.

p. 30 Literary Analysis Sinners are detestable in God's sight; they resemble a spider or a loathsome insect that is held over a fire.

p. 30 Stop to Reflect The repeated word is "nothing." Edwards wishes to emphasize the helplessness and worthlessness of human beings, compared to the almighty power of God.

p. 31 English Language Development Students should circle the quotation marks at the bottom of the page. The quote is from the Bible.

p. 31 Reading Strategy Students may circle *many* and *entering.* The meaning is "gathering" or "crowding."

© **Pearson Education, Inc.**

p. 31 Literary Analysis Edwards wants the congregation to join other sinners who have repented and thrown themselves on Christ's mercy.

p. 31 Reading Check The Biblical quotation is "Haste and escape for your lives, look not behind you, escape to the mountain, lest you be consumed." The quotation is appropriate because, like the sermon, it is a warning to escape from destruction.

p. 32 Review and Assess

1. It is only the power and pleasure of God that prevents sinners from falling into Hell.

2. Image 1: God's anger is like a dreadful storm. Image 2: God's anger is like great waters that are dammed for the moment.

3. Sinners can obtain Christ's mercy and salvation if they repent.

4. Edwards appeals to fear and guilt.

5. (a) The meaning of *abhors* is "hates" or "detests." (b) The meaning of *pining* is "grieving" or "yearning for."

Unit 2
from The Autobiography
by Benjamin Franklin

p. 36 Reading Strategy Students should circle any of the following phrases: Franklin decides to take up a difficult project. He will try to live a perfect life. He knows . . . what is right and wrong.

p. 36 Stop to Reflect It shows that he is organized, methodical, and determined.

p. 36 English Language Development 1. receipt; 2. believe; 3. eighteen; 4. grieve; 5. chief; 6. conceit.

p. 36 Reading Check Students should circle "Lose no time; be always employed in something useful; cut off all unnecessary actions."

p. 37 Vocabulary and Pronunciation Students should write two of the following words: sincerity, tranquillity, chastity, humility.

p. 37 Reading Strategy He might say, "Calm down. Don't get excited. Don't worry."

p. 37 Reading Strategy Students should fill in the blanks with the words *temperance* and *silence*.

p. 37 Reading Strategy Students should circle "more by the use of the ears than of the tongue."

p. 38 Reading Check Students' answers should look like the chart below.

	Mon.	Tues.	Wed.	Thurs.	Fri.	Sat.	Sun.
T							
S							
O							
R							
F							
I							
S							
J							
M							
C							
T							
C							
H							

p. 38 Literary Analysis Students should underline "He is too busy with trips and business in Europe."

p. 39 Reading Strategy The story indicates that Franklin has a good sense of humor. The fact that the man wanted a bright ax, but changed his mind when he realized how much work it was, is funny, especially when he tries to hide his laziness by saying that he likes a speckled ax best.

p. 39 Reading Check Franklin thinks that a good man should keep some faults so that he can keep his friends. People may envy or hate him if he becomes perfect.

p. 40 Literary Analysis Students should underline the following pronouns: *I, I, I, me, me.*

p. 40 Stop to Reflect Students may say that Franklin's attitude seems quite normal and healthy. He isn't upset that he couldn't achieve perfection. Rather, he realizes that, by simply trying to be a better person, he is better off than if he hadn't even tried.

p. 40 Read Fluently Students should read the passage clearly, varying their tone and volume appropriately. They should circle "evenness of temper" and "cheerfulness in conversation."

p. 41 Review and Assess

1. Franklin starts trying to live a perfect life.

2. (1) the name of the virtue; (2) some short notes about it

3. Temperance is first on the list because it helps you keep a clear head. Silence is second on the list because knowledge is obtained more by the use of the ears than of the tongue. Order is third on the list because it would give Franklin more time for his studies. Resolution is fourth on the list because it would help Franklin stick to his plan.

© Pearson Education, Inc.

4. Franklin is serious about his project, and he likes to establish methods and systems for getting things done.

5. Students should check "Franklin is telling the story of his own life" and "Franklin talks about himself, using the pronoun *I*."

from The Crisis
by Thomas Paine

p. 45 Reading Strategy *Possible answer:* Students should circle *glorious* and *Heaven*. They should underline, *conflict, hell, cheap, conquered.*

p. 45 Literary Analysis

1. Britain has a big army.

2. Britain has said that she will keep taxing the colonists.

3. Britain will keep controlling the colonists.

4. Britain has great power over America.

p. 45 English Language Development 1. was not; 2. are not; 3. could not; 4. should not.

p. 46 Stop to Reflect Students may agree or disagree with Paine's view. They should present compelling reasons for either opinion.

p. 46 Reading Check Students should circle the sentence "Wars, with no endings, will break out until that time comes."

p. 47 Read Fluently Students should read the passage clearly, varying their tone and volume appropriately. Paine says that he loves brave, strong men.

p. 47 Vocabulary and Pronunciation Students should circle *fight*.

p. 47 Culture Note Students may say that the early colonists did not like the way Britain controlled them or they didn't like the way Britain taxed them.

p. 48 Review and Assess

1. Students should check "hell."

2. Students should choose "God is."

3. The man said, "Well! give me peace in my day."

4. Paine got angry because he thought that the man was being unfatherly. He said that a generous father would say, instead, "If there must be a war, let it be in my day. That way, my child can have peace."

5. Students may say that Paine is trying to persuade his readers to take up arms against Britain and fight for their freedom.

6. Students should circle the following words: *glorious, tyranny, devils, curse.*

Speech in the Virginia Convention
by Patrick Henry

p. 52 Stop to Reflect Students may agree or disagree that it is best to know the worst. They should present compelling reasons for either opinion.

p. 52 Read Fluently Students should read the passage clearly, varying their tone and volume appropriately. Students should circle "by the past."

p. 53 English Language Development shelves, knives, calves, elves, scarves

p. 53 Reading Strategy Students should put a check before "the British want to treat the colonists like slaves."

p. 53 Reading Check Students should underline "Henry says that the colonists' petitions have been ignored. Their protests have met more violence. Their pleas have been set aside."

p. 53 Literary Analysis Students should underline "When shall we be stronger? Will it be the next week, or the next year? Will it be when we are totally disarmed, and when a British guard shall be stationed in every house?"
question 1: Never
question 2: No
question 3: No

p. 54 Literary Analysis

1. the vigilant, the active, the brave

2. let it come!

p. 54 Vocabulary and Pronunciation *Sample answers:* measurement (action or process of measuring), development (action or process of developing)

p. 54 Reading Strategy

1. Students may say that the persuasive appeal makes them feel excited, all worked up, and ready to take a stand.

2. Students may underline the following three sentences, numbered as follows: 1. I know not what course others may take; but as for me, give me liberty or give me death. 2. Is life so dear, or peace so sweet, as to be purchased at the price of chains and slavery? 3. Our brethren are already in the field!

p. 55 Review and Assess

1. 1. I have but one lamp by which my feet are guided, and that is the lamp of experience. 2. I know of no way of judging of the future but by the past.

2. He thinks they are here "to bind and rivet upon us those chains which the British ministry have been so long forging."

3. Britain has ignored the colonists' petitions and insulted them from the throne.

© Pearson Education, Inc.

4. Paine uses **restatement** when he says, "I have but one lamp by which my feet are guided, and that is the lamp of experience. I know of no way of judging of the future but by the past." He uses **repetition** when he says "The war is inevitable—and let it come! I repeat it, sir, let it come!" He uses **parallelism** when he says, "The battle, sir, is not to the strong alone; it is to the vigilant, the active, the brave." He uses **rhetorical questions** when he asks, "But when shall we be stronger? Will it be the next week, or the next year?"

5. Students should circle the following sentence: There is no retreat but in submission and slavery!

Letter to Her Daughter from the New White House by Abigail Adams

p. 59 Reading Check The land is mostly woods with a few little cottages here and there.

p. 59 Culture Note *Sample answers:* Mississippi River, Ohio River, Hudson River

p. 59 Vocabulary and Pronunciation Sample answers for *scale:* size and proportion; an instrument used for weighing; Sample answers for *order:* state of neatness; to give a command.

p. 60 Literary Analysis (1) fifteen (2) short (3) They had to be short in order to get fifteen done in one day.

p. 60 Read Fluently Students should read the passage clearly, varying their tone and volume appropriately. Students should circle "wood is not to be had because people cannot be found to cut and cart it."

p. 60 Vocabulary and Pronunciation desert (dee ZERT): to leave, abandon; desert (DEZ ert): a barren land area that has very little water

p. 61 Literary Analysis Students may say that they know because Adams is asking her daughter to keep a secret, and she is telling her daughter how to respond to questions about how Adams likes the new White House.

p. 61 Reading Strategy The underlined sentence is an opinion because it cannot be proved. It is what Abigail Adams thinks.

p. 62 Review and Assess

1. Students should check "woods."

2. Students should complete the sentence with the words "light" and "heat."

3. Abigail Adams dries the family's laundry in the White House's "great unfinished audience room."

4. Who: Mrs. Washington; Where: Mount Vernon

5. *Possible answers:*

Good Things	Bad Things
She can see the river from her window	It is difficult to light the inside of the house.
The house is "upon a grand and superb scale."	There are no bells for calling the servants for help.
"It is a beautiful spot."	Not a single apartment is finished.

6. 1. fact; 2. opinion; 3. fact; 4. opinion

from Letters from an American Farmer by Michel-Guillaume Jean de Crèvecoeur

p. 66 Literary Analysis *Possible answers:* 1. The poor worked very hard. 2. The poor were starving. 3. The poor did not own any land.

p. 66 English Language Development leaving, coming, receiving, causing

p. 66 Reading Check Crèvecoeur compares the people who have left Europe to plants. People and plants are similar in that (1) they need certain things to keep them from dying, and (2) if they live in places where they have those things in abundance, they will do very well.

p. 67 Read Fluently Students should read the passage clearly, varying their tone and volume appropriately. Eight countries are represented in this family.

p. 67 Vocabulary and Pronunciation

Word	Meaning of Word
entertain	to amuse
employ	to use
enjoy	to take pleasure in
Word + -ment	**Meaning of New Word**
entertainment	the act of amusing
employment	the act of using
enjoyment	the act of taking pleasure in

p. 68 Vocabulary and Pronunciation
Sample answers:

race 1. a family, tribe, people, or nation belonging to the same stock 2. a contest of speed

long 1. going on for a considerable amount of time 2. to feel a strong desire for

vain 1. useless, having no result 2. having too much pride in one's appearance

p. 68 Reading Strategy The underlined sentence is an opinion. Students should circle the word *ought.*

© Pearson Education, Inc.

p. 68 Culture Note *Sample answer:* Crèvecoeur is suggesting that in some other countries, church and state are not separate and that people are forced to support the church financially.

p. 69 Review and Assess

1. *Sample answers:* (1) The poor European is a wretch who "wanders about." (2) He "works and starves." (3) His "life is a continual scene of sore affliction or pinching penury."

2. *Sample answers:* Box 1— Laws: In America, the laws protect the citizen; Box 2—Rewards for Labor: In America, the worker is rewarded fairly for his labor; Box 3—Ownership of Property: In America, people can save their money and buy property; Box 4—Demands of Religion and Royalty: In America, people do not have to pay high taxes to religions and royalty.

3. Students should check the following items: "you won't believe this, but," "don't tell anyone I said this, but," and "hope to see you soon."

4. *Sample answers:* Here, they are citizens. Here, they are rewarded for their labors and can buy land.

Unit 3
The Devil and Daniel Webster
by Washington Irving

p. 73 Culture Note Students should circle "(forest where) Captain Kidd had supposedly buried his pirate treasure" and "an old fort that Native Americans had once used in fighting the colonists."

p. 73 Vocabulary and Pronunciation Students should say the words aloud and circle the *oarse* (or *oars*) in *coarse,* the *ourse* (or *ours*) in *course,* the *orce* (or *orc*) in *divorce* and *force,* the *orc* in *forcing,* the *oarse* (or *oars*) in *hoarse,* the *orse* (or *ors*) in *horse,* the *orce* (or *orc*) in *porcelain,* and the *ors* in *torso.*

p. 73 Vocabulary and Pronunciation over there

p. 74 Vocabulary and Pronunciation Students may circle *woodland* or *white-faced.*
woodland: land covered with woods
white-faced: having a face that is white, or light-skinned

p. 74 Literary Analysis Students should circle "All her avarice was awakened at the mention of hidden gold." One word to describe Tom's wife is *greedy.*

p. 75 Vocabulary and Pronunciation Accept all real words that end in the suffix *-less. Example:* hopeless; Meaning: without hope; *Example:* childless; Meaning: without children.

p. 75 Stop to Reflect Students should circle *a.*

p. 76 Reading Check Students should circle *c.*

p. 76 English Language Development Students should circle all the quotation marks. They should use the *Devil* label for "You shall open a broker's shop in Boston next month" and "You shall lend money at two per cent a month" and the *Tom* label for "I'll do it tomorrow, if you wish" and "Egad, I'll charge four!" Irving shows a change of speaker by starting a new paragraph.

p. 76 Stop to Reflect Students may answer *yes* or *no* to this question. They should present compelling reasons for either opinion.

p. 77 English Language Development Students should label *thought* with "1-past" and *had made* with "2-past perfect."

p. 77 Reading Check Tom becomes "a violent churchgoer."

p. 77 Culture Note Tom's defense is dishonest because he does not need more money to take care of himself; he is already very rich.

p. 78 Reading Check The devil is knocking on Tom's door.

p. 78 Stop to Reflect Students may answer *yes* or *no* to this question. They should present compelling reasons for either opinion.

p. 78 Literary Analysis Students should circle "Let all griping money brokers lay this story to heart." Students may say that the narrator wants readers to learn any of the following: Do not be so greedy; do not charge high interest rates and gouge your customers; do not behave in an evil way or you will come to an evil end.

p. 79 Review and Assess

1. Students should circle *greedy, selfish,* and *lazy.*

2. Tom's wife goes to the forest to try to bargain with the Devil and is never heard from again.

3. Tom agrees to become a usurer in exchange for Captain Kidd's pirate treasure.

4. Tom forces someone to repay a loan and lies about it, saying "The Devil take me" in his lie. The Devil comes to take him, and Tom is never heard from again.

© Pearson Education, Inc.

5. *Possible responses:*

Different Characters' Thoughts & Experiences	Comments About Events & Characters
"All her avarice was awakened" (wife)	"Being of the same fearless temper as her husband"
"At length she determined to drive the bargain on her own" (wife)	"it was just to Tom's taste" (Tom)
"However Tom might have felt disposed to sell himself to the Devil, he was determined not to do so to oblige his wife" (Tom)	"Let all griping money brokers lay this story to heart."
"he began to feel anxious about those of the next" (Tom).	

6. Students should check these items: Many European colonists distrusted Native Americans; Some people disliked the slave trade; Some moneylenders charged high interest rates; Boston was a center of colonial commerce.

A Psalm of Life
by Henry Wadsworth Longfellow

p. 83 Literary Analysis Students should circle *numbers/slumbers* and *dream/seem* and draw lines between them. Then they should circle *b*.

p. 83 English Language Development Students should say the line aloud and circle *noun*.

p. 83 Reading Strategy Students should circle *c*.

p. 83 Vocabulary and Pronunciation Students should circle "take heart."

p. 84 Review and Assess

1. Students should circle "positive."

2. Students should check "Life is real!" and "Life is earnest!"

3. Students should circle *d*.

4. *Possible responses:*

Stanza	Main Idea
1	Do not give up hope.
2	Life is real and not useless.
3	Be heroic in life.
4	We can be great like others.
5	Our achievements will in turn inspire others.

5. *Possible responses:*

Image	Broader Meaning
to dust returneth	a person dies
dumb, driven cattle	people with no minds of their own
footprints on the sands of time	human achievements, one's legacy
shipwrecked brother	another human being in trouble or alone

The Raven
by Edgar Allan Poe

p. 88 English Language Development a dreary midnight

p. 88 Culture Note Students should write *January, February, March, April, May, June, July, August, September, October,* and *November.*

p. 88 Vocabulary and Pronunciation Students should read the line and circle the *s* in *silken, sad,* and *rustling* and the *c* in *uncertain.* Then they should circle *a*.

p. 89 Reading Check Students might circle "Darkness," "nothing," or the whole line, "Darkness there and nothing more."

p. 89 English Language Development Students should circle *made* and label it *V* and *he* and label it *S*.

p. 90 Reading Check Students should circle "Tell me what thy lordly name is" and label it *Q*. They should circle "Nevermore" and label it *A*.

p. 90 Reading Strategy Students should circle *a*.

p. 91 Reading Check *Possible response:* The Raven will not leave the next day, as the speaker said he would. The Raven will never leave.

p. 91 Literary Analysis *Possible response:* The repetition adds to the feeling of hopelessness. It makes it seem that no matter what the speaker does or says, he is doomed. It is very negative and absolute. Students might circle any two of "thing of evil," "bird or devil," "bird or fiend," "the tempest," "the Night's Plutonian shore," "black plume as a token" and/or "Take thy beak from out my heart!"

p. 92 Vocabulary and Pronunciation Students may circle the *e* in *Be*, the *ie* in *fiend* and *shrieked*, the *ee* in *thee*, the *ea* in *Leave* (which occurs twice), and the *ea* in *beak*.

p. 92 Reading Check *Possible responses:* The Raven is still there, and the speaker is still miserable. The Raven is still affecting the speaker's life, and the speaker is miserable.

© Pearson Education, Inc.

1. Students should circle "sad," "brooding," "hopeless," and "superstitious."

2. T—The speaker misses Lenore.
   F—Lenore is away visiting her parents for the holidays.
   F—The speaker is reading a book about bird watching.
   T—The Raven enters through the window.
   F—The Raven has an extensive vocabulary.
   T—The Raven perches on a bust of an ancient Greek goddess.
   T—The Raven is still perched on the bust when the poem ends.

3. Possible responses include the Raven's name, the impossibility of the speaker reuniting with Lenore in the hereafter, and the Raven's plans of never leaving.

4. Possible examples include end rhyme such as *lore/more* in the first stanza; internal rhyme such as *dreary/weary* and *napping/tapping/rapping* in the first stanza; alliteration such as "weak and weary," "quaint and curious," and "nodded, nearly napping" in the first stanza; and assonance such as "weak and weary" in the first stanza or "bleak December" in the second.

5. *Possible answers:*

Setting
midnight dreary, bleak December
Characters
speaker in mourning for a lost loved one, eerie black Raven
Events
mysterious knocking, echo in the darkness, Raven flying in and perching on a bust, Raven saying the same word over and over, Raven never leaving
Word Choice
"wrought its ghost," "fantastic terrors," "ghastly grim and ancient Raven wandering from the Nightly shore," "Night's Plutonian shore," "thing of evil," "bird or devil," "bird or fiend," "the tempest," "black plume as a token," "Take thy beak from out my heart," "pallid bust of Pallas," "eyes have all the seeming of a demon's that is dreaming,"

6. Students might put lines after *Raven, bust,* and the first *word.* They should underline *Raven* and label is *S,* spoke and label it *V,* and the first word and label it *O.*

from Walden
by Henry David Thoreau

p. 97 Culture Note Thoreau chose the fourth of July to show his own independence by living alone in the woods.

p. 97 Reading Check Students may circle "to live deliberately" or "to front only the essential facts of life."

p. 97 Stop to Reflect Living in the woods would force Thoreau to concentrate only on the essentials of life. It would enable him to learn how to enjoy the enjoyable and face the awful things about life.

p. 98 Vocabulary and Pronunciation Students should circle *Simplicity* and label it *N.* They should circle *Simplify* and label it *V.*
noun: simplicity
meaning: the state of being simple
verb: simplify
meaning: to make simple

p. 98 Reading Strategy Thoreau says, "Simplify, simplify." He believes in reducing life to its essentials.

p. 99 English Language Development Students should circle *a-fishing.* On the line, they should write *fishing.*

p. 99 Stop to Reflect Students should circle *c.*

p. 99 Vocabulary and Pronunciation The word here means "a path, a road, or a direction of travel."

p. 100 English Language Development Students should circle the exclamation point at the end of the sentence.

p. 100 Literary Analysis Students might circle "If a man does not keep pace with his companions, perhaps it is because he hears a different drummer" or "Let him step to the music which he hears, however measured or far away." They should circle *b.*

p. 100 English Language Development Students should circle *richest* and *most independent.*

p. 101 Stop to Reflect Students should circle *b.*

p. 101 Reading Check Students should circle "thoughts."

p. 101 Reading Strategy Possible response for students who circle *agree:* Poor people do not have as many responsibilities as rich people and can concentrate on the most valuable part of life: love, family, having fun, etc. Possible response for students who circle *disagree:* Poor people do not have as many options as rich people and must spend most of their time just struggling to get by.

p. 102 Literary Analysis Students should check "images from nature" and "figurative language."

© **PEARSON** Education, Inc.

p. 102 Stop to Reflect Students may say that the sentence means that no day is real to us unless we are aware of it and paying attention.

p. 103 Review and Assess

1. *Possible response:* Thoreau went to live in the woods because <u>he wanted to face the essentials of life and not get bogged down in trivial detail.</u> Thoreau left the woods because <u>his life there had become too much of a routine and it was time to move on to other things.</u>

2. Students should circle *b.*

3. Students should circle *independence, nature,* and *simplicity.*

4. *Possible responses:*

	Example 1	**Example 2**
Simple Language	"An honest man has hardly need to count more than his ten fingers"	Time is but the stream I go a-fishing in"
Images from Nature and Everyday Life	three meals a day	symbol of the bug in the table
Short Sentences	"Simplicity, simplicity, simplicity!"	"My head is hands and feet"
Figurative Language	"In the midst of this chopping sea of civilized life"	"Time is but the stream I go a-fishing in"

5. Students should circle one of the three sentences and then evaluate it. They should discuss whether the statement presents its idea clearly and supports it with enough examples and reasons. They should also compare the idea to their own knowledge and experience.

Unit 4
An Episode of War
by Stephen Crane

p. 107 Reading Strategy Students may circle "rubber blanket" and "breast-work" as examples of historical details.

p. 107 Culture Note In today's military, a special division of the army, rather than regular officers, would be responsible for handling food supplies.

p. 107 Stop to Reflect Students may speculate that the lieutenant has been shot.

p. 108 Literary Analysis Students should circle the word *helplessness.*

p. 108 English Language Development The repetition of the word *then* produces emphasis and underlines the men's numbed shock and their feelings of apprehension.

p. 108 Literary Analysis The passage exemplifies Realism in the use of point of view. Only now can the lieutenant see sights that were unknown to him when he was a participant in the fight. True-to-life details include the general on a black horse, the lines of infantry, the green woods, and the aide who gallops up, salutes, and presents a paper. Finally, the narrator compares the scene to a "historical painting."

p. 108 Reading Check Students should circle the word *schoolhouse.*

p. 109 Read Fluently Students should read the passage clearly, varying their tone and volume appropriately. Conditions are primitive and chaotic.

p. 109 Vocabulary and Pronunciation Students may name the verb *terminate.*

p. 109 Vocabulary and Pronunciation Students' responses will differ, depending on their native language and the expressions they choose. Make sure they supply a formal equivalent for each slang expression.

p. 109 Stop to Reflect The doctor is condescending and insensitive, perhaps because he is overworked and upset.

p. 110 Reading Strategy The lieutenant stoically accepts the loss of his arm. Compared to other injuries he has seen, he is not so badly off.

p. 111 Review and Assess

1. The lieutenant is shot in the arm.

2. People who offer help include the orderly-sergeant, the man who asks the lieutenant if he wants to lean on his shoulder, the stragglers who tell the lieutenant where to find the field hospital, and the officer who uses his handkerchief to bandage the lieutenant's wound.

3. Two ambulances have interlocked wheels in the mud.

4. Students may mention the frequent use of amputation, the crowded and filthy conditions, or the overworked doctors.

5. The nameless lieutenant symbolizes the unfortunate Everyman, helpless to prevent his injury, sheathe his own sword, or avoid amputation. He is wounded by chance, then swept toward a fate he is powerless to escape. His horrible experience is just one more in a string of such tragedies that humanity is powerless to avoid; it is just "an episode of war."

© Pearson Education, Inc.

from My Bondage and My Freedom
by Frederick Douglass

p. 115 Reading Check Douglass had a hard time learning to read. Students should circle the word *disadvantages*.

p. 115 English Language Development The comparison suggests that she became hard and uncompromising.

p. 116 English Language Development *Sample rewriting:* She had a tear for every sorrow or suffering, and she had a smile for every innocent joy.

p. 116 Stop to Reflect Students should underline these phrases: *divest her of her excellent qualities* and *her home of its early happiness.*

p. 116 Literary Analysis Douglass's owners thought he was secretly reading a book.

p. 117 Read Fluently Students should read the passage clearly, varying their tone and volume appropriately. Douglass learned to read from his playmates, the white boys.

p. 117 Reading Strategy The white boys will be free when they become twenty-one, while Douglass will always remain a slave.

p. 117 Reading Check Students should underline the phrase *fresh and bitter condemnation.*

p. 118 Vocabulary and Pronunciation The modern equivalent is *trumpet.*

p. 118 Reading Strategy Everything reminds Douglass that as a slave, he does not possess liberty, which should be the birthright of every man. He is constantly aware of being a slave.

p. 118 English Language Development The repeated words/sentence parts are verbs and prepositional phrases.

p. 119 Stop to Reflect Douglass's mistress was a victim because slavery dehumanized her.

p. 119 Vocabulary and Pronunciation *But* usually means "yet" or "in spite of this."

p. 120 Review and Assess

1. Mrs. Auld's husband persuades her to stop teaching Douglass.

2. Douglass learns how to read from his playmates, the white boys.

3. The white boys are ashamed of slavery and condemn it.

4. Douglass reads a book about liberty and realizes he can no longer live without it.

5. Students should point out that slavery is dehumanizing for both the slave and the slaveholder, as is shown by the changes in Douglass and in Mrs. Auld. By nature, human beings are alien to slavery, as is shown by the attitude of the young white boys. Finally, every human being has liberty as a natural birthright, as is shown by

Douglass's reaction when he reads a book about liberty.

6. Mrs. Auld would probably have denied any change in her personality and would have seen her actions as proper.

The Notorious Jumping Frog of Calaveras County
by Mark Twain

p. 124 Reading Check Students should underline the phrase *always betting on anything that turned up.*

p. 124 Literary Analysis The exaggerated details are the bets on which bird would fly first and the teaching of the frog to catch flies.

p. 125 Reading Strategy *Sample rewriting:* He used to go downtown sometimes and try to make a bet.

p. 125 English Language Development The adverb is *carefully.*

p. 125 Read Fluently Students should read the passage clearly, varying their tone and volume appropriately. The stranger seems to be cool and calm.

p. 125 Literary Analysis Students should underline the word *maybe.*

p. 126 Reading Strategy Students should circle the words *set* (dialect for "sat") and *hisself* (dialect for "himself").

p. 126 Literary Analysis The details add to the humor by being improbable and exaggerated.

p. 126 English Language Development *Sample rewriting:* I don't see anything about that frog that makes it better than any other frog.

p. 127 English Language Development *Sample answer:* "How did you possibly get here?"

p. 127 Culture Note The tale suggests that the pioneers and miners of the West enjoyed having a good laugh at improbable, exaggerated stories. The tellers and listeners of such tales were freewheeling and imaginative.

p. 127 Literary Analysis Wheeler is about to tell another long-drawn-out tale. Suggesting that Wheeler has yet another story to tell contributes to the humor because it is another exaggeration.

p. 128 Review and Assess

1. Smiley always wanted to place a bet.

2. Smiley thought his frog could outjump any frog in the county.

3. The stranger lured Smiley into leaving his frog and then loaded the frog with quailshot.

4. By relating Wheeler's dialect and mannerisms, the story does succeed in giving us a portrait of him.

5. *Example:* Smiley's maniacal betting at every conceivable opportunity, or his "teaching" of the frog, or the way he is outwitted by the stranger, who fills Dan'l Webster with quailshot. *Why It Is*

© Pearson Education, Inc.

Amusing: Each example appeals to our sense of the improbable, the ridiculous, or the absurd.

6. *Sample rewriting:* Smiley had a yellow, one-eyed cow that had no tail, but a short stump like a banana instead.

The Story of an Hour
by Kate Chopin

p. 132 Vocabulary and Pronunciation The word means "news" in the underlined sentence.

p. 132 Stop to Reflect Richards does not want to risk upsetting Mrs. Mallard with an inaccurate report on such a grave matter.

p. 132 Reading Strategy Ironic details include the new spring life in the treetops, the delicious breath of rain in the air, the peddler crying his wares, the notes of a distant song, and the twittering of countless sparrows in the eaves.

p. 133 Read Fluently Students should read the paragraph clearly, varying their tone and volume appropriately. The phrase about the clouds suggests that Mrs. Mallard may soon experience happiness or relief.

p. 133 English Language Development Possible answers include *watches, buses, axes,* and *churches.*

p. 133 Literary Analysis We expected Mrs. Mallard's grief for her husband to last longer. Instead, she feels newly free and independent.

p. 134 Reading Check The accident report was inaccurate. Brently Mallard was nowhere near the train wreck.

p. 134 Literary Analysis Students should underline the phrase "joy that kills."

p. 135 Review and Assess

1. The narrator might mean that Mrs. Mallard is unhappy or that her heart is not in her marriage.

2. Students may include any of the following details in their charts: the tops of trees aquiver with new spring life, the delicious breath of rain in the air, the peddler crying his wares, the notes of a distant song, the twittering of sparrows in the eaves, and patches of blue sky showing through the clouds.

3. The sights, smells, and sounds, which all have vibrant associations of happiness or renewal, foreshadow the change in Mrs. Mallard from grief to exhilaration.

4. Mrs. Mallard has apparently resented Brently Mallard's imposition of his will upon her.

5. We had expected that Brently Mallard was killed, but he was actually far away from the railroad disaster. We had also expected Mrs. Mallard to live a long life "for herself," but the shock of seeing her husband return leads to a fatal heart attack.

6. The detail is the deliberate care with which Richards verifies the accident report with a "second telegram."

Unit 5
The Turtle
by John Steinbeck

p. 139 Literary Analysis We can tell that the turtle is determined to get across the road because he does the following things: he turns aside for nothing, and he threshes slowly through the grass, dragging his shell along.

p. 139 Vocabulary and Pronunciation clover: *k;* insect: *k;* climb: *k;* fierce, *s;* faces: *s;* braced: *s*

p. 140 Reading Check The turtle crushes the ant between its body and legs.

p. 140 Vocabulary and Pronunciation pushed: *t;* upraised: *d;* peered: *d;* braced: *t*

p. 140 English Language Development suddenly: in a sudden manner; finally: in a final manner

p. 140 Reading Strategy Students should circle the following section on page 140: "She saw the turtle and swung to the right, off the highway, the wheels screamed and a cloud of dust boiled up." Students should circle the following section on page 141: "the driver saw the turtle and swerved to hit it." (1) The woman symbolizes people who are kind, considerate, and helpful. (2) The man symbolizes people who are mean, cruel, and thoughtless.

p. 141 English Language Development four-inch-thick concrete; a hard-shell (or hard-shelled) turtle

p. 141 Culture Note Answers will vary depending on a student's native country, but examples might include cars, buses, trains, motorcycles, and bicycles.

p. 141 Stop to Reflect (1) The turtle helps the wild oat seeds by taking them to the other side of the highway and allowing them to plant themselves in the soil. Then he covers them with a layer of soil. (2) Steinbeck is saying that various life forms help one another survive.

© Pearson Education, Inc.

1. seeds, insects, grass, the land turtle (any three)
2. *Sample answers:*

Problems	How the Turtle Deals with Them
the highway embankment	climbs up the embankment very slowly
the concrete of the highway	pulls himself up the concrete slowly
the red ant	snaps his head and legs in, crushing the ant

3. He carries the oat seeds across the highway and then covers them with dirt.
4. He caused the turtle to roll across the highway quickly, thus avoiding being run over by another vehicle.
5. The theme Steinbeck is expressing is that the creatures on earth help one another to survive.
6. Students should check the following details: The turtle turned aside for nothing; the turtle stared straight ahead, and the turtle grabs onto a piece of quartz and pulls itself over.

The Far and the Near
by Thomas Wolfe

p. 146 Read Fluently Students should read the paragraph clearly, varying their tone and volume appropriately. Then they should underline the following: "as the train had approached this house, the engineer had blown on the whistle."

p. 146 English Language Development days, countries

p. 146 Culture Note Answers will depend on the native language of the student.

p. 147 Reading Strategy Students may say that the engineer has very high expectations for the women—that they are "beautiful and enduring, something beyond all change and ruin, and something that would always be the same." They may predict that the man will find out that the women, like everything else, have changed over time—or perhaps were never what he thought they were.

p. 147 Vocabulary and Pronunciation

g	green	g	grape
g	signal	j	change
g	sagged	j	gesture
j	strange	j	visage
j	magic	j	imagined
g	gone	g	again

p. 147 Reading Check Students may say that the engineer begins to feel strange and confused and becomes more and more puzzled.

p. 148 Literary Analysis *Suggested answer:* The man is disappointed when he meets the woman because she looks at him with a mistrustful eye. Her face is harsh and pinched and meager. Her eyes are filled with timid suspicion and uneasy doubt. He had thought she was warm and friendly, but now he finds her cold and unfriendly.

p. 148 Stop to Reflect *Possible answer:* Their reaction to the man seems normal. After all, they don't know him, they are alone in the house, and they haven't been expecting any visitors. They probably think it is a bit scary that a strange man would expect to be invited in for a visit.

p. 148 Culture Note *Possible answers:*
living room, parlor, sitting room, lounge

p. 149 Review and Assess

1. The cottage is white with green shutters. It has vegetables, grapes, flowers, and oak trees growing outside.
2. *Sample answer:*

First, the engineer blew the whistle.
↓
Then, the woman heard the whistle.
↓
Then, the woman and her daughter appeared on the back porch.
↓
After that, the woman and her daughter waved to the engineer.

3. Students should check the following words: beautiful, enduring, warm, and affectionate.
4. Students may say that the engineer is a bit of a dreamer. He has a picture in his mind of what the women are like, and he thinks that they will never change. This tells us that the engineer is a hopeful, optimistic person.
5. We know that the engineer's meeting is the anticlimax of the story because it is a disappointment to the character and to the reader. We have been expecting a high point, but it is the low point of the story. Up until that moment, the man has been expecting to have a wonderful, warm meeting with the women. When he sees that they are not friendly, he is let down.
6. Students should check the following details: The engineer thought that the women would always stay the same. The engineer begins to think that he knows the women well. The woman has an unfriendly tone when she answers the door.

 © Pearson Education, Inc.

In Another Country
by Ernest Hemingway

p. 153 Vocabulary and Pronunciation

oo	wounded	ow	about
ow	bounce	ow	shouted

p. 153 Reading Strategy Students may say that they would feel very fortunate and grateful that their injuries would heal completely, or they may say that they would not believe the doctor.

p. 153 English Language Development Students should circle the quotation marks around the following passages: "Very interesting, very interesting," and "No."

p. 154 Reading Check The boy wears a black handkerchief across his face because he has no nose.

p. 154 Vocabulary and Pronunciation

e	instead	ee	treatment
e	leather	e	death
ee	speaks		

p. 154 English Language Development *Sample answers:* Mexican, Russian, Egyptian, Japanese, Ukrainian

p. 155 Literary Analysis The narrator says that he is very much afraid to die, he wonders what it will be like when he goes back to the front.

p. 155 Literary Analysis Students should circle the following words: *I, my, I, me.*

p. 156 Stop to Reflect Students may say that the major is upset about his wound. Some may guess that some loss associated with his own marriage causes him to snap at the narrator.

p. 156 Reading Check The major explains his behavior by telling the narrator that his wife has just died.

p. 157 Read Fluently Students should read the paragraph clearly, varying their tone and volume appropriately. The major walks proudly out of the hospital, crying and biting his lips as he walks.

p. 157 Culture Note Answers will depend on the student's native country. Black, yellow, and white are most commonly used.

p. 157 Reading Check The major's wife had been sick for only a few days.

p. 157 Reading Strategy *Sample answers:* (1) He is thinking about his wife and how much he loved her. (2) He is thinking about his hand and wondering if it will ever be healed.

p. 158 Review and Assess

1. The narrator and the other men go to the hospital every day to receive treatment for the wounds they received in World War I.

2. The narrator: a leg injury; the major: a hand injury; the boy with the black handkerchief: a face (or nose) injury

3. The characters are being treated with various kinds of experimental machines.

4. Students should check the following passages: We all had the same medals . . . I had been wounded, it was true . . . "Oh—" I said, feeling sick for him.

5. *Sample answer:* I would be afraid of being on the front, but I would hope that I wouldn't endanger any of my fellow soldiers by acting in a cowardly manner.

A Worn Path
by Eudora Welty

p. 162 Literary Analysis We know that the point of view is limited third person because the narrator tells the story as an outside observer and reveals the thoughts and emotions of one character, Phoenix Jackson.

p. 162 Vocabulary and Pronunciation

silent	bright	silent	through
silent	straight	silent	thought
f	laughter	silent	high
f	laughed	f	enough
silent	lights		

p. 162 English Language Development scarecrow—something meant to scare crows; overhead—in a position over one's head; windmill—a mill that is powered by the wind

p. 163 Literary Analysis The narrator is suggesting that Phoenix lives in a fantasy world sometimes.

p. 163 Reading Check Phoenix thinks she sees a ghost.

p. 164 Read Fluently Students should read the paragraph clearly, varying their tone and volume appropriately. Then they should underline the following text: "Sweet gum makes the water sweet" and "Nobody know who made this well, for it was here when I was born."

p. 164 Reading Check A black dog knocks her down into the ditch.

p. 165 English Language Development Answers will depend on the student's native language and may include *abuela* and *abuelita.*

p. 165 Literary Analysis Students should underline the following sentence: "Without warning, she had seen with her own eyes a flashing nickel fall out of the man's pocket onto the ground."

p. 166 Reading Strategy *Sample answer:* Yes. I would have told the man he had dropped a nickel.

p. 166 Stop to Reflect Phoenix seems to think the man is pointing his gun at her because she picked up the nickel.

p. 167 English Language Development Here I **am.** Here you **are.** Here he **is.** Here we **are.** Here they **are.**

p. 167 Read Fluently Students should read the paragraph clearly, varying their tone and volume appropriately. *Possible answers:* (1) patient (2) kind

p. 167 Reading Check Students should circle the following passages: "Swallowed lye." "Every little while his throat begin to close up again, and he not able to swallow. He not get his breath. He not able to help himself."

p. 168 Stop to Reflect *Sample answer:* No. It makes it more interesting to wonder why Phoenix is taking such a difficult walk during December.

p. 168 Reading Strategy *Sample answers:* (1) She feels sorry for Phoenix. (2) She is a generous woman who wants to do something nice for Phoenix for Christmas.

p. 168 Reading Check Students should circle the following text: "a paper windmill."

p. 169 Review and Assess

1. The time of year is December, near Christmas.

2. Students should check the following words: small, old, blue-eyed, and wrinkled.

3. The purpose of Phoenix's journey is to get some medicine for her grandson.

4. Students should check the following sentences: Far out in the country there was an old Negro woman with her head tied in a red rag, coming along a path through the pinewoods. But when she went to take it there was just her own hand in the air. "The doctor said as long as you came to get it, you could have it," said the nurse.

5. *Sample answer:* Her grandson is the most important thing in life to Phoenix. She is willing to do whatever she needs to do to help him and to make him happy.

Unit 6

The First Seven Years
by Bernard Malamud

p. 173 Culture Note
• the Great Depression and World War II
• *Sample answers:* comfort, security, traditional roles, wealth, success, leisure, conformity
• *Sample answers:* atomic energy, computers, franchises, television, rock and roll

p. 174 Reading Strategy Students should circle "nervously alert."

p. 174 Reading Check Feld hopes that his daughter and Max will hit it off, fall in love, and get married.

p. 175 Reading Strategy Students may say that Max wants to see what Feld's daughter looks like before he goes out with her.

p. 175 Read Fluently Students should read the paragraph clearly, varying their tone and volume appropriately. Students might circle *violent, pounding,* and *torn.*

p. 176 Reading Check Feld has to hire a new assistant, who turns out to be neither as trustworthy nor as skilled as Sobel.

p. 176 Vocabulary and Pronunciation The word *received* in this paragraph means "welcomed."

p. 177 Reading Check Students may underline "It was all right" and "You can't really tell much the first time."

p. 177 Reading Strategy Students may say that Miriam delays because she is teasing her father or because she realizes how much her father wants her to like Max.

p. 177 Reading Strategy After their second date, Miriam says Max bores her and she has no interest in going out with him again.

p. 178 English Language Development Students may write either "So when you will come back to work" or "Why you don't think of me?"

p. 178 Reading Strategy Students might say Sobel is angry because he loves Miriam and does not want her father to find a husband for her. They might also say that he resents working hard for Feld for five years in return for low wages.

p. 179 Reading Check Sobel is in love with Miriam.

p. 179 Literary Analysis Students should underline "Feld had a sudden insight."

p. 179 Literary Analysis Students might say that Feld stops planning that Miriam will marry Max. He sadly accepts the fact that Sobel loves his daughter and that she might agree to marry him.

p. 180 Stop to Reflect 1. Feld hopes that his daughter will marry an educated man or go to college herself. 2. Miriam hopes to work rather than get an education. 3. Sobel hopes that Miriam will marry him.

p. 181 Review and Assess

1. Max is appealing to Feld because he is a hard-working college student who will likely become successful. Feld believes that he would make a good husband for his daughter, Miriam.

2. Miriam is bored by Max because he is too interested in material things.

3. Sobel becomes angry because Feld is trying to find a suitable husband for Miriam and has arranged

© PEARSON Education, Inc.

for Max and Miriam to go out on a date. Sobel is in love with Miriam and resents Feld's meddling.

4. In the chart, students should supply the name of one character and two or three examples of his or her thoughts, actions, feelings, and situation in the first column. In the second column, they should list emotional, physical, spiritual, or intellectual connections they can make to this character.

5. *Sample answers:* (1) Feld bitterly gives up his dream of a better life for his daughter. (2) Feld agrees to let Sobel propose marriage to Miriam in two years.

Everyday Use
by Alice Walker

p. 185 Reading Check Maggie is Dee's sister.

p. 185 Literary Analysis Students may circle "chin on chest, eyes on ground, feet in shuffle." They might underline "ever since the fire that burned the other house to the ground."

p. 186 Reading Strategy Students should underline "Dee is lighter than Maggie, with nicer hair and a fuller figure."

p. 186 Stop to Reflect Dee went to school in Augusta and moved away. Maggie has stayed with her mother.

p. 186 Vocabulary and Pronunciation The word *bright* in this paragraph means "intelligent."

p. 187 Literary Analysis Students may say that Dee doesn't bring her friends home because she hates her house and is ashamed of her family.

p. 187 Reading Strategy Students should circle the description of Dee's dress and jewelry and her activity of taking photographs. They should underline that fact that Maggie doesn't want to shake Dee's friend's hand. The sisters seem very different: Dee is flamboyant and active, while Maggie is shy and quiet.

p. 187 Reading Check Dee has changed her name to better reflect her African heritage. She feels her old name reflects the history of slavery.

p. 188 Culture Note Some students may say that Dee is interested in folk art because she has learned to appreciate her heritage and wants to preserve it. Others may think that folk art from her home will give Dee a chance to show off in front of her friends.

p. 188 Vocabulary and Pronunciation Students might say that they can picture Dee speaking very quickly.

p. 189 Stop to Reflect Some students may say that Dee wants the pieces of the churn to remember her family and her childhood home. Others may say that she wants to display her now-fashionable country heritage to her new friends.

p. 189 Read Fluently Students should read the sentence clearly, varying their tone and volume. Maggie may feel surprised, upset, and angry.

p. 189 English Language Development Possible singular subjects and verbs: narrator offers, she explains. *That's (that is), I don't.* Plural subject and verb: *They are, These are.*

p. 189 Literary Analysis Students might underline "pieces of dresses Grandma used to wear" and "did all this stitching by hand."

p. 190 Reading Check Students might circle "can't appreciate," "backward," or "everyday use."

p. 190 Stop to Reflect Some students will agree with Dee and others will disagree. Students should offer compelling reasons for either opinion.

p. 190 Reading Strategy Maggie views the quilts as something practical to be used to keep warm. The quilts remind her of her grandmother. Dee views the quilts as something priceless to be hung on a wall. The quilts remind her of her African American heritage.

p. 190 Stop to Reflect Some students will think that Dee would appreciate the quilts better and others will think that Maggie would. Students should offer compelling reasons for either opinion.

p. 191 Literary Analysis Students may say that Mama gives Maggie the quilts because she has promised them to her or because she is offended by Dee's assumption that she can just walk away with them, especially since she didn't want them when they were offered to her.

p. 191 English Language Development Students should circle *sat.*

p. 191 Stop to Reflect Maggie feels relaxed and happy after her sister leaves.

p. 192 Review and Assess

1. Their house burned down in a fire. They lost their home, and Maggie suffered burn scars.

2. Dee and a friend named Hakim-a-barber come to visit.

3. (1) "I never knew how lovely these benches are." (2) "Can I have these old quilts?"

4. Students might say that the narrator knows more about her heritage because she appreciates the history of the butter churn and remembers how her mother made the quilts from clothing scraps.

5. Maggie: she is thin and awkward. She is embarrassed by her scars. She is not bright but has a kind heart. She speaks quietly and slowly. Dee: "is lighter than Maggie, with nicer hair and a fuller figure." She wears brightly colored clothes and jewelry. She is bright, educated, and feels that she is better than her mother and sister. She usually gets what she

wants and has a temper. She speaks quickly and confidently.

6. Students might say that narrator gives the quilts to Maggie (1) because she feels sorry for her and (2) because she realizes that Maggie will truly appreciate them.

**Mother Tongue
by Amy Tan**

p. 196 Literary Analysis Students may underline "I cannot give you much more than personal opinions on the English language," "I spend a great deal of my time thinking about the power of language," and "Recently, I was made keenly aware of the different Englishes I do use."

p. 196 Reading Check Tan's mother comes to hear her give a talk about her writing. With her mother in the room, Tan realizes that her language changes when she speaks to her mother.

p. 197 Reading Check Students might say that when she speaks with her mother, Tan uses a kind of nonstandard English that reflects how her mother speaks.

p. 197 English Language Development Not waste money that way.

p. 197 Literary Analysis Students should underline "Lately, I've been giving more thought to the kind of English my mother speaks."

p. 198 Reading Check Students may circle "ashamed" or "because she expressed them imperfectly her thoughts were imperfect."

p. 198 Stop to Reflect Tan saw that people in stores, banks, and restaurants did not take her mother seriously. That evidence seemed to support her idea that her mother's thoughts are imperfect.

p. 199 Reading Strategy Tan believes the language spoken in immigrant families plays an important role in shaping the language of the children. As evidence, Tan points to how her mother's "limited" English shaped her own use of English and the fact that her test results in math were better than those in English. Some students might agree because they feel Tan's evidence is strong or because they have had similar experiences. Others might disagree because they feel Tan does not provide enough convincing evidence.

p. 199 Culture Note *Sample answers:*
• The overall purpose of standardized tests is to measure the level of skills that a student has in a certain subject, such as math or English.
• Types of standardized tests include state assessments, SATs, and ACTs.

p. 199 Vocabulary and Pronunciation *Sample answers:* Speaking Standard English was not Mrs. Tan's strong suit. Amy Tan's strong suit is writing fiction.

p. 200 Culture Note *Possible answers:*
• Gish Jen, Li-Young Lee
• *Typical American, The City in Which I Love You*
• Garrett Hongo, Hisaye Yamamoto
• *The River of Heaven, Seventeen Syllables and Other Stories*

p. 200 Read Fluently Students should read the paragraph clearly, varying their tone and volume appropriately. The four kinds of Englishes include 1. the "simple" English Tan speaks to her mother; 2. the "broken" English her mother uses with Tan; 3. Tan's "watered down" translation of her mother's Chinese; 4. Tan's translation of her mother's internal language, or her Chinese if she could speak in perfect English.

p. 201 Stop to Reflect *Possible answers:* 1. supportive 2. affectionate 3. inspirational

p. 202 Review and Assess

1. Language is important to Tan because she is a writer and because she has seen its influence in her mother's life and her own.

2. *Sample answer:* Tan uses Standard English when she speaks in public and nonstandard English with her mother.

3. *Sample answers:* (Effect 1) Tan had to call people for information on her mother's behalf. (Effect 2) Tan had better test results in math and science than she had in English. (Effect 3) Tan was steered away from writing by her teachers.

4. Students might say that Tan's mother inspired some of the stories that Tan wanted to write and also influenced her use of four different kinds of "Englishes" to capture the way her mother thinks and speaks.

5. *Sample answer:* Tan explores why her test results on achievement tests in English were lower than those in math or science.

6. *Sample answer:* Tan believes people who do not use Standard English often face prejudice. Some students will agree because they are convinced by Tan's evidence or have had similar experiences. Others will disagree because they do feel not convinced by the evidence Tan presents.

© **Pearson Education**, Inc.

Answers: Part 2

"The Earth on Turtle's Back" (Onondaga)

"When Grizzlies Walked Upright" (Modoc)

from **The Navajo Origin Legend (Navajo)**

from **The Iroquois Constitution (Iroquois) (p. 207)**

Summarize Main Idea

Sample Responses:

"The Earth on Turtle's Back:" Paragraph beginning "The Duck dove first"

Main Idea: All the animals tried to bring the Earth up, but failed.

Supporting Details: The duck dove first. He swam down and down, far beneath the surface, but floated back up. The beaver tried. He went even deeper, so deep that all was dark, but he could not reach the bottom either. The Loon tried. He was gone a long, long time, but he too failed.

"When Grizzlies Walked Upright:" Paragraph beginning "Then the Sky Spirit took his walking stick"

Main Idea: The Sky Spirit created the earth, as we know it.

Supporting Details: He began to put his finger to the ground here and there. Wherever he touched, a tree grew. The snow melted in his footsteps, and the water ran down in rivers.

The Navajo Origin Legend: Paragraph beginning "The white ear of corn had been changed"

Main Idea: The wind gives life.

Supporting Details: It was the wind that gave them life. It is the wind that gives life now. When this ceases to blow, we die.

The Iroquois Constitution: Paragraph beginning "If any man or any nation"

Main Idea: Anyone who follows the constitution is welcome.

Supporting Details: If any man or nation obeys the laws of the Great Peace and makes known their disposition to the lords of the confederacy; if their minds are clean and they are obedient and promise to obey the wishes of the confederate council.

"A Journey Through Texas" by Alvar Núñez Cabeza de Vaca

"Boulders Taller Than the Great Tower of Seville" by García López de Cárdenas (p. 208)

Sequence of Events

Sample Responses:

"A Journey Through Texas:"

While waiting for the women to return, a number of the Native Americans died.

After that, Castillo and Estevanico left with the two women to find the Native American inhabitants the women had found.

When Castillo and Estevanico returned, they said that they had found permanent houses with inhabitants and food.

The explorers then thanked God for the news.

After that, they separated from the first group of Native Americans.

The next place the group went, they were met with food and shelter.

Finally, the explorers left to go in search of maize.

"Boulders Taller Than the Great Tower of Seville:"

After Don Pedro de Tovar gave his report to the general, Don García López de Cárdenas was sent to explore the river.

After receiving provisions from the natives, he traveled 20 days to the river.

After three days trying to get down to the river, three explorers went down.

They returned later that afternoon, unable to get down.

After exploring for several more days, the group turned back because they could not get water.

from The Interesting Narrative of the Life of Olaudah Equiano by Olaudah Equiano (p. 209)

Classify Descriptive Details

Sample Responses:

Sights: perspirations, galling of the chains, scene of horror

Sounds: sickness, galling of the chains, groans

Smells: unfit for respiration, filth

Other details: almost suffocated, almost inconceivable

from Journal of the First Voyage to America by Christopher Columbus (p. 210)

Break Down Sentences

Sample Responses:

1. Sentence: It was a great affliction to me to be ignorant of their natures, for I am very certain they are all valuable; specimens of them and of the plants I have preserved.

   Sentence broken into parts: I was sorry not to know more about the different trees. I am certain they are all valuable. I have kept specimens of the trees and plants.

2. Sentence: Going round one of these lakes, I saw a snake, which we killed, and I have kept the skin for your Highnesses; upon being discovered he took to the water; whither we followed him, as it was not deep, and dispatched him with our lances; he was seven spans in length; I think there are many more such about here.

Sentence broken into parts: We saw a snake about seven spans in length. When we saw the snake, he took off in the water. We followed him, since the water was not deep. We killed him with our lances. We kept it for the king and queen. There are probably more snakes like him.

3. Sentence: I discovered also the aloe tree, and am determined to take on board the ship tomorrow, ten quintals of it, as I am told it is valuable.

   Sentence broken into parts: I discovered the aloe tree. I am planning to take some of it on board tomorrow. I am told it is valuable.

4. Sentence: We asked him in return, for water, and after I had gone on board the ship, the natives came down to the shore with their calabashes full, and showed great pleasure in presenting us with it.

   Sentence broken into parts: We asked him for water in return. I went on board the ship. The natives came with their calabashes full of water, and happily gave it to us.

from The General History of Virginia
by John Smith

from Of Plymouth Plantation
by William Bradford (p. 211)

Paraphrase

Sample Responses:

Sentence 1: But now was all our provision spent, the sturgeon gone, all helps abandoned, each hour expecting the fury of the savages; when God, the patron of all good endeavors, in that desperate extremity so changed the hearts of the savages that they brought such plenty of their fruits and provision as no man wanted.

Sentence 1 paraphrase: When all the food was gone and we expected the natives to attack us, God changed the hearts of the natives, and they brought enough food for everyone.

Sentence 2: Notwithstanding, within an hour after, they tied him to a tree, and as many as could stand about him prepared to shoot him, but the King holding up the compass in his hand, they all laid down their bows and arrows and in a triumphant manner led him to Orapaks where he was after their manner kindly feasted and well used.

Sentence 2 paraphrase: They tied him to a tree and prepared to shoot him. But when the King held up the compass, they all laid down their weapons and took him to Orapaks where he was well treated.

Sentence 3: Now every once in four or five days, Pocahontas with her attendants brought him so much provision that saved many of their lives, that else for all this had starved with hunger.

Sentence 3 paraphrase: Every few days Pocahontas and her helpers brought enough food to save the lives of many people.

"To My Dear and Loving Husband"
by Anne Bradstreet

"Huswifery" by Edward Taylor (p. 212)
Restate Poetic Language
Sample Responses:

1. Poetic Language: I prize thy love more than whole mines of gold
   More Familiar Language: I prize your love more than gold

2. Poetic Language: Thy love is such
   I can no way repay
   More Familiar Language: I cannot repay you for your love

3. Poetic Language: Then while we live, in love let's persevere
   More Familiar Language: While we live, let's keep our love strong.

4. Poetic Language: That when we live no more, we may live ever
   More Familiar Language: So that when we die, our love will live on

5. Poetic Language: Make me, O Lord, Thy spinning wheel complete
   More Familiar Language: Make me your spinning wheel, Lord

6. Poetic Language: Then weave the web Thyself. The yarn is fine.
   More Familiar Language: Then weave the web yourself. The yarn is fragile.

7. Poetic Language: Then dye the same in heavenly colors choice.
   More Familiar Language: Then dye the fabric in wonderful colors.

8. Poetic Language: Then clothe therewith mine understanding, will,
   More Familiar Language: Control my understanding and will

9. Poetic Language: Then mine apparel shall display before Ye/ That I am clothed in holy robes for glory
   More Familiar Language: Then I will be dressed for your glory

from Sinners in the Hands of an Angry God by
Jonathan Edwards (p. 213)
Question Author's Purpose
Sample responses:

4. Q: What is God's wrath like?
   A: God's wrath is like rushing water that is dammed but will overflow when he releases it.

© **PEARSON** Education, Inc.

5. Q: What prevents God from releasing his wrath?
   A: God's will and pleasure keeps him from releasing his wrath.

6. Q: When did destruction come upon similar people?
   A: It came when they were not expecting it.

7. Q: What does God think of you?
   A: He loathes you.

8. Q: What does the writer want you to think about?
   A: He wants you to think about the potential of Hell.

9. Q: When God sees your suffering, will he stop his wrath?
   A: No, he will not.

10. Q: When does God want to show pity?
    A: He is always ready to show pity.

11. Q: What happens if you stay unconverted?
    A: You will suffer in front of all the heavenly creatures.

12. Q: What is the duration of the suffering?
    A: The suffering is forever.

13. Q: Who is being addressed?
    A: People in the congregation who have not been born again.

14. Q: What is the extraordinary opportunity?
    A: Christ's mercy is available today.

15. Q: What does the speaker want everyone to do?
    A: He wants them to fly from God's wrath and come to Christ.

from The Autobiography and *from* Poor Richard's Almanack by Benjamin Franklin (p. 214)

Identify Paragraph Topics

Sample Responses:

Topic for second paragraph: Franklin has to define the virtues for himself.

Supporting details: 1. Franklin finds that different people define the virtues differently. 2. Temperance meant food and drink for some people, but applied to all pleasures for other people. 3. Franklin chooses 13 virtues and defines them.

The Declaration of Independence by Thomas Jefferson

from The Crisis, Number 1, by Thomas Paine (p. 215)

Simplify Long Sentences

Sample Responses:

from "The Declaration of Independence"

Long sentence: And for support of this declaration, with a firm reliance on the protection of divine providence, we mutually pledge to each other our lives, our fortunes and our sacred honor.

Simplified sentence: We pledge to support this document with all that we have.

from The Crisis, Number 1

Long sentence: I have as little superstition in me as any man living, but my secret opinion has ever been and still is, that God Almighty will not give up a people to military destruction, or leave them unsupportedly to perish, who have so earnestly sought to avoid the calamities of war, by every decent method which wisdom could invent.

Simplified sentence: Because we have tried so hard to avoid war, I believe that God will not allow us to be destroyed.

"An Hymn to the Evening" and "To His Excellency, General Washington" by Phillis Wheatley (p. 216)

Restate Poetic Language

Sample Responses:

from "To His Excellency, General Washington"

Poetic Language: Enough thou know'st them in the fields of fight

More Familiar Language: You know about his battle successes

Poetic Language: Proceed, great Chief, with virtue on thy side

More Familiar Language: Go forward in your virtue

from "An Hymn to the Evening"

Poetic Language: Soon as the sun forsook the eastern main

More Familiar Language: As the sun began to set

Poetic Language: Let placid slumbers soothe each weary mind

More Familiar Language: Let everyone have peaceful sleep

"Speech in the Virginia Convention" by Patrick Henry

"Speech in the Convention" by Benjamin Franklin (p. 217)

List Key Ideas

Sample Responses:

from "Speech in the Virginia Convention"

Key idea of final paragraph #6: We should go to war.

Supporting details: We will not grow stronger by inaction. If we depend on God, we are not too weak. Our cause makes us invincible. God and other friends will fight the battle for us. The battle is not always won by the strongest party. Our only options now are slavery.

from "Speech in the Convention"

Key idea of first paragraph: Though I don't agree with everything in the Constitution, I may someday.

Supporting details: In the past I have changed my opinion after further thought. The older I am the more I doubt my own judgments. Many people think they know everything, but do not.

"Letter to Her Daughter From the New White House" by Abigail Adams

from Letters From an American Farmer by Michel-Guillaume Jean de Crèvecoeur (p. 218)

Summarize Main Idea

Sample Responses:

"Letter to Her Daughter From the New White House"

Main idea of second paragraph: Mrs. Adams would be happy with a warm place, but they are having trouble with heat.

Supporting details: With forests around, there is no wood because no one is around to cut it. One man supplied enough wood to dry out the place. But he cannot do any more. They do not even have grates so they can use coal.

from Letters From an American Farmer

Main idea of second paragraph: The laws and industry of the new country have made rightful citizens of many people.

Supporting details: In other countries, many of these people were poor, but not citizens. The laws of the United States give them protection. They receive payment for their work. They are free people.

"The Devil and Tom Walker" by Washington Irving (p. 219)

Summarize Paragraphs

Sample Responses:

Main idea of third paragraph: Tom Walker and his wife were a poor and miserly couple.

Supporting details: They were so miserly that they cheated each other. His wife hid everything. Tom Walker always looked for her hidden belongings. Their house was forlorn-looking. No one came to visit. A starving horse lived in their yard.

"A Psalm of Life" and "The Tide Rises, The Tide Falls" by Henry Wadsworth Longfellow (p. 220)

Recognize Metaphors

Sample Responses:

2. They are both temporary.
3. They are both living creatures.
4. They both leave something to show behind.
5. They both are moving forward.
6. They both are moving backward.
7. They both wipe something away.

"Thanatopsis" by William Cullen Bryant
"Old Ironsides" by Oliver Wendell Holmes
"The First Snowfall" by James Russell Lowell
from Snowbound by John Greenleaf Whittier (p. 221)

Explain Poetic Phrases

Sample Responses:

5. Line from "Thanatopsis:" So live, that when thy summons comes to join/The innumerable caravan

   Explanation: "Thy" means "your." "Summons" refers to a call. The innumerable caravan refers to all the people that have gone before in death. The line refers to when you die.

6. Line from "Old Ironsides:" No more shall feel the victor's tread

   Explanation: The boat will not have anyone walking on it again.

7. Line from "The First Snowfall:" That my kiss was given to her sister. /Folded close under deepening snow.

   Explanation: "Folded close under" means "lying beneath." The poet is referring to a dead child buried in the ground.

8. Line from Snowbound: The cock his crested helmet bent

   Explanation: A cock is a rooster. His crest looks like a helmet.

"Crossing the Great Divide" by Meriwether Lewis

"The Most Sublime Spectacle on Earth" by John Wesley Powell (p. 222)

Outline Main Idea and Supporting Details

Sample Responses:

from "Crossing the Great Divide"

Main idea of first paragraph: The travelers are ready to travel again.

Details about the main idea: An Indian reported that the white men were coming. They arrived happily. The canoes arrived at noon. They found out they would be able to get more horses.

"The Fall of the House of Usher" and "The Raven" by Edgar Allan Poe (p. 223)

Sequence of Events

Sample Responses:

"The Fall of the House of Usher"

One stormy night, Roderick and the narrator hear many sounds, and Madeline reappears out of her coffin.

© Pearson Education, Inc.

Finally, Madeline and Roderick both die, and their house collapses on itself.

"The Raven"

One night there was a tapping at the door, and the narrator is frightened.

A Raven flies in.

The Raven speaks the word "Nevermore" to answer all the narrator's questions.

The narrator begins to think the Raven is there to taunt him about his lost love, Lenore.

The narrator begs the Raven to leave, but it stays forever.

"The Minster's Black Veil" by Nathaniel Hawthorne (p. 224)
Analyze Characters' Behavior

Sample Responses:

Character: The people of the congregation

What the character does: Turn around in their seats

Why the character does it: To see Mr. Hooper

Character: Several women

What: Left the church

Why: They were upset by the veil

Character: Elizabeth

What: Walked out of the door

Why: Because Mr. Hooper would not lift the veil one time

from Moby-Dick by Herman Melville (p. 225)
Identify Chain of Events

Sample Responses:

Event 3: The crew chases the whale for three days.

Event 4: Starbuck wonders if he is doing the right thing.

Event 5: Smaller boats are lowered to chase the whale.

from Nature, from Self-Reliance, "The Snowstorm," and "Concord Hymn" by Ralph Waldo Emerson (p. 226)
Reword Author's Ideas

Sample Responses:

From *Nature*: Crossing a bare common, in snow puddles, at twilight, under a clouded sky, without having in my thoughts any occurrence of special good fortune, I have enjoyed a perfect exhilaration.

Reworded: Sometimes walking across the land in the early evening, I have experienced an unexpected thrill.

From *Self-Reliance:* Whoso would be a man must be a nonconformist.

Reworded: Whoever wants to be fully human cannot conform to all of society's expectations.

"The Snowstorm:" Come see the north wind's masonry.

Reworded: See what the snow has done.

"Concord Hymn:" And fired the shot heard round the world

Reworded: Started a war that changed the whole world

from Walden and from Civil Disobedience by Henry David Thoreau (p. 227)
Identify Key Ideas

from Walden

5. As long as possible live free and uncommitted.

6. The morning wind forever blows, the poem of creation is uninterrupted; but few are the ears that hear it.

7. I wanted to live deep and suck out all the marrow of life.

8. I say, let your affairs be as two or three, and not a hundred or a thousand.

9. How worn and dusty, then, must be the highways of the world, how deep the ruts of tradition and conformity!

10. Only that day dawns to which we are awake.

from Civil Disobedience

1. Government is at best but an expedient; but most governments are usually, and all governments are sometimes, inexpedient.

2. The character inherent in the American people has done all that has been accomplished.

3. I ask for, not at once no government, but at once a better government.

Emily Dickinson's Poetry (p. 228)
Form a Mental Picture

Students should continue jotting down notes on their mental images. Sketches should attempt to accurately capture these images.

Walt Whitman's Poetry (p. 229)
Identify Theme

Sample Responses:

from "Song of Myself"

Theme: Every individual is worth celebrating.

Details relating to theme:

1. An individual's good qualities belong to everyone.

2. Everyone lives on in some way.

3. Many experiences—like harvesting—are inspiring.

4. Everyone fills up his or her life with experiences that make that person unique.

© Pearson Education, Inc.

from "I Hear America Singing"

Theme: America is filled with many kinds of people.

Details relating to theme:

1. America sings different songs, including those of mechanics, carpenters, masons, boatmen, mothers, wives, girls, and so on.
2. Each person sings a song specific to his or her individuality.

"A Noiseless Patient Spider"

Theme: Each soul is venturing forward trying to make a life.

Details relating to theme:

1. A spider ventures forth to explore its surroundings.
2. Human souls are similar to the spider.
3. A soul ventures forth wondering, venturing, and making bridges.

"An Episode of War" by Stephen Crane

"Willie Has Gone to the War" words by George Cooper, music by Stephen Foster (p. 230)

Form a Mental Picture

Students should continue jotting down notes on their mental images. Sketches should attempt to accurately capture these images.

"Swing Low, Sweet Chariot" and "Go Down, Moses" Spirituals (p. 231)

Explain Poetic Phrases

Sample Responses:

Poetic Phrase: Jordan

What It Means or Symbolizes: The crossing over Jordan brought the Israelites out of slavery. The reference symbolizes freedom from slavery.

Poetic Phrase: band of angels

What It Means or Symbolizes: A band of angels would come to take someone "home"—through death.

Poetic Phrase: The story of Moses

What It Means or Symbolizes: The whole song uses the story of Moses taking the Israelites out of Egypt as a metaphor for the American slaves being freed.

from My Bondage and My Freedom by Frederick Douglass (p. 232)

Reword Author's Ideas

Sample Responses:

1. Actual: In attaining this knowledge, I was compelled to resort to indirections by no means congenial to my nature, and which were really humiliating to me.

   Reworded: To learn to read and write I had to do some things that I am not proud of doing.

2. Actual: She either thought it unnecessary, or she lacked the depravity indispensable to shutting me up in mental darkness.

   Reworded: She was not cruel enough to prevent me from learning.

3. Actual: How could she, then, treat me as a brute, without a mighty struggle with all the noble powers of her own soul.

   Reworded: Her soul told her that she could not treat me as ignorant.

4. Actual: There was no sorrow nor suffering for which she had not a tear, and there was no innocent joy for which she did not a smile.

   Reworded: She cried over sad things and rejoiced over the good.

5. Actual: Seized with a determination to learn to read, at any cost, I hit upon many expedients to accomplish the desired end.

   Reworded: Determined to read, I found ways to do it.

"An Occurrence at Owl Creek Bridge" by Ambrose Bierce (p. 233)

Plot a Story Map

Sample Responses:

Setting: Northern Alabama

Characters: Peyton Farquhar

What the characters want: He wants to escape and be reunited with his wife and children

What blocks their wants: He is being hanged for a crime

Main events: Peyton hears that the Yankees may cross Owl Creek bridge. He determines to destroy the bridge. He is caught. The soldiers prepare to hang him. He imagines an escape

Climax (high point): He believes he is ready to run into his wife's arms

Conclusion: He is dead.

"The Gettysburg Address" and "Second Inaugural Address" by Abraham Lincoln

"Letter to His Son" by Robert E. Lee (p. 234)

Summarize Main Idea

Sample Responses:

"The Gettysburg Address"

Original: Now we are engaged in a great civil war, testing whether that nation, or any nation so conceived and dedicated, can long endure.

Summary: This war is testing whether a nation with these principles can last.

© Pearson Education, Inc.

"Second Inaugural Address"

Original: Both parties deprecated war; but one of them would *make* war rather than let the nation survive; and the other would *accept* war rather than let it perish.

Summary: One side made war to destroy the nation, and the other side fought to keep it together.

"Letter to His Son"

Original: Still, a Union that can only be maintained by swords and bayonets, and in which strife and civil war are to take the place of brotherly love and kindness, has no charm for me.

Summary: A country that requires war rather than love and kindness
is no place for me.

from Civil War Diaries, Journals, and Letters (p. 235)

Identify Chain of Events

Sample Responses:

from Mary Chesnut's Civil War

2. Seven hundred men were sent over to demand the surrender.
4. That night, the troops fire on Fort Sumter.
5. April 13, 1861; Fort Sumter is on fire.
6. April 15, 1861; Fort Sumter surrenders.
7. Finally, Colonel Chestnut returns home.

"Recollections of a Private"

1. The writer shaved.
2. He enlisted.
3. His uniform didn't fit.
4. The activity was less exciting than he anticipated.
5. Finally word came that they were to head to Washington.

"A Confederate Account of the Battle of Gettysburg"

1. Orders came to attack.
2. The troops attacked with spirit, even though their numbers had been decreased.
3. One group of soldiers went ahead of the others.
4. Finally the soldiers are beaten back.

"An Account of the Battle of Bull Run"

1. Yesterday a victory was won.
2. Stonewall Jackson was wounded, but not seriously.
3. His horse was hurt, too.
4. God gave the victory.

"Reaction to the Emancipation Proclamation"

1. Reverend Turner heard about the Proclamation.
2. He ran to the newspaper office to read a copy of it.

3. People were grabbing it, so he grabbed part and ran off.
4. As people saw him coming, they cheered.
5. As it was read, people were very excited.
6. Finally, many people passed the White House to thank the President.

"An Account of an Experience With Discrimination"

1. A streetcar conductor will not stop for Sojourner Truth, so she is dragged several yards.
2. Her friend Josephine gets them to stop, and reports the conductor.
3. The conductor is fired.
4. Later, another conductor tells her to get off.
5. Again, the conductor is reported and then fired.

"The Boys' Ambition" *from* Life on the Missisippi and "The Notorious Jumping Frog of Calaveras County" by Mark Twain (p. 236)

Recognize Humor

Sample Responses:

from "The Boys' Ambition"

"He would speak of the lapboard side of a horse in an easy, natural way that would make one wish he was dead." This is funny because it is an exaggeration—the listener would not really wish the boy were dead.

"The Notorious Jumping Frog of Calaveras County"

"Simon Wheeler backed me into a corner and blockaded me there with his chair, and then sat down and reeled off the monotonous narrative which follows this paragraph." This is funny because it means Simon trapped him. The word "monotonous" is funny, too, because the story is not monotonous at all.

"The Outcasts of Poker Flat" by Bret Harte (p. 237)

Make a Character Chart

Sample Responses:

Several men exchange glances as John Oakhurst steps outside because they are considering hanging him.

Duchess cries and Mother Shipton and Uncle Billy swear because they have been removed from Poker Flat.

The Duchess gets off her horse because she refuses to go any further.

Uncle Billy becomes less angry because he is drunk.

"Heading West" by Miriam Davis Colt
"I Will Fight No More Forever" by Chief Joseph (p. 238)

Use a Chain-of-Events Organizer

Sample Responses:

"Heading West"

Event 2: They say goodbye to everyone and travel to Kansas City.

Event 3: They travel out into the prairie to join the Vegetarian Group.

Event 4: When they finally arrive they discover that the settlement is not developed properly.

"I Will Fight No More Forever"

Event 1: Chief Joseph is tired of fighting.

Event 2: Many important chiefs are dead.

Event 3: They have nothing to keep them warm.

Event 4: They are out of food.

Event 5: Chief Joseph is too tired and sad to fight anymore.

"To Build a Fire" by Jack London (p. 239)

Identify Sensory Images

Sample Responses:

Sight: pure white; dark hairline; curved and twisted; protruding bundle; gray-coated; roaring fire

Sound: sharp, explosive crackle; roaring fire

Touch: cold and uncomfortable; warm moccasins; hot supper; naked skin; numb nose; fire

Taste: hot supper; bacon grease; tobacco

Smell: hot supper; bacon; tobacco

"The Story of an Hour" by Kate Chopin (p. 240)

Analyze Characters' Behavior

Sample Responses:

Richards rushes to get the information to Mrs. Mallard because he doesn't want her to find out from someone less caring.

Mrs. Mallard weeps with wild abandon because she is overwhelmed at the news.

Mrs. Mallard collapses in a chair because she is exhausted.

Josephine kneels by the door listening because she is worried about her sister.

Mrs. Mallard dies because she is shocked to see her husband living.

"April Showers" by Edith Wharton (p. 241)

Identify a Chain of Events

Sample Responses:

Event 2: She sends it off for publication.

Event 3: Theodora receives an acceptance letter.

Event 4: The magazine comes out, but another author is given credit.

Event 5: She travels to Boston for an explanation.

Event 6: The editor tells her it was a mistake.

Event 7: Finally, her father meets her at the train and comforts her by telling her of a similar experience.

"Douglass" and "We Wear the Mask" by Paul Laurence Dunbar (p. 242)

Rephrase Poetry as Prose

Sample Responses:

"Douglass"

You saw the future and the country heard your voice. The battle was not over, and is still not. Now the battle continues, and we need your guidance and comfort.

"We Wear the Mask"

Our faces lie because they hide the pain in our hearts. Why should the world notice our pain? We cry to God from tortured souls, but the world only sees the mask.

"Luke Havergal" and "Richard Cory" by Edwin Arlington Robinson
"Lucinda Matlock" and "Richard Bone" by Edgar Lee Masters (p. 243)

Gather Evidence About Characters

Sample Responses:

"Lucinda Matlock"

was a hard worker: "I spun, I wove, I kept the house, I nursed the sick, I made the garden"

loved life: "It takes life to love Life."

"Luke Havergal"

loves a woman who has died: "The leaves will whisper there of her"

is grieved: "there is not a dawn in eastern skies/To rift the fiery night that's in your eyes"

"Richard Cory"

was a gentleman: "We people on the pavement looked at him"

was appealing: "he fluttered pulses when he said, 'Good-morning'"

was wealthy: "richer than a king"

was unhappy: "Went home and put a bullet through his head."

"Richard Bone"

he questions things: "I did not know whether what they told me/Was true or false"

he believed the epitaphs were not true: "made myself party to the false chronicles"

© Pearson Education, Inc.

"A Wagner Matinée" by Willa Cather (p. 244)

Outline Main Idea and Supporting Details

Main idea of second paragraph:

The narrator has a wave of memories of his aunt.

Details about the main idea.

1. The aunt's name reminds him of her physical appearance.
2. He feels like a stranger among his things.
3. He feels like he is a young boy again, living with his aunt.
4. He remembers playing the organ in her parlor while she knitted mittens for the workers.

Main idea of third paragraph:

The narrator meets his aunt at the station and takes her home.

1. He has trouble finding her among the crowd.
2. She is the last to get off the train.
3. She is covered with dust and soot.
4. The narrator's landlady puts her to bed right away.

"The Love Song of J. Alfred Prufrock" by T. S. Eliot (p. 245)

Paraphrase

Sample Responses:

The silent streets lead you to ask questions.

The yellow fog settles silently over everything.

Imagist Poets (p. 246)

Identify Sensory Images

Sample Responses:

"This is Just to Say"

Sight: plums; icebox

Touch: icebox; cold

Taste: plums; delicious; sweet; cold

Smell: plums

"Pear Tree"

Sight: silver dust; great mass; flower; white leaf; silver; white pear; flower-tufts; thick; purple hearts

Touch: higher than my arms reach

Taste: ripe fruits

Smell: ripe fruits

"Winter Dreams" by F. Scott Fitzgerald (p. 247)

Respond to Characters' Actions

Students should list characters and their significant actions. Following each action they should say whether they agree or disagree with the way the character handled the situation and why or they could say what they would have done in the same situation.

"The Turtle" *from* The Grapes of Wrath by John Steinbeck (p. 248)

Outline Main Idea and Supporting Details

Sample Responses:

Main idea of final paragraph:

The turtle plants the seeds.

Details about the main idea:

1. A truck comes along and flips the turtle off the highway.
2. The turtle lies on its back.
3. The turtle sticks out its legs and flips itself over, dumping the seeds into the ground.
4. The turtle drags dirt over the seeds.

"anyone lived in a pretty how town" and "old age sticks" by E. E. Cummings

"The Unknown Citizen" by W. H. Auden (p. 249)

Interpret Poetic Images

Sample Responses:

2. The words represent the seasons and the times of day.
3. She felt what he felt; his happiness was hers, and his grief was hers, too.
1. The image is one of old people putting up signs to keep people off a yard.
2. The young people pull the signs off. The feeling is one of youthful disrespect and energy.
3. They laughed at the old people for yelling about the signs.
1. He was reliable. He may not have enjoyed his work, but people depended on him.
2. His actions were predictable and steady.
3. He had all the things that "normal" people had. He was an everyman.

"The Far and the Near" by Thomas Wolfe (p. 250)

Identify Key Ideas

Sample Responses:

Paragraph 2: A few minutes after two every day, the train went by.

Paragraph 3: Every day for twenty years the woman in the cottage waved to the train engineer.

© Pearson Education, Inc.

"Of Modern Poetry" and "Anecdote of the Jar" by Wallace Stevens

"Ars Poetica" by Archibald MacLeish

"Poetry" by Marianne Moore (p. 251)

Explain and Respond to Poetry

2. Poetry has to apply to the people who read it.
3. I put a jar on a hill in Tennessee.
4. Grass grew up around it.
5. A poem should be real and useful to people.
6. A poem should be beautiful in itself.
7. I also dislike poetry that isn't about real things.
8. One sees that there is a place for the real.

"In Another Country" by Ernest Hemingway

"The Corn Planting" by Sherwood Anderson

"A Worn Path" by Eudora Welty (p. 252)

Make a Character Chart

Sample Responses:

"In Another Country"

The doctor asks the narrator what sport he played best before the war because he wants the narrator to play it again.

The major cried because his wife had died.

"The Corn Planting"

Hal wanted the narrator to go with him to the Hutchenson's because he had to tell them that Will was dead.

Hal and the narrator went for a walk to put off telling the Hutchenson's.

The Hutchenson's plant corn in the night as a way of coping with their son's death.

"A Worn Path"

Phoenix Jackson walks to town to buy medicine for her grandson.

"Chicago" and "Grass" by Carl Sandburg (p. 253)

Reword Poet's Ideas

Sample Responses:

"Chicago," Lines 6–9: Chicago is full of hardships and wickedness.

Lines 10–15: Chicago is also full of people that are happy to be alive and who work hard to build the city into something great.

Lines 20–22: The strong city is happy to be what it is.

"Grass," Lines 1–3: The grass covers the bodies buried from the wars.

Lines 7–9: After a few years, the grass hides the battlegrounds.

"The Jilting of Granny Weatherall" by Katherine Anne Porter (p. 254)

Make a Timeline

Sample Responses:

20: She was jilted by George on her wedding day; She was married to John and kept house and cared for her children.

40: She had milk leg and pneumonia.

60: She thought she was going to die, and made trips to see all her family members.

80: Doctor Harry checks her; Father Connelly comes; her children arrive; she dies.

"Race at Morning" and "Nobel Prize Acceptance Speech" by William Faulkner (p. 255)

Understand Dialect/Summarize the Main Idea

Sample Responses:

2. It was just getting dark.
3. I had fed the horse, climbed down the bank to the boat, and shoved off when I saw him.
4. I could see the rocking chair he was carrying
5. and I knew it was him going back to the fork in the bayou.
6. as if the game wardens had told him how he could disappear without anyone knowing where.

Robert Frost's Poetry (p. 256)

Restate Poetry as Prose

Sample Responses:

"Birches"

Lines 1–3: When I see birch trees bending, I think a boy has been swinging on them.

Lines 50–53: I hope I will not die.

"Mending Wall"

Lines 5–9: Hunters also destroy walls when they hunt for rabbits.

"Out, Out—"

Lines 1–3: The buzz saw cut sticks, making sweet-smelling dust.

Lines 10–13: I wish they would let me stop working so that I could enjoy some freedom.

"Stopping by Woods on a Snowy Evening"

Lines 1–4: I know whose property this is, but he lives in the village,
so I can be here.

Lines 5–8: The horse probably thinks it's strange to stop in a deserted place.

"Acquainted With the Night"

Lines 1–3: I have spent a lot of time out in the night.

Lines 5–6: I have walked by the watchmen and avoided looking at him so I didn't have to explain where I had been.

© Pearson Education, Inc.

"The Gift Outright"

Lines 1–3: The land possessed us before we knew it.

Lines 8–11: We were weak until we realized that we had to give ourselves to the land.

"The Night the Ghost Got In" by James Thurber

from Here Is New York by E. B. White (p. 257)

Identify Paragraph Topics

Sample Responses:

"The Night the Ghost Got In"

Paragraph 2: The ghost's footsteps kept going around the dining room table.

Paragraph 3: The narrator and his brother went to see the ghost, but both ended up running back to their rooms in fright.

from Here Is New York

Paragraph 1: New York City is unlike any other city in the world.

Paragraph 2: Manhattan's height makes it unique.

from Dust Tracks on a Road by Zora Neale Hurston (p. 258)

Analyze Characters

Sample Responses:

The white women came to town to visit Zora's school.

Mrs. Calhoun held a switch in her hand to make sure that the children behaved.

Zora read dramatically because she loved the story and wanted to show off.

The women bring her clothes and books because she does not have any of her own.

"The Negro Speaks of Rivers," "Ardella," "Dream Variations," and "Refugee in America" by Langston Hughes

"The Tropics in New York" by Claude McKay (p. 259)

React to Poetry

Students should continue listing lines from various poems. They should then record their reactions to the lines and what the poem has made them feel.

"From the Dark Tower" by Countee Cullen

"A Black Man Talks of Reaping" by Arna Bontemps

"Storm Ending" by Jean Toomer (p. 260)

Explain Poetic Images

Sample Responses:

2. Seeds require work. This image gives me the impression of slow growth and lots of labor.

1. Picking cotton is hard work. In this case, the hard work isn't even done on their own land. It is unjust that the children have to always work for other people.

2. Bitter fruit is not satisfying. People never want to feed something bitter to their children.

1. The image makes me think of times I have been in storms.

"The Life You Save May Be Your Own" by Flannery O'Connor (p. 261)

Analyze Characters' Behavior

Sample Responses:

The girl jumps up because she is excited.

Mr. Shiftlet tips his hat to say hello.

Mr. Shiftlet gives the girl chewing gum to be friendly.

The daughter made loud sounds because she thought he was going to burn himself.

"The First Seven Years" by Bernard Malamud (p. 262)

Make a Timeline

Sample Responses:

Section 1: Feld admires Max for his diligence. Feld is grieved by Miriam's indifference. Max brings some shoes to be repaired. Feld encourages him to ask Miriam out for a date.

Section 2: Feld loses Sobel. Max and Miriam go out twice. Miriam is not impressed. Feld discovers that his new assistant is stealing from him and has a heart attack.

Section 3: Feld drags himself to see Sobel to ask him to return to work. Sobel says he won't. Sobel says he loves Miriam. Feld says Miriam won't marry him. Sobel cries. Feld says he can talk to Miriam in two years. Sobel returns to work.

"The Brown Chest" by John Updike (p. 263)

Form a Mental Picture

Students should record notes on the various scenes mentioned. Sketches should attempt to depict these scenes as Updike describes them.

"Hawthorne" by Robert Lowell

"Gold Glade" by Robert Penn Warren

"Traveling Through the Dark" by William Stafford

"The Light Comes Brighter" and "The Adamant" by Theodore Roethke (p. 264)

Restate Poetry as Prose

Sample Responses:

"Gold Glade"

Lines 5–10: By the limestone edge of the gorge, was rushing water that went down and down.

Lines 11–15: Above the gorge, the sky showed through the leaves and it drew me on. I found the gold glade.

"Hawthorne"

Lines 1–8: The streets of Hawthorne's Salem are ordinary, flat, with old wooden houses.

"Traveling Through the Dark"

Lines 1–4: I found a dead deer and planned to roll it into the canyon so no cars would run into it.

"The Light Comes Brighter"

Lines 1–4: The light from the east is brighter. The sound of crows and thawing ice is sharper.

"The Adamant"

Lines 1–4: Truth cannot be crushed by anything.

"Average Waves in Unprotected Waters" by Anne Tyler (p. 265)

Identify Chain of Events

Sample Responses:

1. Bet wakes Arnold, feeds him his breakfast, and gets him dressed.

3. Bet buys train tickets, and she and Arnold get on the train.

6. They go to the hospital and Bet leaves Arnold there.

7. Bet returns to the train station and listens to the mayor give a speech while she waits for her train.

from The Names by N. Scott Momaday

"Mint Snowball" by Naomi Shihab Nye

"Suspended" by Joy Harjo (p. 266)

Summarize Paragraphs

Sample Responses:

"The Names"

Paragraph beginning "I sometimes think:" I have to acknowledge my racial heritage so I can really be myself.

Paragraph beginning "It happened so:" When I was thirteen I got a horse named Pecos that changed my life.

"Mint Snowball"

Paragraph beginning "My great-grandfather had:" My grandfather's specialty, Mint Snowball, was a favorite of everyone.

Paragraph beginning "Before my great-grandfather died:" My great-grandfather sold the recipe and disappointed his family because they never knew how to make Mint Snowball.

"Suspended"

Paragraph beginning "One I was so small:" When I was small I heard music that was magical.

Paragraph beginning "My rite of passage:" The jazz I heard made me recognize myself as a human being.

"Everyday Use" by Alice Walker (p. 267)

Analyze Characters

Sample Responses:

Maggie walks with a shuffle because she was burned in a fire.

Maggie tries to go back to the house because she is nervous about seeing Dee.

Maggie falls back because she is nervous about Dee's boyfriend.

Mama keeps the quilt for Maggie because she thinks it is rightfully hers.

from The Woman Warrior by Maxine Hong Kingston (p. 268)

Identify Paragraph Topics

Sample Responses:

Paragraph 2: Brave Orchid's children were not sitting with their mother.

Paragraph 3: Brave Orchid had a lot of food with her.

Paragraph 4: Brave Orchid thinks about her son who is a soldier somewhere in southeast Asia.

"Antojos" by Julia Alvarez (p. 269)

Sequence Events

Event 2: Yolanda travels north looking for guava stands.

Event 3: Yolanda stops at a cantina and asks a woman for guavas.

Event 4: A group of boys says they will show her guavas, and they go off in the car.

Event 5: They find, gather, and eat many guavas.

Event 6: They have a flat tire and a group of men approaches carrying machetes.

Event 7: The men are friendly and change the tire for Yolanda.

"Freeway 280" by Lorna Dee Cervantes

"Who Burns for the Perfection of Paper" by Martín Espada

"Most Satisfied by Snow" by Diana Chang

"Hunger in New York City" by Simon Ortiz

"What For" by Garrett Hongo (p. 270)

Reword Poet's Ideas

"Who Burns for the Perfection of Paper"

Lines 1–5: When I was sixteen I worked making legal pads.

Lines 22–27: When I was in law school ten years later, I remembered all the work that went into making a legal pad.

"Most Satisfied by Snow"

Lines 1–5: Fog and space are everywhere, but hard to see.

© Pearson Education, Inc.

Lines 6–11: But snow is visible and makes everything beautiful.

"Hunger in New York City"

Lines 1–4: Hunger will always find you; it cannot be avoided.

Lines 5–11: Hunger makes you want many things like food, wisdom, and friends.

from The Mortgaged Heart
by Carson McCullers

"Onomatopoeia" by William Safire

"Coyote v. Acme" by Ian Frazier (p. 271)

Paraphrase

Sample Responses:

from The Mortgaged Heart

Paragraph 1: The loneliness of Americans comes from trying to establish an identity.

Paragraph 2: The desire to be an individual seems to be one of the most fundamental human qualities.

"Coyote v. Acme"

Paragraph 1: Mr. Coyote is suing the Acme Company for bad products.

Final paragraph: Mr. Coyote sues for thirty-eight million seven hundred and fifty thousand dollars.

"Straw Into Gold" by Sandra Cisneros

"For the Love of Books" by Rita Dove

"Mother Tongue" by Amy Tan (p. 272)

Summarize Main Idea

"For the Love of Books"

Main idea of paragraph 1: I have always loved books.

Supporting details: I loved to feel their heft in my hand, I loved the crisp whisper of a page turning, I even loved to gaze at a closed book and daydream about the possibilities inside.

"Mother Tongue"

Main idea of paragraph 3: I used a different English from the English my mother uses.

Supporting details: I was saying things like . . ., speech filled with carefully wrought grammatical phrases.

"The Rockpile" by James Baldwin (p. 273)

Rephrase Characters' Speech

Sample Responses:

2. You know Mama doesn't want you to go downstairs.

3. I will be right back.

4. She won't know I am gone unless you tell her.

from Hiroshima by John Hersey

"Losses" and "The Death of the Ball Turret Gunner" by Randall Jarrell (p. 274)

Question Author's Purpose

Sample Responses:

from Hiroshima

4. Q: Why was Mr. Tanimoto uneasy?
   A: He fears that he is under suspicion because of his American affiliations.

5. Q: What was Mr. Tanimoto doing that day?
   A: He was carrying a Japanese cabinet to a man's house with another man.

6. Q: What did Mr. Tanimoto do when the bomb went off?
   A: He jumped between two large rocks.

"Losses"

1. Q: How many people died?
   A: Many people died. So many died that it seemed normal.

2. Q: How did the soldiers handle their missions?
   A: They treated it like it was normal for the time.

"The Death of the Ball Turret Gunner"

1. Q: What woke the speaker when he was six miles from Earth?
   A: Enemy fire

"Mirror" by Sylvia Plath

"In a Classroom" by Adrienne Rich

"The Explorer" by Gwendolyn Brooks

"Frederick Douglass" and "Runagate Runagate" by Robert Hayden (p. 275)

Interpret and Explain Poetry

Sample Responses:

2. A dusty ray of light makes me think of being in school on a sunny day.

3. Since satin is smooth, the image is restful.

4. It sounds like lots of people talking at once but not saying anything.

5. The darkness is full of thick shapes everywhere. The image is scary.

"For My Children" by Colleen McElroy

"Bidwell Ghost" by Louise Erdrich (p. 276)

Identify Sensory Words

Sample Responses:

Sight: floats, narrow, alabaster, crowns, dancer, fire, thin white dress, embroidered with fire, blackened nest of hair, cold white blossoms

Sound: Beatles tunes, oboe and flute, cracked

Touch: crowns, fire, heat, blackened nest of hair

Smell: cold white blossoms

Taste: honey and cocoa, wine

"The Writer in the Family"
by E. L. Doctorow (p. 277)

Respond to Characters' Actions

Grandmother bragged about her son's new life because she thought he had moved to Arizona.

Aunt Frances called because her mother wondered why she wasn't hearing from Jack.

The narrator writes to his grandmother because he is pretending to be Jack.

"Camouflaging the Chimera"
by Yusef Komunyakaa

"Ambush" *from* The Things They Carried
by Tim O'Brien (p. 278)

Form a Mental Picture

Students should record notes on the various scenes mentioned. Sketches should attempt to depict these scenes as the authors describe them.

The Crucible, Act I, by Arthur Miller
(p. 279)

Make a Character Chart

Sample Responses:

Tituba: She danced in the forest. She says she gave the girls chicken blood to drink. Mr. Parris says he saw her waving her hands and screeching.

Reverend Parris: He cries about his sick daughter Betty. He says "Oh, my God! God help me!" Mr. Proctor says that he does not like Mr. Parris's sense of authority.

Abigail Williams: She danced in the forest. She says Goody Proctor is a liar. There are rumors that she was dismissed from Goody Proctor's service for doing something wrong.

Mrs. Ann Putnam: She comes to visit the Parrises. She says that her dead babies were all murdered. Rebecca Nurse does not believe Mrs. Putnam about the murdered babies.

Mercy Lewis: She comes to see how Betty is doing. She says that Ruth walks like a dead one. Abigail says that Parris saw Mercy naked.

Mary Warren: She visits Abigail and Mercy. She cries that they have to confess. Mercy says Mary is a coward.

John Proctor: He comes to the Parris house. He tells Abigail to put their relationship out of her mind. Abigail says he is strong.

Rebecca Nurse: She calms Betty down. She says this is childishness. Mr. Hale has heard of her good works.

Giles Corey: He comes to the Parris'. He says that he admires Parris' strength. Mr. Proctor says Giles is old and cannot hear well.

Reverend John Hale: He comes bringing many books. He says that the people have to accept his verdict if there is no witchcraft involved. The Putnams say he found a witch in Beverly last year

Betty Parris: She jumps out of bed. She says that Abigail drank a charm to kill John Proctor's wife. Abigail says she loves Betty dearly.

The Crucible, Act II, by Arthur Miller
(p. 280)

Paraphrase Dialogue

Sample Responses:

Sentence 1: Hale: No man may longer doubt the powers of the dark are gathered in monstrous attack upon this village.

Paraphrase: It is clear that dark powers are attacking this village.

Sentence 2: Proctor: It may be I have been too quick to bring the man to book, but you cannot think we ever desired the destruction of religion.

Paraphrase: I may have accused him too quickly, but we did not want to destroy our religion.

Sentence 3: Cheever: The court bid me search your house, but I like not to search a house.

Paraphrase: The court told me to search your house, but I don't want to.

The Crucible, Act III, by Arthur Miller
(p. 281)

Use a Story Map Organizer

Sample Responses:

Problem: The girls have been caught dancing in the forest and they begin to accuse other citizens of witchcraft.

Event 2: Abigail and John Proctor talk.

Event 3: The girls call out the names of townspeople.

Event 4: John and Elizabeth talk.

Event 5: Townspeople are arrested.

Climax: The trial of the townspeople is the turning point.

The Crucible, Act IV, by Arthur Miller
(p. 282)

Prepare a Reader's Theater

Students should assign roles, jot down ideas about their performance, and finally present their performance to the class. The class should evaluate the performance.

© **Pearson Education, Inc.**